"The Day when neither wealth nor children will be of any benefit. Only those who come before Allāh with a pure heart (will be saved)"

[Qur'ān: As-Shu'arā' 26: 88-89]

A Handbook of SPIRITUAL MEDICINE

Ibn Daud

A Handbook of Spiritual Medicine

Comments & Suggestions
Allāh ﷻ says, "(The believers pray,) Our Lord! Do not punish us if we forget or make a mistake." [Al-Baqarah 2:286]

The author would appreciate hearing comments and suggestions from any readers. If you find any errors in this book, these are solely due to his shortcomings. Please email the author directly and he will do his best to correct them in the next edition inshā'Allāh.

British Library
A catalogue record for this book is available from the British Library.
www.bl.uk

Publishing
Published by Ibn Daud Books, Leicester, UK and printed by SOFIAPRINT, Istanbul, Turkey.

Ibn Daud Books
theauthor@ibndaudbooks.com
www.ibndaudbooks.com
Leicester, UK

ISBN 978-18380492-1-8

TABLE OF CONTENTS

	The Author's Journey	6
	Introduction	10
	Recommendations	14
	Acknowledgements	18
	Self-Purification	20
	A Continual Cycle of Self-Purification	24
	How to Use this Book	28
1.	Anger	30
2.	Antipathy Towards Death	44
3.	Blameworthy Modesty	50
4.	Boasting, Arrogance & Pride	56
5.	Displeasure with Blame or Disapproval	70
6.	Displeasure with the Divine Decree	76
7.	Envy	84
8.	Extravagance	92
9.	False Hope	100
10.	Fantasizing	108
11.	Fear of Poverty	116

12. Fraud 126

13. Hard-Heartedness 140

14. Hatred 152

15. Heedlessness 160

16. Iniquity 172

17. Love of the World 180

18. Miserliness 190

19. Mockery 200

20. Negative Feelings 208

21. Obliviousness to Blessings or Ingratitude 218

22. Ostentation or Showing Off 226

23. Relying on Other than Allāh ﷻ 240

24. Seeking Reputation 248

25. Vanity 258

26. Wantonness or Greed 266

Index 275

Bibliography 289

The Handbook Team 292

THE AUTHOR'S JOURNEY

Being a British-born Muslim, I have been a seeker of faith from my adolescent years. A son of practising parents who came from Pakistan as immigrants, I had a blessed childhood. The nurturing (tarbiyyah) in our home life was all about practice and exemplification – in the 1970s and 80s there was no accessible formal Islāmic education near our country village in the northeast of England. Thus it was left to my parents to give us some means to unlock the treasures of the Qurān and to describe to us how much could be gained through the pillars of prayer, fasting and charity. I have fond memories of being shown and taught how to 'do the right thing', offer genuine kindness to strangers, give generously from the heart, value our elders, and have compassion for those less fortunate. All of this impressed a strong sense of faith and integrity upon me and my siblings, and it served as our Islāmic upbringing.

Outside the home, I received both public and private schooling. In a community inhabited by people of all faith, but with primary schools committed to the Christian tradition, I learnt the Lord's Prayer, and sang hymns with enough proficiency and gusto to be included in a choir run jointly by school and church.

Negotiating the hormonally hectic years of secondary (high) school, college and university wasn't easy (when is it ever?). Without doubt, the most dazzling of distractions danced their way across my field of vision as a young person setting up as an undergraduate on a degree course. Suddenly, I was away from the trappings and security of home life. The course I had chosen was business and information technology, but the great majority of new faces among the 'freshers' had their wide-eyed selves set on the business of partying and flaunting themselves. The information that was constantly on offer was that such-and-such was having a party, or that a large bunch of friends wanted to see me at the club, bar or function. The struggle was very real, and so many colleagues on the course were soon bewildered when it came to their studies. I pondered the excesses of the swathe of free-spirited folk, and at first viewed their repeated calls to revelry as a curious kind of imposition, but this thought was soon overtaken by more insecure ones such as 'Shouldn't I be behaving in the same way?' or 'Isn't this entirely normal?' Thankfully, I was suitably 'switched on' to be able to make it through this four-year minefield relatively unscathed, and was fortunate indeed when I came across the book 'Purification of the Heart: Signs, Symptoms and Cures of the Spiritual Diseases of the Heart' by Shaykh Hamza Yusuf Hanson. If I remember rightly, I was in the third year of university study. Whenever and wherever I opened this book, it shook my conscience, gripping me with a new cause. Quite stark was the message: 'Pull yourself together young man! Become a meaningful contributor before it is too late!' It was a profound directive to seek a solution to the illnesses of my heart, and it was so achingly obvious to me at the time that there were no real external factors. All was 'at sea', but the distance to shore was of my own making.

Roughly around the same time, towards the end of my MBA studies, I lived with a medic whose particular quirk was to reference the 'Oxford Handbook of Clinical Medicine' with zeal: like some sort of charm, he would lift this cheese-and-onion coloured textbook from his pocket on a daily basis to pore over notes which ran the whole gamut of the known medical and surgical world. If you will pardon the pun, it is the memory of the efficacy of this small book coupled with my long-term preoccupation with the concept of 'tazkiyah' ('self / character purification') which brings me to this point. If a handbook could illustrate the maladies of the human spiritual condition, and offer up the remedies too, then I too could use something like that to direct my own self to a purer path. Aided by distant memories of the Seven Deadly Sins from my younger school days, I could appreciate the categorisations that ran through Shaykh Hamza Yusuf's work and utilise them to provide a definitive structure, a plan for my own guidance. I could see a flickering light on the shore.

Still, the idea for this hybrid handbook lay dormant for a decade or more. In my forties, and a family man, I moved to the East Midlands in the UK for two main reasons: for my children to be enrolled in schools with an Islāmic ethos, and for me to find comfort in regular daily prayers in the masājid. The Prophet's ﷺ hijrah from Makkah to Madīnah, as well as being a flight from a hostile situation, was a move to a better social and moral surrounding. Our relocation to Leicester was by no means as weighty, testing or secretive as the journey of our Beloved Prophet ﷺ, but it was certainly a move to a better situation, morally strengthening and conducive to production for the sake of Allāh ﷻ.

Somewhere down the line, out of these six years of living in Leicester, and from talking and reasoning with a great many people, there came a more ardent desire to create this handbook that would help people overcome boundaries to living their best. The desire was now coupled with the means to produce something to cultivate improvement and good manners in myself and others. Perhaps it was a case of the plan being strengthened considerably by the new location, or more accurately it was the galvanising personalities within that new situation who would benefit me with their knowledge, and push me to shore. These good people and respected scholars are mentioned in the 'acknowledgements' section of this book. At this point, it is enough to say that the entire experience of taking a rough idea through all the stages of creative endeavour, editing, proofing and finally publication on an independent basis has been fulfilling to say the least. The process of seeking full authentication and accurate cross-referencing of works from among the seminal texts of Islām, the Glorious Qur'ān and the words of our Honourable Prophet ﷺ has brought me closer to these truths and to the Lord and Master of the Universes. By means of wise words and advice from both Muslim and non-Muslim brothers and sisters, Allāh ﷻ has kept me constantly 'in touch' with His wisdoms. May Allāh ﷻ honour these people and love them for their love of His dīn, and for their sincere consultation:

"And those who have responded to their Lord (in submission to Him), and have established ṣalāh, and whose affairs are (settled) with mutual consultation between them." [As-Shūrā 42:38]

Indeed, with Allāh's ﷻ blessing and permission, what we find here is a kind of handbook that I hope will grant us the means to wrestle ourselves free from the lower self, the 'nafs ul-ammārah', defined as that part of the self that overwhelmingly commands us towards sin. In the same way that we pray and read the Qur'ān, or engage in regular remembrance of Allāh ﷻ on a daily basis, then if we reflect on this book and others like it, we can apply its advices to our busy lives in this modern, hi-tech era. I hope that the accessibility and brevity of the language means that this is a book capable of soothing the pains of people of all ages, all denominations: believers and non-believers alike.

Again, I would like to offer sincere thanks to the countless generous people who have devoted time and effort in helping me towards this goal. The foremost of these, however, are my devoted and inspirational mother, Hameeda and late father Mohammed Daud Parekh: it is to them that I dedicate this book. Without their love and prayers, these pages would be blank leaves and I would not be able to say so wholeheartedly: "this is the upstanding and unshakeable religion."

اَللّٰهُمَّ آتِ نَفْسِي تَقْوَاهَا وَزَكِّهَا أنتَ خَيْرُ مَنْ زَكَّاهَا
أَنْتَ وَلِيُّهَا وَمَوْلَاهَا

Allāhumma āti nafsī taqwāhā wa zakkihā anta khayru man zakkāhā anta Waliyyuhā wa Mawlāhā

O Allāh! Grant me the sense of piety and purify my soul as You are the Best to purify it. You are its Guardian and its Protecting Friend.

Āmīn.

Ibn Daud
Leicester, UK
Ramaḍān 1441 (May 2020)

INTRODUCTION

مقدمة محمد وائل الحنبلي

بسم الله الرحمن الرحيم الحمد لله رب العالمين و صلى الله على سيدنا محمد و على آله و صحبه أجمعين، سبحانك لا علم لنا إلا ما علمتنا فعلمنا ما ينفعنا وانفعنا بما علمتنا وزدنا علما وعملا وفقها و إخلاصا في الدين يا رب العالمين.

طلب مني المصنف من بريطانيا أن اكتب له مقدمة لكتاب جمعه يتعلق بالتربية والسلوك والآداب والأخلاق التي ينبغي أن تمني ليتحلى بها حياة المسلم. و هذا التحسين في ثلاثة مواضع: فيما بينه وبين إخوانه من المؤمنين، و فيما بينه وبين الله، وفيما بينه وبين المخلوق كله

بداية أقول قال الله تعالى «وأما من خاف مقام ربه و نهى النفس عن الهوى فإن الجنة هي المأوى» أيها الأخوة الله سبحانه وتعالى في هذه الآية بيّن لنا أن الطريقة في هذه الدنيا الطريق الذي يُوصِل الى الجنة هو أن تخاف مقام ربك وأن تنهى النفس عن الرذائل، أن تخاف مقام ربك بحسن العبادة بالتفقه بالإخلاص، و نهى النفس عن الهوى ان يبتعد عن رذائل الأمور و عن النواهي وأن يبتعد عما فيه إثم يُغضب الله وأن يبتعد عما فيه إثم يُسيء الى عباد الله. وقال تعالى «يوم لا ينفع مال ولا بنون الا من اتى الله بقلب سليم». تأمّلوا معي هذه الآية، هي علم الاخلاق والتربيه كله، كل علم الأخلاق والتربية في هذه الآية، كيف؟ لأنّه يقول الله سبحانه وتعالى في هذه الآية لم ينتفع أحد يوم القيامة إلا إذا كان قلبه سليما، وعلم التربية وعلم السلوك وعلم الآداب عن ماذا يبحث؟ كله يبحث عن القلب وعن اصلاحه وعن تأديبه وهذا ما قال الله سبحانه في هذه الآية «من اتى الله بقلب سليم».

ولو انتقلنا إلى حديث النبي صلى الله عليه وسلم عن اصلاح القلب و عن التربية وعن السلوك، سنجد هذا في كثير من الأحاديث. قال صلى الله عليه وسلم «ألا وإن في الجسد مضغة إذا صلحت صلح الجسد كله» في رواية «صلح العمل كله» «وإذا فسدت فسد العمل كله» أيها الإخوة. القلب إذا صلح حاله بالتربية بالاوراد والاذكار بالطاعات صلح العمل كله. هذا بالنسبة إلى القلب بشكل عام، وأما إذا أردنا أن نخصّص الآداب والأخلاق في السنة النبوية فنرجع إلى الحديث الذي في البخاري ومسلم قال صلى الله عليه وسلم «لا تحاسدوا ولا تناجشوا ولا تباغضوا ولا تدابروا ولا يبع بعضكم على بيع بعض، كونوا عباد الله إخوانا». هذه هي الآداب التي يبحثها علم التربية وهذه هي الأخلاق التي يُوصي بها العلماء الربّانيّون. وقال أيضا صلى الله عليه وسلم «اتق الله حيثما كنت واتبع السيئة الحسنة تمحها و خالق الناس بخلق حسن». في هذا الحديث يبيّن النبي صلى الله عليه و سلم المعاملة بين العبد وربه «اتق الله حيثما كنت». و يبين المعاملة بين المؤمن وبين عباد ربه بقول «وخالق الناس بخلق حسن»، وهذا هو كله علم التربية و الأخلاق.

وأما هذا الكتاب و مؤلفه، جزاه الله تعالى خيرا وسهل فيه علم التربية لكل قارئ، فهذا، كما ذكرت، أهم الأمر للمسلم. يقول العلامة ابن عابدين رحمه الله تعالى في مقدمة حاشيته «إن علم الإخلاص والعجب والحسد والرياء فرض عين، مثل غيرها من آفات النفوس كالكبر والشح والحقد والغش والغضب والعداوة والبغضاء والطمع»، ثم يقول «مما هو مبين في إحياء علوم الدين» اذاً العلامة ابن عابدين رحمه الله يلفت الإنتباه إلى الموضوع الأصلي في أشهر كتب العلماء، أن علوم التزكية والتربية هي فرض عين على كل مسلم لأنّ به يصحح العبادة و يصحح المعاملة. و كذلك العلامة السيوطي قال في كتابه الأشباه والنظائر «وأما علم القلب ومعرفة أمراضه من الحسد والعجب والرياء فرض عين.» ونسبه أيضا إلى الإمام الغزالي.

ونختم هذه المقدمة بكلام العلامة الشرنبلالي رحمه الله تعالى عندما كان يتكلم عن الطهارة في كتابه مراقي الفلاح شرح نور الإيضاح قال «لا تنفع الطهارة الظاهرة إلا مع الطهارة الباطنة». فالإمام الشرنبلالي يرى أن المسلم ينبغي عليه أن يصحح الطهارة الظاهرة التي تكون بالتطهير الذي يوافق السنة النبوية و الطهارة الباطنة التي تكون بذكر الله في كل أحيان، و تكون بمراقبة القلب، و تكون بصحبة الصالحين ورفقة الأولياء . و ينصر المؤمن بتوفر الكتب على سير الصحابة و النبي صلى الله عليه وسلم.

ختاما نسأل الله سبحانه الإخلاص في القول والعمل و أسأل الله أن ينفع بهذا الكتاب وأن يوفق كل من نفع بقرائته بالهداية و الإصلاح و نسأل الله الثبات في الدين وأن يوفقنا التأسي بأخلاق النبي محمد ﷺ

قاله وكتبه محمد وائل الحنبلي الدمشقي
في النصف في الثاني من شعبان عام ١٤٤١
و لا تنسوني من دعواتكم

I begin in the name of Allāh ﷻ, the Most Kind, the Most Merciful. All praise is due to Allāh ﷻ, the Lord of the Worlds. May He send salutations upon our leader Muḥammad and upon all of his family and companions. Glory be to You (Allāh ﷻ), we have no knowledge except which You have taught us, so grant us knowledge that will benefit us and give us benefit from that which You teach us, and increase us in knowledge, action, understanding and sincerity in religion O Lord of the Worlds.

The author from Britain has asked me to write a foreword for a book he has compiled which concerns the science of upbringing and education (tarbiyyah), conduct (sulūk), etiquette (ādāb) and good character (akhlāq), all of which should be cultivated, to adorn a Muslim's life. This essential improvement is in three areas: in his or her conduct and attitude towards fellow believers; in the relationship between the believer and Almighty Allāh ﷻ; and in the conduct shown towards the rest of the creation.

Firstly, Allāh ﷻ says, "And as for those who were in awe of standing before their Lord and restrained themselves from (evil) desires, Paradise will certainly be (their) home." [An-Nāzi'āt 79: 40-41] In this verse Allāh ﷻ is explaining to us the path of this world, the path that leads to Paradise. It is that you be in awe of standing before your Lord and restrain yourself from all vice. You are in awe of standing before your Lord via superb worship, devotion to study and sincerity. You restrain yourself from (evil) desires by distancing yourself from vice and the forbidden, by distancing yourself from anything that involves sin and angers Allāh ﷻ, and by distancing yourself from anything potentially harmful to the servants of Allāh ﷻ, again through sin.

Allāh ﷻ says, "the Day when neither wealth nor children will be of any benefit. Only those who come before Allāh ﷻ with a pure heart (will be saved)." [As-Shu'arā' 26: 88-89] Ponder over this verse with me. This (verse) is the entirety of the science of good character, upbringing and education. How? Because Allāh ﷻ says in this verse that none will benefit on the Day of Judgement unless their heart is pure. And the science of upbringing, education, conduct and etiquette discusses what? They all discuss the heart and its rectification and disciplining. And this is what Allāh ﷻ says in this verse "those who come before Allāh with a pure heart (will be saved)."

If we look to the ahādīth of the Prophet ﷺ regarding rectification of the heart, upbringing, education and conduct, we will find plenty of it within the ahādīth.

The Prophet ﷺ said, "In the body there is a morsel of flesh, if it is sound, the whole body is sound (in a narration "all actions are sound"). If it is corrupted, the whole body is ("all actions are") corrupted. Indeed, it is the heart." [Ṣaḥīḥ Al-Bukhārī 52] When the state of the heart is sound due to good teaching, the habit of performing nawafil (supererogatory, more than is considered a 'duty') actions and the remembrance of Allāh ﷻ, then all (of one's) actions will be sound. This is in relation to the heart in a general sense. If we wish to specify etiquette and good character in the prophetic practice then we turn to the ḥadīth which is in Ṣaḥīḥ Al-Bukhārī and Ṣaḥīḥ Muslim: The Prophet ﷺ said, "Don't nurse grudges and don't bid each other out for raising the price and don't nurse aversion or hatred and don't enter into a transaction when others have already entered into that transaction, and be fellow-brothers and servants of Allāh" [Ṣaḥīḥ Al-Bukhārī 6066, Ṣaḥīḥ Muslim 2564:32]. These are the etiquettes discussed by the science of upbringing and education and this is the good character with which the pious scholars have bestowed. The Prophet ﷺ has also said: "Be wary of Allāh wherever you are, and follow an evil deed with a good one to wipe it out, and treat the people with good character" [At-Tirmidhī 1987]. In this ḥadīth the Prophet ﷺ has explained the conduct between the slave and his Lord: "Be wary of Allāh wherever you are". And he explains the conduct between the believer and the servants of Allāh ﷻ in saying "and treat the people with good character". This, in its entirety, is the science of upbringing, education and good character.

As for this book, and its author, I ask Allāh ﷻ to reward him with good, and to make the science of upbringing and education within it easy to understand for all readers. It is, as I have mentioned, the most important matter for a Muslim. Allāmah Ibn 'Ābidīn says in the foreword to his commentary (Radd Al-Muhtār 'ala Ad-Durr Al-Mukhtār), "(Having) knowledge of sincerity, vanity, envy and ostentation is mandatory (farḍ 'ayn) just like the other spiritual diseases such as arrogance, avarice, fraud, anger, enmity, hatred and ambitious desire." He then says, "As mentioned in Ihyā 'Ulūm Ad-Dīn". Allāmah Ibn 'Ābidīn is thus drawing our attention to the central and repeated theme amongst the most celebrated works of scholars that these sciences of tazkiyah and teaching the soul's improvement are compulsory (fard 'ayn) upon every Muslim, as via these one's worship and conduct will be corrected. Similarly, Allāmah Suyuṭī says in his book 'Al-Ashbāh wa An-Nadhāir' that "knowledge of the heart and recognising its diseases such as envy, vanity and ostentation is compulsory (farḍ 'ayn)." Again, he cites Imam Al-Ghazalī as his source.

I will end this foreword with the words of Allāmah Shurunbulālī in his discussion of purity in the book 'Marāqiy Al-Falāḥ: a Commentary on Nur Al-Īḍāḥ', "The outer purity will not be of benefit without the inner purity." Imām Shurunbulālī expresses with certainty that the practising Muslim must perfect his outer purity (by means of water) in the act of washing in accordance with the Sunnah of the Prophet ﷺ, and he or she must seek to attain inner purity by emulating the Sunnah of the Prophet ﷺ in this inward sphere also: this is done through remembrance of Allāh ﷻ in all actions, through deep inspection of one's heart and soul, and through keeping excellent company. Here, the believer is helped by the availability of the written biographies and accounts of the Prophet ﷺ and his Companions.

Lastly, I ask Allāh ﷻ for sincerity in deeds and action, and I ask Allāh ﷻ that He provides benefit through this book, and that He enables the guidance and rectification of all who benefit from opening its pages. With Allāh's ﷻ assistance, may we be blessed with steadfastness in religion, and towards practice of the good character of the Prophet Muḥammad ﷺ. Āmīn.

Mohammed Wail Al-Hanbali Al-Hanafi Ad-Dimashqi
Istanbul, Turkey
Sha'bān 1441 (April 2020)

Do not forget me in your prayers.

RECOMMENDATIONS

Most illnesses that we have today emanate from diseases of the heart, therefore it's essential to try and rectify the unseen realms of our hearts and exert maximum efforts in self-purification.

This body of work is arranged in a unique way, where signs and symptoms of spiritual ailments are addressed with various treatments in light of sources of sharī'ah as well as advice and counsel from other reliable sources.

It is colour-coded which will be very beneficial to the reader, especially in an educational setting.

The author has put in a lot of hard work to ensure that the reader can reflect and ponder over his shortcomings, which is a continuing duty upon a Muslim. This work will enable the reader to self-analyse and assist him or herself in meeting their Creator with a 'sound heart'.

There are some very relevant issues mentioned and I'm certain that those who will read the work with a view to correcting their inner souls will be benefited immensely from the work.

Dr Shaykh Ashraf Makadam
Director of Trust, Madani Schools Federation

Leicester, UK
Ramaḍān 1441 (April 2020)

RECOMMENDATIONS

A beautifully structured and well-presented work, highlighting one of the most important aspects of Islāmic teachings - purifying the heart from blameworthy character traits and replacing them with praiseworthy ones.

May Allāh ﷻ accept the efforts of the author and team and make it beneficial.

Āmīn.

Mufti Muhammad ibn Adam Al-Kawthari
Director and researcher at the Institute of Islāmic Jurisprudence (Darul Iftaa)

Leicester, UK
Ramaḍān 1441 (April 2020)

Alhamdulillāh, I was pleased to see the book '**A Handbook of Spiritual Medicine.**'

Mashā-Allāh, it has been compiled in great detail yet in an easy-to-follow format. If read with the guidance of a shaykh (spiritual guide) then inshā'Allāh it will aid greatly, be of much benefit and ease the path to the attainment of tazkiyah.

I pray Allāh ﷻ accepts the work of brother Jamal and makes it a means of attaining His everlasting pleasure.

Āmīn.

(Mawlānā) Muhammad Yahya
(Director) An Nasihah Publications

Leicester, UK
Sha'bān 1441 (April 2020)

RECOMMENDATIONS

The importance of spiritual wayfaring cannot be emphasised enough, particularly in our times where the material realm is emphasised as the only means to human happiness and progress.

Allāh ﷻ clearly informs us after more than ten oaths are undertaken to emphasise the centrality of internal rectification by the words "Successful indeed is the one who purifies their soul" [As-Shams 91:9]. Countless verses of the Qur'ān and Prophetic narrations attest to this, such as those that set about demarcating the state of iḥsān (spiritual perfection) with the words: "Worship Allāh as if you see Him; if not that, then He sees you" [Ṣaḥīḥ Al-Bukhārī 50, Ṣaḥīḥ Muslim 9:5].

Making this science accessible to a new generation is of utmost importance especially in times of a spiritual vacuum. The 'Handbook of Spiritual Medicine' is to be commended as a clear presentation of the science of internal purification in a format which enables easy access to symptoms of spiritual illnesses and their cures. This is all the more important as many maladies that plague the modern world in essence emanate from the spiritual maladies within our own collective 'selves' and communities.

We pray that Allāh ﷻ accepts this work as a fresh exposition of an ancient science and rectifies the Muslim community and the wider community by novel presentations such as the method adopted by this work.

Shaykh Zaqir
Director of Darul Arqam Educational Trust

Leicester, UK
Sha'bān 1441 (April 2020)

RECOMMENDATIONS

In the Name of Allāh, Most Gracious, Most Merciful.

The author has made a great contribution to this field through his work. The presentation and layout employed in presenting the spiritual diseases and their remedies are highly effective and make this book comprehensible for the readers. Inshā Allāh, it will be a spiritual medicine for the seekers of the spiritual path. I asked the author to make a few corrections, and it is testament to the idea that he has adopted the very spirit of the book that he was very quick to agree to them. May Allāh ﷻ reward him abundantly.

Shaykh Imran bin Adam
Principal, Jame'ah Uloom Al Qur'an

Leicester, UK
Sha'bān 1441 (April 2020)

ACKNOWLEDGEMENTS

The Prophet ﷺ said, "He who does not thank the people is not thankful to Allāh." [Sunan Abī Dawūd 4811]

All praise be to Allāh ﷻ, Lord and Sustainer of the universe, for helping me fulfil this work, and salutations and peace be upon the Messenger of mercy and guidance, and upon his family, righteous Companions and those that follow him.

This work is the result of the collaboration of many special people from amongst the respected Ulamā of Leicester and further afield, to whom I wish to express my deepest gratitude, notably Mawlānā Yahya ibn Faruq, Director of An Nasihah Publications, who held my hand through the challenging process of self-publishing. I also thank both Mawlānā Imran bin Adam, Principal of Jame'ah Uloom Al Qur'an, and Shaykh Muhammed Zaqir, Director of Darul Arqam Educational Trust, both of whom saw the importance of a book of this nature and hence encouraged me and guided this effort through to completion. May Allāh ﷻ protect and elevate their positions. Āmīn.

I am indebted to my editing team, Mawlānā Uthmaan Hafejee, Mawlānā Amaan Muhammad, Mustafa Abid Russell and Irfan Chhatbar, without whom I would not have had the support, patience, skills and expertise to bring this book to fruition. I am truly honoured and deeply grateful to have found the company of such God-conscious individuals.

I would also like to express my gratitude to my sweet daughter, Ammaarah, for helping me gain valuable insights into the world of social media, and my kind and loving sister, Henna, for reviewing my first draft paper and for her energetic streams of advice and encouragement.

Along my journey, I have received invaluable support from many other kind and generous individuals. May Allāh ﷻ compensate them with the best of rewards in both worlds. Āmīn.

Finally, my immense gratitude goes to the mother of my children, Sana, whose guidance and wisdom during this journey has been a great source of strength for me. And I am extremely indebted to my loving parents, Hameeda Parekh and the late Mohammed Daud Parekh for their teaching and my upbringing. They led by example.

I pray to Allāh ﷻ for the best of rewards for our Prophet ﷺ, his inheritors - the scholars of Islām, and those who follow their path to happiness and salvation in this life and in the Hereafter. Āmīn.

Ibn Daud

Leicester, UK
Ramaḍān 1441 (April 2020)

SELF-PURIFICATION

The Importance of Spiritual Wellbeing

Just as you seek the best medical treatment to avoid illnesses and improve your physical health and wellbeing, whether that be paracetamol to treat a mere headache or something more substantial like chemotherapy to treat cancer, your soul can also suffer from spiritual illnesses such as riyā (ostentation), takabbur (pride and arrogance), ḥasad (envy), lack of shukr (ingratitude), ḥubb al-jāh (love of fame), ḥubb al-māl (love of wealth), and the like.

Spiritual health is fundamentally different however, and in some respects more important. Why is this?

- The detrimental consequences of a physical illness will come to an end upon death; whereas, the evil result of a spiritual illness will begin upon death, and will last for eternity
- Imām Al-Ghazālī ﵀ said that "the science of the states of the heart ('ilm aḥwāl al-qalb) is an individual obligation, not just a collective one"; in other words, this is a responsibility for every adult Muslim (farḍ 'ayn), according to capacity, and not a responsibility left to specially qualified individuals within the community (farḍ al-kifāyah) [Letter to a Disciple/Ayyuhāl Walad, p. 58-59]

Allāh ﷻ further declares:

- "Successful indeed are those who purify themselves" [A'laa 87:14]
- "As for those who struggle in Our cause, We will surely guide them along Our Way. And Allāh is certainly with the good-doers" [Al-'Ankabūt 29:69]
- "The Gardens of Eternity, under which rivers flow, where they will stay forever. That is the reward of those who purify themselves" [Ṭāhā 20:76]

The Messenger of Allāh ﷺ has also said:

- "The mujāhid is he who strives in the obedience of Allāh" [Al-Bayhaqī in Shu'ab Al-Īmān 10611]
- "The believers most perfect in faith are those best in character and those best to their spouses" [At-Tirmidhī 2612]
- "There is nothing heavier than good character put in the scale of a believer on the Day of Resurrection" [Sunan Abī Dawūd 4799]

Numerous other Qur'ānic verses and an untold number of ahādīth explicitly indicate the obligation (farḍiyya) of purifying the heart: the significance of abstinence (zuhd), contentment (qanā'ah), humility (tawāḍu'), sincerity (ikhlāṣ), patience (ṣabr), gratitude (shukr), love of Allāh ﷻ (ḥubb Allāh), contentment with the Decree (riḍā bil-qaḍā), trust (tawakkul), submission (taslīm), and so on.

A man came to the Prophet ﷺ and asked, "What is tazkiyah an-nafs (purification of the soul)?" The Prophet ﷺ replied, "That a person knows Allāh is with him wherever he is." [Al-Mu'jam Aṣ-Ṣaghīr Aṭ-Ṭabarānī 555]

What are your Objectives?

Allāh ﷻ says that the Prophet Ibrahīm ﷺ prayed to Him, "And do not disgrace me on the Day all will be resurrected, the Day when neither wealth nor children will be of any benefit. Only those who come before **Allāh** with a pure heart (will be saved)." [As-Shu'arā', 26: 87-89]

On the Day of Judgement, you will be presented 'inside out', so to speak. The people who have taken the greatest care to preserve their soul will be the most beautiful, regardless of their physical appearance on Earth. Contrastingly, those who have neglected to follow His instructions will turn up as ugly as the hearts and souls they harboured on Earth. Then only good beings will enter Paradise, while the perverse will not.

Just as with the medical treatment of physical illnesses, for a spiritually sick person, the objectives of self-purification therefore are to:

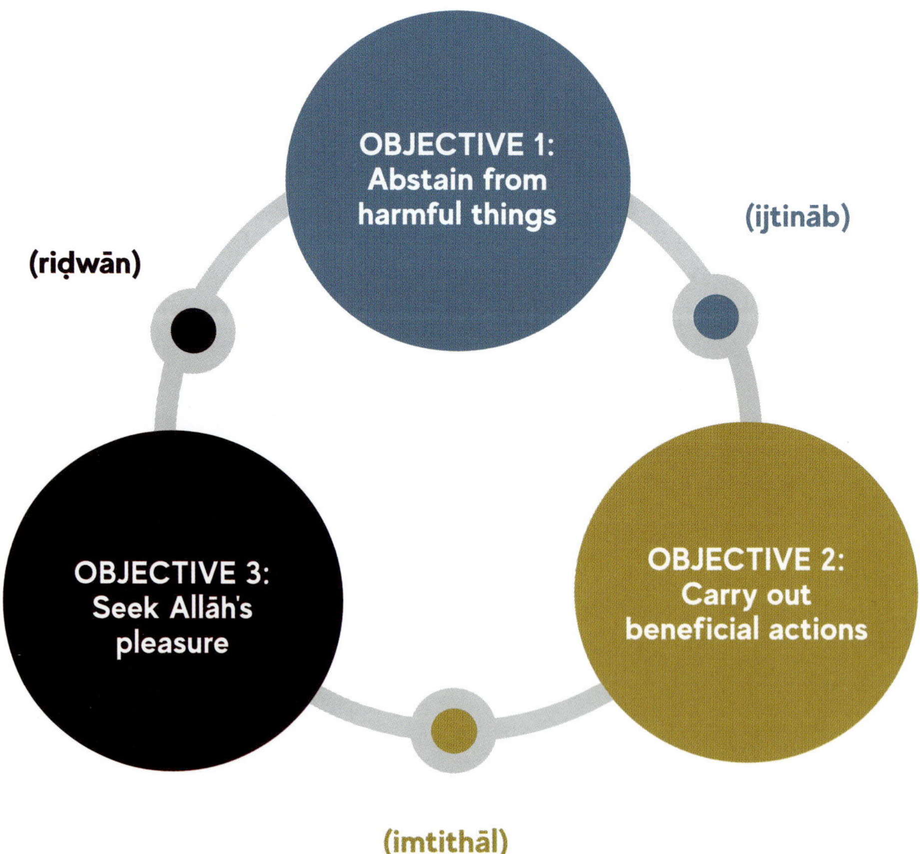

1. Abstain **(ijtināb)** from those things that harm you by ridding your heart (bāṭin) of vile, unrefined attributes such as lust, anger, malice, jealousy, love of the world, love of fame, stinginess, greed, ostentation, vanity, deceit, calamities of the tongue, and the like
2. Carry out the actions required **(imtithāl)** to benefit you by adorning your heart with the lofty attributes of perseverance, gratitude, fear of Allāh ﷻ, hope, abstention, unity, trust, love, truthfulness, remorse, reflection, reckoning, contemplation, and so on
3. Seek the good pleasure **(riḍwān)** of Allāh ﷻ

Imām Al-Ghazālī رحمه الله said, "Just as if you learned that your life would only last another week, inevitably you would not spend it in learning about law, ethics, jurisprudence, scholastic theology and suchlike, because you would know that these sciences would be inadequate for you. Instead, you would occupy yourself with inspecting your heart, discerning the features of your personality, giving worldly attachments a wide berth, purging yourself in adoring God the Exalted, worshipping Him and acquiring good qualities. And not a day or night passes for (any) worshipper without his death during it being a possibility!" [Letter to a Disciple/Ayyuhāl Walad, p.56-57]

A CONTINUAL CYCLE OF SELF-PURIFICATION

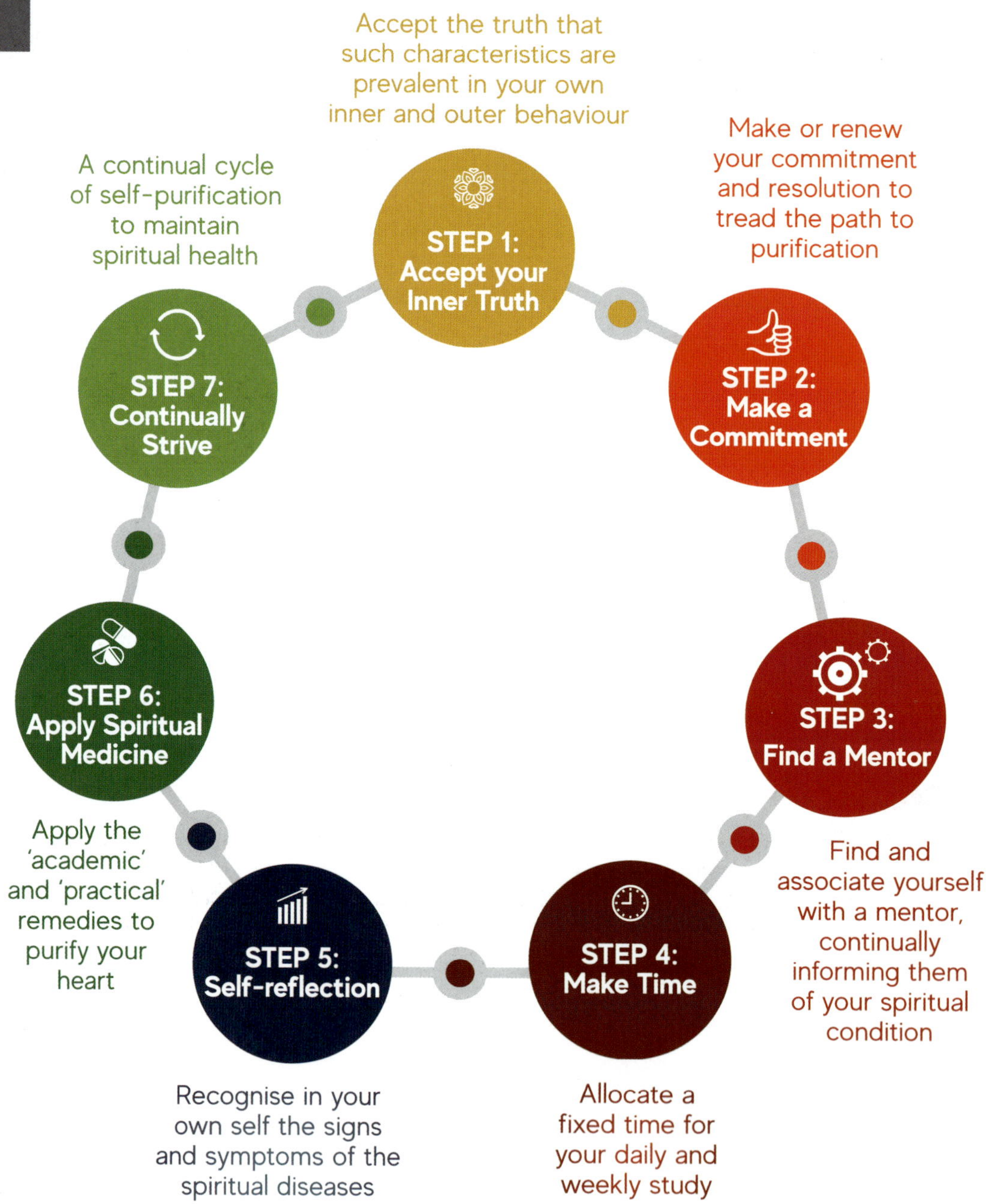

INITIATING A CONTINUAL CYCLE OF SELF-PURIFICATION

Step 1: Accept your Inner Truth

In order to purify yourself, you must accept the truth that such characteristics are present in your own inner and outer behaviour. You can then open your heart and mind and begin to understand and apply the 'academic' remedies, in terms of better understanding the principles of your faith and what constitutes right and wrong, before implementing the 'practical' remedies in earnest.

The ultimate objective of self-purification (and therefore this text) is to seek the divine pleasure (ridwān) of Allāh ﷻ, by undergoing a spiritual struggle to adorn the heart with the lofty attributes of perseverance, gratitude, fear of Allāh ﷻ, hope, abstention, unity, trust, love, truthfulness, remorse, reflection, reckoning, contemplation, and so on.

Indeed, Allāh ﷻ says, "Surely, Allāh would never change a people's state (of favour) until they change their own state (of faith)." [Ar-Ra'ad 13:11]

The Prophet ﷺ said:

- "There is no disease that Allāh has created except that He also has created a treatment" [Ṣaḥīḥ Al-Bukhārī 5678]
- "The one who sent down the disease sent down the remedy" [Al-Muwaṭṭa 744:3474]

Step 2: Make a Commitment

Once you have accepted the truth, you need to make a commitment and a firm resolution to tread the path to purification (a lifelong endeavour). Make constant du'ā to Allāh ﷻ that He eradicates spiritual illnesses from your heart, for in reality He is the real healer of the illnesses.

The Prophet ﷺ said:

- "O Allāh! Grant me the sense of piety and purify my soul as You are the Best to purify it. You are its Guardian and its Protecting Friend" [Musnad Aḥmad 19308]
- "There is a remedy for every malady, and when the remedy is applied to the disease it is cured with the permission of Allāh, the Exalted and Glorious" [Ṣaḥīḥ Muslim 2204:69]

Step 3: Find a Mentor

In the same way that you seek the help and advice of a doctor, you should also find a mentor and stick closely by them, continually informing them of your spiritual condition, discussing your spiritual illnesses and cures, and following their instruction to the best of your ability.

The Prophet ﷺ said, "Scholars are the inheritors of the Prophets." [At-Tirmidhī 2682, Sunan Abī Dawūd 3641]

Imām Al-Ghazālī said, "Know that the traveller should have a master as a guide and instructor, to rid him of bad traits through his instruction and replace them with good ones. The significance of instruction is comparable to the work of the farmer who uproots thorn-bushes and removes weeds from the rest of his crops. Consequently, his plants are in a proper condition, and his yield is brought to perfection." [Letter to a Disciple/Ayyuhāl Walad, p.34-35]

Step 4: Make Time

One of the main reasons for laziness is that you do not set a fixed time for your daily practices; the notable successes in your life are invariably the result of application, timetabled discipline and conscientiousness, so you must allocate a fixed time for daily and weekly study. Keep a close eye on yourself, constantly assessing the condition of your heart throughout the day.

Allāh says, "As for those who struggle in Our cause, We will surely guide them along Our Way. And Allāh is certainly with the good-doers." [Al-'Ankabūt 29:69]

Imām Al-Ghazāli exhorts on the importance of routines, "Your time should not be without structure, such that you occupy yourself arbitrarily with whatever comes along. Rather, you must take account of yourself and order your worship during the day and the night, assigning to each period of time an activity that must not be neglected nor replaced by another activity. By the ordering of this time, the blessing will show in itself." [The Beginning of Guidance/Bidāyah Al-Hidāyah, p.60-61]

Step 5: Self-reflect

You must then review the definitions of all of the diseases alongside the associated signs and symptoms in detail, looking at where such characteristics are present in your own inner and outer behaviour, and select the disease(s) with which you can most closely correlate. Remember that in order to purify yourself, you must begin to recognise and accept the truth.

The Prophet ﷺ said, "In the body there is a morsel of flesh, if it is sound, the whole body is sound. If it is corrupted, the whole body is corrupted. Indeed, it is the heart." [Ṣaḥīḥ Al-Bukhārī 52, Ṣaḥīḥ Muslim 1599:107]

Step 6: Apply Spiritual Medicine

You should then begin to understand and apply the 'academic' remedies, in terms of better understanding your faith and adjusting your mindset, before implementing the 'practical' remedies in earnest.

Allāh ﷻ says, "Successful indeed is the one who purifies their soul." [As-Shams 91:9]

Step 7: Continually Strive

The Prophet ﷺ said, "The one who strives in the way of Allāh the Exalted is he who strives against his soul in the obedience of Allāh." [Musnad Aḥmad 23967]

But just like medical prescriptions, if you apply the techniques that have been compiled from the vast teachings of the Qur'ān and the exemplary model of the Prophet ﷺ, only then will you see results. If you work on your heart by steadily and consistently implementing what is suggested here, you will begin to see changes in your life, your condition, your society, and even within your own family dynamics.

It is a blessing that we have the science of purification, and that this teaching exists in the world today. What remains is for us to take these teachings seriously.

"Successful indeed is the one who purifies their soul, and doomed is the one who corrupts it!" [As-Shams 91: 9-10]

May Allāh ﷻ grant us all the tawfīq and make us from His chosen friends.

Āmīn.

HOW TO USE THIS BOOK

Diseases and Their Definitions
Each spiritual disease has been defined at the start of each chapter to help the reader understand and recognise its characteristics.

Traffic Light Approach
Red, green and amber colours have then been used across each chapter for ease of reference. Hopefully, everyone recognises these universal indicators, but here is a little more in the way of explanation:

- **Red** is used to highlight problem areas, i.e. the signs and symptoms of a spiritual disease and how they manage to creep up on a person
- **Green** is used to highlight where action is required to turn things around, i.e. the potential remedies, both academic or conceptual (e.g. correcting our mind-set or belief system) and practical (day-to-day actions that can be taken to begin to address spiritual ailments). Ultimately, either or both of the two remedies gives each of us an opportunity to move closer to Allāh ﷻ, our Loving Cherisher
- **Amber** is used as a reminder to the reader that there may be exceptions, instances where certain feelings or actions may be permissible (e.g. where anger is felt towards impermissible acts)

Qur'ān & Aḥādīth sources
Throughout the book, the author has used 'The Clear Qur'ān' by Dr Mustafa Khattab and authentic ahādīth sources (such as Ṣaḥīḥ Al-Bukhārī and Ṣaḥīḥ Muslim) with their clear and miraculous insights to spiritual ailments, remedies and exceptions.
The beneficial advice of famous scholars, such as Imām Al-Ghazālī ؒ, has also been incorporated directly from their most famous works. Please note that references have been used more than once where required.

All the sources used have been verified and validated by qualified scholars. Please refer to 'The Handbook Team' and 'Bibliography' sections for further details.

TRANSLITERATION KEY

Vowels

A	Short Vowel as in "Ago"	I	Short Vowel as in "Sit"
Ā	Long Vowel as in "Heart"	Ī	Long Vowel as in "See"
AY	Diphthong as in "Page"	AW	Diphthong as in "Home"
'	Abrupt start or pause	U	Short vowel as in "Put"
Ū	Long Vowel as in "Food"		

Consonants

ب	B	"B" no "H" attached	ص	Ṣ	"S" with full mouth
ت	T	Soft "T", no "H" attached	ض	Ḍ	"D" with full mouth, using sides of tongue
ث	TH	"TH" as in "Thin"	ط	Ṭ	"T" with full mouth
ح	Ḥ	"H" Guttural sound	ظ	Ẓ	"DH" as in "Dhuhr" with full mouth
خ	KH	"KH" Very guttural, no usage of tongue	ع	'	Guttural sound - accompanies vowel
د	D	Soft "D", no "H" attached	غ	GH	"GH" Very guttural, no usage of tongue
ذ	DH	"DH" as in "Adhān"	ق	Q	"K" with back of the tongue raised
س	S	"S" only, not "Z"	و	W	"W" read, not silent
ش	SH	"SH" as in "Shin"	ي	Y	"Y" only, not "I"

NOTE: Double consonants must be pronounced with emphasis on both letters without pause, e.g. Allāhumma should be read al-lāhum-ma.

Allāh is the Arabic word for God, the One True God shared by all classical monotheistic faiths, such as Judaism, Christianity and Islām. Throughout this book the Arabic word for God, Allāh, will be used.

Subhānahū wa ta'āla - May He be glorified

Sallalāhu 'alayhi wa sallam - Allāh's peace and mercy be upon him

'Alayhis salām - Peace be upon him

Radiyallāhu 'anhu - May Allāh be pleased with him

Rahimahullāh - May Allāh have mercy on him

الغَضَب

Anger

TREATMENTS

- Recognise Allāh's ﷻ Power & Rights
- Recognise Your Own Shortcomings
- Recognise Others' Rights (including Social Media)
- Follow the Prophetic Example
- Counsel Children at a Young Age
- Maintain Balance between Anger & Mercy
- Understand Pitfalls of Anger
- Silence, Sitting, Reclining & Ablution
- Diversion & Withdrawal
- Seek Refuge in Allāh ﷻ & Repentance
- Exercise Your Willpower & Take Control (including Social Media)
- Seeking Forgiveness & Pardon
- Controlled Decision-Making
- Forbearance & Humility
- Greater Wisdom in Forgiving

SIGNS & SYMPTOMS

- Rising Tempers & Evils of the Tongue
- Rage & Hatred
- Cutting off Family (& Friendly) Ties
- Creating an Oppressive Environment
- Displeasure with the Divine Decree
- Angry Comments on Social Media

EXCEPTIONS

- Addressing Injustices
- Witness to Impermissible Acts
- Lacking Basic Needs
- Belittlement
- Protective Jealousy

CHAPTER 1

Anger [Ghadab] الغَضَب

Anger can be compared to a chained, restless beast imprisoned in the heat of the midday sun: near-impossible to restrain once it breaks its chains, and doubtless of no benefit to its owner once unleashed. Intense anger or wrath is known as 'ghadab'.

A man asked the Prophet ﷺ "What will keep me away from the anger of Allāh?" The Prophet ﷺ said, "Do not become angry." [Musnad Aḥmad 6635]

The Messenger of Allāh ﷺ became angry at times. He ﷺ once said, "I am one of the sons of Ādam; I get angry as you get angry" [Sunan Abī Dawūd 4659]. The Prophet's ﷺ anger could be seen on his face. But his anger was always in response to a deviation from 'normal' human character and behaviour that would be offensive to Allāh ﷻ.

Scholars agree that anger is not prohibited per se. Indeed it is part of the wisdom behind the Qur'ānic commandment to enjoin what is right and forbid what is evil. However, as much as anger remains an essential quality of the human creation, if is not guided to something useful - if used recklessly and left untamed - it can possess, consume, and ultimately destroy a person.

ANGER

Anger

Signs & Symptoms

Rising Tempers & Evils of the Tongue

Due to your anger, and that of another, a quarrel is stirred and heated to the point of conflict. As is the nature of all things heated, you are both given to stand, rising with feelings of fury

You flare up in anger at the slightest annoyance, and you are even prepared to make the other person non-existent

Rage & Hatred

Your anger also gives rise to hatred, jealousy, evil thoughts, etc. making you detest the other person's enjoyment and happiness (you even feel happiness at the other's pain and suffering)

You have spoilt or ruined your life because of a rash act or statement made in a fit of rage

Cutting off Family (& Friendly) Ties

You have deeply offended and unjustly violated others by your argumentative nature

You have become entirely estranged from your family because of your inability to control your anger

Creating an Oppressive Environment

You have created oppressive environments because of the fear you instill in others, because of your irrational and wild anger

Displeasure with the Divine Decree

You react severely when trials come upon you, because you forget that nothing takes place without Allāh's ﷻ leave and that this life is a testing ground of trials

Angry Comments on Social Media

You send angry comments over social media (e.g. X, Facebook) - an unknown and potentially vast audience reads your ill-judged remarks - instead of contacting the person directly or talking face-to-face

Qur'ānic, Prophetic & Scholarly Evidence

Allāh ﷻ says, "Be moderate in your pace. And lower your voice, for the ugliest of all voices is certainly the braying of donkeys. Have you not seen that Allāh has subjected for you whatever is in the heavens and whatever is on the earth, and has lavished His favours upon you, both seen and unseen? (Still) there are some who dispute about Allāh without knowledge, or guidance, or an enlightening scripture." [Luqmān 31: 19-20]

A man came to the Prophet ﷺ and said, "Advise me" He ﷺ said, "Do not become angry". The man repeated (his request) several times and he ﷺ said, "Do not become angry." [Ṣaḥīḥ Al-Bukhārī 6116]

The Prophet ﷺ said:

- "Whoever thinks highly of himself, or walks with an arrogant attitude, will meet Allāh when He is angry with him" [Al-Adab Al-Mufrad 549]
- "There are no people who went astray after having been guided except for indulging in disputation" [At-Tirmidhī 3253]
- "Do not dispute with your brother, ridicule him, nor promise him and then break your promise" [At-Tirmidhī 1995]
- "The most hated person with Allāh is the most quarrelsome person" [Ṣaḥīḥ Al-Bukhārī 2457, 4532]
- "When two persons indulge in hurling (abuses) upon one another, it would be the first one who would be the sinner so long as the oppressed does not transgress the limits" [Ṣaḥīḥ Muslim 2587:68]

Imām Al-Ghazālī رحمه الله said, "O disciple...do not argue with anyone regarding any issue, insofar as you are able, since there is much that is harmful in it, and 'its evil is greater than its utility.' For it is the origin of every ugly character trait, such as insincerity, envy, haughtiness, resentment, enmity, boastfulness and so on." [Letter to a Disciple/Ayyuhāl Walad, p.42-43]

Anger

Academic Treatment	Qur'ānic, Prophetic & Scholarly Evidence
Recognise Allāh's ﷻ Power & Rights	
You repel or keep your anger under control by recognising that nothing takes place without the leave of Allāh ﷻ	Allāh ﷻ says, "Whatever (pleasure) you have been given is no more than a fleeting enjoyment of this worldly life. But what is with Allāh is far better and more lasting for those who believe and put their trust in their Lord; who avoid major sins and shameful deeds, and forgive when angered." [Ash-Shūrā 42: 36-37]
You have come to recognise that there is no power or might except with Allāh ﷻ, that not an atom moves without the express permission and will of Allāh ﷻ	
You contemplate at the time of anger as to the reason for your outburst, that it was actually because of some divine intervention that 'interfered' with your desires	
Recognise Your Own Shortcomings	
You remind yourself that Allāh ﷻ is your Master, Benefactor, Creator and Sustainer, and that you yourself disobey and commit a multitude of sins and errors, day and night	
You remind yourself that your true Master, who has every right over you, tolerates you and your imperfections, and therefore question where you will be if He punishes you for every mistake	
Recognise Others' Rights (including Social Media)	Allāh ﷻ says, "And hasten towards forgiveness from your Lord and a Paradise as vast as the heavens and the earth, prepared for those mindful (of Allāh). (They are) those who donate in prosperity and adversity, control their anger, and pardon others. And Allāh loves the good-doers." [Āli 'Imrān 3: 133-134] The Prophet ﷺ said: o "A judge should not decide between two parties while angry" [Ṣaḥīḥ Al-Bukhārī 7158, Ṣaḥīḥ Muslim 1717:16] Allāh ﷻ will claim from the tyrannical ruler the rights he usurped even from his non-Muslim subjects o "The most perfect of believers in belief is the best of them in character. The best of you are those who are the best to their women" [At-Tirmidhī 1162] o "None of you truly believes until he loves for his brother what he loves for himself" [Ṣaḥīḥ Al-Bukhārī 13]
You remind yourself that you are not the owner of the person with whom you are angry, that you are not his creator, that you do not sustain him, that you did not give him life, and that you have no right or control over him	
You treat others how you want to be treated in all types of interaction, including online, by doing your best to constantly think of others and empathise with them	
You consider how you would like Allāh ﷻ to deal with you and therefore you lean towards a more compassionate approach in dealing with the person with whom you are angry	

Anger

Academic Treatment	Qur'ānic, Prophetic & Scholarly Evidence
Follow the Prophetic Example	
You remind yourself that out of the thousands of reports about the smallest details of the Prophet's ﷺ life, never has anyone related that the Prophet ﷺ ever did anything unwise or rash	A man came to the Prophet ﷺ and said, "Advise me" He ﷺ said, "Do not become angry". The man repeated (his request) several times and he ﷺ said, "Do not become angry." [Ṣaḥīḥ Al-Bukhārī 6116] The Prophet ﷺ said: o "The believer does not curse" [At-Tirmidhī 2019] o "The believer does not defame, nor curse, nor be indecent, nor is he immodest" [At-Tirmidhī 1977] According to scholars such as Imām An-Nawawī رحمه الله, when the Messenger of Allāh ﷺ said, "Do not become angry," he meant that the preferred behaviour is to be mindful and to guard against anger that overpowers and distorts one's words or actions to the point of dysfunction.
You understand that the Prophet ﷺ never applied his intellectual gifts and Prophetic status for anything other than guiding humanity aright	
You remind yourself that the Prophet ﷺ was the most forbearing and forgiving of people, and that all the Prophets were characterised by these same qualities (none was known to be arrogant or easily angered)	
You come to recognise that the preferred behaviour is to be mindful and to guard against anger that overpowers and distorts one's words or actions to the point of dysfunction	

Academic Treatment	Qur'ānic, Prophetic & Scholarly Evidence
Counsel Children at a Young Age	
You understand that according to one model, the soul has three stages, the second of which is the 'middle' 7 years (8 to 14), the age of anger, when children react strongly to stimuli and are annoyed easily, hence you counsel your children, focusing on training and discipline	The Prophet ﷺ said, "Teach and make things easy, do not make them difficult. If any of you becomes angry, let him keep silent." [Musnad Aḥmad 3448]

Anger

Academic Treatment	Qur'ānic, Prophetic & Scholarly Evidence
Maintain Balance between Anger & Mercy	
You realise that in order to adopt the straight way and not to draw the wrath of Allāh ﷻ upon yourself, you must demonstrate a balance between ghadab (wrath and stern justice) and raḥmah (mercy or the spirit of the law) towards others	The Prophet ﷺ said: o "O 'Uqbah, reconcile with whoever cuts you off, give to whoever deprives you, and turn away from whoever wrongs you" [Musnad Aḥmad 17334] o "O Allāh, You are forgiving and generous. You love to forgive" [Musnad Aḥmad 25384]
You remind yourself that the Messenger of Allāh ﷺ never allowed his anger to get the better of him. He was in control of himself, secure, and always in a state of spiritual certainty	'Āishah (may Allāh be pleased with her) said, "The Prophet ﷺ was not indecent, he was not obscene, he would not shout in the markets, and he would not respond to an evil deed with an evil deed, but rather he would pardon and overlook." [Musnad Aḥmad 25417]
You learn to strike a balance between impulsiveness (that people ultimately regret) and cowardice, knowing that foul words and deeds delivered on impulse are a major cause of shame and regret	
You remind yourself of the reward for when you control yourself in an argument, notwithstanding your being right, that you will be granted a palace in the highest portion of Paradise	
You remind yourself that refraining from any argument, although extremely difficult to do, is regarded as a (sign of) perfection of faith. The preferred state of mind must be: "I might be right and know it, but I do not need to show it," even with the slightest body language or facial expression	The Prophet ﷺ said, "Do not become angry and Paradise will be yours." [At-Targhīb wa At-Tarhīb by Al-Mundhirī 4158]
Understand Pitfalls of Anger	
You realise that you must guard against anger (that is baseless), and that if it is not guided to something useful, it will possess, consume, and ultimately destroy you	The Prophet ﷺ said, "Whoever controls his anger at the time when he has the means to act upon it, Allāh will fill his heart with contentment on the Day of Resurrection." [Al-Mu'jam Aṣ-Ṣaghīr Aṭ-Ṭabarānī 861, Al-Mu'jam Al-Kabīr Aṭ-Ṭabarānī 13646]
You realise that what is mercifully veiled (by Allāh ﷻ) in you can be exposed when you display anger	

Anger

ANGER

Practical Treatment

Qur'ānic, Prophetic & Scholarly Evidence

Practical Treatment	Qur'ānic, Prophetic & Scholarly Evidence
Silence, Sitting, Reclining & Ablution	
If you are overcome by anger, you sit down if you happen to be standing, and lie down if sitting, which will lessen your anger	The Prophet ﷺ advised: o "If any of you becomes angry, let him keep silent." [Musnad Aḥmad 2556, 3448] o "When one of you becomes angry while standing, he should sit down. If the anger leaves him, well and good; otherwise he should lie down" [Sunan Abī Dawūd 4782] o "Verily, anger comes from Satan and Satan was created from fire. Fire is extinguished with water, so if you become angry then perform ablution with water" [Sunan Abī Dawūd 4784] o "I guarantee a house on the outskirts of Paradise for one who leaves arguments even if he is right, and a house in the middle of Paradise for one who abandons lies even when joking, and a house in the highest part of Paradise for one who makes his character excellent" [Sunan Abī Dawūd 4800]
If your anger still does not cool down, then you perform ablution (wuḍū) with cold water, or you drink cold water	
You understand that anger often manifests itself in the face, which becomes red and flushed, and therefore the actual act of splashing water on the face can alter your mood	
Diversion & Withdrawal	
You look to divert your attention by immediately engaging in some other activity, especially reading, which is very effective in curbing anger	
You realise that anger can be entirely irrational and requires nothing more than a change of posture to reconstitute the mind	
You withdraw from the presence of the one who is the object of your anger	
Seek Refuge in Allāh ﷻ & Repentance	Once a person grew very angry before the Prophet ﷺ, who then noticed how when the face shows extreme anger it resembles Satan; the Prophet ﷺ then said, "I have a word, if spoken, will remove it from him. It is, 'I seek refuge in Allāh from Satan the accursed.'" [Ṣaḥīḥ Al-Bukhārī 6115, Ṣaḥīḥ Muslim 2610:109]
You realise that Satan whispers feelings of despair to make you grow despondent of Allāh's ﷻ mercy	
You understand clearly that one of the deceptions of Satan is to make what is easy appear difficult or even impossible	
You do not surrender yourself to the insidious view that you can never repent, so you seek refuge in Allāh ﷻ ('A'ūdhubillāh'), which dissipates the effects of anger	

Anger

Practical Treatment	Qur'ānic, Prophetic & Scholarly Evidence
Exercise Your Willpower & Take Control (including Social Media)	Allāh ﷻ says: o "The (true) servants of the Most Compassionate are those who walk on the earth humbly, and when the foolish address them (improperly), they only respond with peace" [Al-Furqān 25:63] o "(They are) those who do not bear false witness, and when they come across falsehood, they pass (it) by with dignity" [Al-Furqān 25:72] o "No calamity befalls (anyone) except by Allāh's Will. And whoever has faith in Allāh, He will (rightly) guide their hearts (through adversity). And Allāh has (perfect) knowledge of all things" [At-Taghābun 64:11] The Prophet ﷺ said: o "A strong man is not one who defeats (another) in physical combat. Verily, a strong man is he who controls his self at the time of anger" [Ṣaḥīḥ Al-Bukhārī 6114, Ṣaḥīḥ Muslim 2609:107] o "Whoever curbs his anger, while being able to act, Allāh will fill his heart with certainty of faith" [Al-Jāmi' Aṣ-Ṣaghīr 8997] o "Whoever avoids lying while he is doing so wrongly, a house will be built for him on the outskirts of Paradise. Whoever avoids arguing while he is in the right, a house will be built for him in its midst. And whoever has good character, a house will be built for him in its heights" [At-Tirmidhī 1993]
You realise that Allāh ﷻ has endowed you with willpower to control your anger to ensure that it is not misdirected and unjustly employed	
You repeatedly exercise your willpower to curb your anger, and this steadily weakens its demands, and as a consequence curbing your anger becomes a simpler task	
You do not lose hope when losing anything, neither do you display excessive happiness when receiving anything, because you accept that everything you gain or lose has already been decreed before your birth	
You do not display anger or complain or whine when faced by any calamity or difficulty; you are determined not to let this trial or tribulation affect your iman (faith)	
You never act spontaneously in accordance with the dictates of your anger	
You avoid haste at all times, including curbing your desire to respond in anger to a post or comment with which you disagree: instead you adopt patience	

Anger

Practical Treatment	Qur'ānic, Prophetic & Scholarly Evidence
Seeking Forgiveness & Pardon	
Where you have carried out an injustice in the state of anger, it is essential that, after your anger has subsided, you (as the aggressor) apologise publicly You humble yourself in the presence of the one whom you have wronged and seek their pardon, in an effort to restore your anger to a point of equilibrium	Similarly, the Prophet ﷺ said: o "It is not lawful for a Muslim to desert (stop talking to) his brother beyond three nights, the one turning one way and the other turning to the other way when they meet, the better of the two is one who is the first to greet the other" [Ṣaḥīḥ Al-Bukhārī 6077] o "Have taqwā (fear) of Allāh wherever you may be, and follow up a bad deed with a good deed which will wipe it out, and behave well towards the people" [At-Tirmidhī 1987] o "And whoever covers the shortcomings of his brother, Allāh will cover his shortcomings in the Hereafter" [Ṣaḥīḥ Al-Bukhārī 2442, Ṣaḥīḥ Muslim 2580:58]
Controlled Decision-Making	
Where you have authority over people (e.g. as a parent, teacher, ruler or judge), you are not permitted to issue a verdict, make a decision or mete out a punishment while angry, so you postpone it for later You remember that Allāh ﷻ is the defender of the rights of those who have no defender, and He will therefore demand from the aggressor (yourself) the rights of the oppressed	The Prophet ﷺ said: o "A judge should not decide between two parties while angry" [Ṣaḥīḥ Al-Bukhārī 7158, Sunan Abī Dawūd 3589]. Allāh ﷻ will claim from the tyrannical ruler the rights he usurped even from his non-Muslim subjects o Mūsa ﷺ asked Allāh "Who is the most honourable of your servants?" Allāh said: "He who forgives having the power to release (his anger and take revenge)" [Al-Bayhaqī in Shu'ab Al-Īmān 7974] Anas ibn Mālik ؓ said "I never saw a case involving legal retaliation being referred to the Messenger of Allāh ﷺ except that he would recommend pardoning the criminal." [Sunan Abī Dawūd 4497]

Anger

Practical Treatment	Qur'ānic, Prophetic & Scholarly Evidence
Forbearance & Humility	
You strive to remove the factor of anger from the immediate situation because you realise that the main reason you have become angry is because you are filled with yourself; your ego has got in the way You act with wisdom, take time, and think deeply before reacting to something, and then respond to harm with generosity You simply let go by forgiving those who wronged you, even if it is your right to be upset You do not allow insult to penetrate and manipulate your emotion You do not become angry such that people only see your rage; instead, you remain calm and never lose control	Allāh ﷻ says, "Be moderate in your pace. And lower your voice, for the ugliest of all voices is certainly the braying of donkeys. Have you not seen that Allāh has subjected for you whatever is in the heavens and whatever is on the earth, and has lavished His favours upon you, both seen and unseen? (Still) there are some who dispute about Allāh without knowledge, or guidance, or an enlightening scripture." [Luqmān 31: 19-20] The Prophet ﷺ said: o "Whoever humbles himself one degree for the sake of Allāh, Allāh will raise him in status one degree, and whoever behaves arrogantly towards Allāh one degree, Allāh will lower him in status one degree, until He makes him among the lowest of the low" [Ibn Mājah 4176] o "Spreading peace and feeding (the hungry) guarantee you Paradise" [Al-Mu'jam Al-Kabīr Aṭ-Ṭabarānī 467] o "Indeed in Paradise there are chambers whose outside can be seen from their inside, and their inside can be seen from their outside – for those who speak well and feed others" [At-Tirmidhī 2527] o "You have two characteristics that Allāh likes: forbearance and modesty" [Ibn Mājah 4188]
You remind yourself of the extensive praise and goodness associated with forbearance and humility	In their persecution of the Prophet ﷺ, the Quraysh mocked him like children would, but the Prophet ﷺ did not become angry. 'Umar ibn Al-Khattāb رضي الله عنه was known to grow angry, but over the course of his development in Islām, his anger ceased to get the better of him. In fact, it was the opposite. He tended to be forgiving and compassionate, especially near the end of his life.

Anger

Practical Treatment	Qur'ānic, Prophetic & Scholarly Evidence
Greater Wisdom in Forgiving	Allāh ﷻ says: o "Whatever (pleasure) you have been given is (no more than a fleeting) enjoyment of this worldly life. But what is with Allāh is far better and more lasting for those who believe and put their trust in their Lord; who avoid major sins and shameful deeds, and forgive when angered" [Ash-Shūrā 42: 36-37] o "(They are) those who donate in prosperity and adversity, control their anger, and pardon others. And Allāh loves the good-doers" [Āli 'Imrān 3:134] o "We have sent you (O Prophet) only as a mercy for the whole world" [Al-Anbiyā' 21:107] o "The reward of an evil deed is its equivalent. But whoever pardons and seeks reconciliation, then their reward is with Allāh. He certainly does not like the wrongdoers" [Ash-Shūrā 42:40] o "Do not let the people of virtue and affluence among you swear to suspend donations to their relatives, the needy, and the emigrants in the cause of Allāh. Let them pardon and forgive. Do you not love to be forgiven by Allāh? And Allāh is All-Forgiving, Most Merciful" [An-Nūr 24:22] o "And whoever endures patiently and forgives – surely this is a resolve to aspire to" [Ash-Shūrā 42:43] o "O believers! Indeed, some of your spouses and children are enemies to you, so beware of them. But if you pardon, overlook, and forgive their faults , then Allāh is truly All-Forgiving, Most Merciful" [At-Taghābun 64:14] o "Good and evil cannot be equal. Respond (to evil) with what is best, then the one you are in a feud with will be like a close friend" [Fuṣṣilat 41:34] o "Be gracious, enjoin what is right, and turn away from those who act ignorantly" [Al-A'rāf 7:199] o "O believers! Stand firm for Allāh and bear true testimony. Do not let the hatred of a people lead you to injustice. Be just! That is closer to righteousness. And be mindful of Allāh. Surely Allāh is All-Aware of what you do" [Al-Mā'idah 5:8] Similarly, the Prophet ﷺ: o Said that when Allāh ﷻ created the creation as He was upon the Throne, He wrote in His Book: "My mercy overwhelms My Anger" [Ṣaḥīḥ Al-Bukhārī 3194, Ṣaḥīḥ Muslim 2751:14] o Asked the Companions: "What do you consider good wrestling?" to which the Sahabah replied: "The man who is not taken down by others (in wrestling)." The Prophet ﷺ countered with "It is not that, rather it is the one who can control himself when he is angry" [Ṣaḥīḥ Muslim 2608:106]
You understand that Allāh ﷻ regards kindness and mercy as being closer to taqwā (God-consciousness) than wrath and severity	
When you deal with other Muslims, you incline towards leniency and forgiveness, not wrath and severity	
You realise that an act of mercy on your part is more praiseworthy than revenge or retaliation	
You realise that when love is present and is allowed to override your anger, your demand for retribution is calmed	
You learn that mercy issues from wisdom (ḥikmah) and you therefore recognise a greater wisdom in forgiveness and a greater good in being lenient and mild (when you are wronged)	

Anger

Exceptions

Exceptions	Qur'ānic, Prophetic & Scholarly Evidence
Addressing Injustices	
You understand that anger is acceptable only at the right time, in the right place, for the right reasons, and with the right intensity	
You use anger as a positive motivator to address the injustices of the world	The Messenger of Allāh ﷺ became angry at times. He ﷺ once said, "I am one of the sons of Ādam; I get angry as you get angry." [Sunan Abī Dawūd 4659]
You use anger to oppose tyranny and prevent wicked acts and corruption (e.g. exploitation, oppression, personal threats, wrongdoing), however this form of anger is something that needs to be trained	With regard to these causes of anger (e.g. food, shelter), Imām Al-Ghazālī (raḥimahullāh) says that this is healthy if it is not taken to an extreme (e.g. an extreme would be when a person steals from others in order to secure his food and shelter). [Iḥyā 'Ulūm Ad-Dīn 3:57]
You respond with anger when someone threatens your life or family	Imām Al-Ghazālī (raḥimahullāh) said, "O disciple...if an issue arises between you and an individual or a group, and your intention in regard to it is that the truth become known and not lost sight of, discussion is allowed. However there are two indications of this intention. The first is that you make no distinction between the truths being disclosed on your own tongue or that of someone else. The second is that discussion in private is preferable to you than in public." [Letter to a Disciple/Ayyuhāl Walad, p.42-43]
Witness to Impermissible Acts	
When you witness impermissible acts being carried out then you feel anger at such abominations	
Lacking Basic Needs	
When your anger is related to basic needs, such as food, shelter, and life, you feel vulnerable and threatened	

Anger

Exceptions	Qur'ānic, Prophetic & Scholarly Evidence
Belittlement	
You detect when others try to belittle you or when you are the object of contempt and scorn (spoiling your dignity)	Imām Al-Ghazālī says that this (related to dignity) is also healthy, with the similar caveat of avoiding two extremes: haughtiness or pride and abject humiliation. The Prophet ﷺ said, "The believer does not humiliate himself." [Iḥyā 'Ulūm Ad-Dīn 1:46]
Protective Jealousy	
You become angry due to your particular sense of values (dignity). For instance, as a scholar in your field, you become angry when you see a book is being abused; as a labourer, your anger grows when someone damages your tools You show a protective sense of jealousy or ghairah regarding your spouse, or when your honour and prestige is challenged or injured. Your protective jealousy however never extends to oppression of your spouse	The Prophet ﷺ said that he himself exhibited jealousy in the sense of guarding and protecting something or someone important to him; Sa'd ibn 'Ubāda once said, "If I saw a man with my wife I would strike him with the sharp edge of the sword." The Prophet ﷺ said (to his Companions), "Are you astonished by Sa'd's (ghīrah) sense of honour? (By Allāh) I have a greater sense of **ghairah** than he has, and Allāh has a still greater sense of ghīrah than mine." [Ṣaḥīḥ Al-Bukhārī 6846]

كَرَاهِيَةُ المَوْت

Antipathy Towards Death

SIGNS & SYMPTOMS

- Strong Aversion to Death
- Clutching and Grasping at Past Times
- Death & the Hereafter Hold Little Importance

TREATMENTS

- Reality of Death
- Remembrance of Death, Pursuit of Good Deeds & Taking Oneself to Account

EXCEPTIONS

- Fear of Not Being Prepared for the Day of Judgement

CHAPTER 2

Antipathy Towards Death

[Karāhiyat al-Mawt] كَرَاهِيَةُ الْمَوْت

Antipathy towards death is when one flees from the ending that befalls every creature, and becomes annoyed when it is even mentioned. It is as if one chooses to remain completely ignorant of Allāh's ﷻ abundant statements describing the temporary nature of this life. This may be due to an excessive love for dunyā (the world) and chasing after the temporary things of this world.

Allāh ﷻ states:

- "Every soul will taste death" [Āli 'Imrān 3:185]
- "Say, 'The death you are running away from will inevitably come to you. Then you will be returned to the Knower of the seen and unseen, and He will inform you of what you used to do'" [Al-Jumu'ah 62:8]

Fear of death is natural, so one naturally protects oneself from it. When the angels, in the form of human beings, visited the Prophet Ibrāhīm ﷺ, he offered them food. When he saw that they did not reach for the food, he grew fearful. Scholars say that Ibrāhīm ﷺ thought they had come to take his life.

Antipathy Towards Death

Signs & Symptoms

Strong Aversion to Death

You have a strong aversion to death to the point that the mere mention of it makes you feel anxious

When death is mentioned, you consider it a morbid topic that is ill-mannered to discuss

You do not accept the reality of life after death, and deny the concept of reward and punishment for your actions

Clutching and Grasping at Past Times

You have an excessive fondness or weakness for mourning

You might have created a shrine of photographs on social media, or gathered trinkets, mementos and belongings of the deceased in a physical space

Memories of a dead friend or loved one reduce you to regular (yearly) tearful outbursts; sometimes, your heartbreak is so disproportionate that living friends and family call upon you to rein in your emotions and 'pull yourself together', looking at you and wondering if you'll ever shake the grief

Death & the Hereafter Hold Little Importance

You have no or little feeling of guilt in doing wrong, since death, and the afterlife which follows, are not important factors in your life

You view the Day of Judgement as some distant and unremarkable event: to you, ideas such as this stem from stories and fairytales from long ago

Your definition of death is quite vague: it is some sort of indistinct 'never to happen' event before which you are supposed to squeeze in all of life's pleasures

Qur'ānic, Prophetic & Scholarly Evidence

Allāh ﷻ says:

- "Say, 'The death you are running away from will inevitably come to you. Then you will be returned to the Knower of the seen and unseen, and He will inform you of what you used to do'" [Al-Jumu'ah 62:8]
- "Surely Allāh will admit those who believe and do good into Gardens under which rivers flow. As for the disbelievers, they enjoy themselves and feed like cattle. But the Fire will be their home." [Muḥammad 47:12]; the objective (the be-all and end-all) of such people is limited to the life on this earth, and they endeavour to eke out whatever pleasures they can before death
- "But they will never wish for that because of what their hands have done. And Allāh has (perfect) knowledge of the wrongdoers" [Al-Jumu'ah 62:7]
- "Indeed, those who do not expect to meet Us, being pleased and content with this worldly life, and who are heedless of Our signs, they will have the Fire as a home because of what they have committed" [Yūnus 10: 7-8]

The Prophet ﷺ said, "Live as long as you want, but you must die; love whatever you want, but you will become separated from it; and do what you want, but you will be repaid for it!" [Al-Mu'jam Al-Awsaṭ Aṭ-Ṭabarānī 4278]

Antipathy Towards Death

Academic Treatment

Reality of Death

You remind yourself that disliking or glossing over the reality of death in no way distances you from its closeness

You are content with what Allāh, the Exalted, has decreed

You understand that for the believer, there is comfort in death, that it takes you from an abode of difficulty and trial to one of peace and infinite freedom

You realise that everyone will experience the loss of a loved one, and that people who believe in Allāh and the afterlife handle calamities and tribulations capably, including the grimness of death

Qur'ānic, Prophetic & Scholarly Evidence

As Allāh states:

- o "Every soul will taste death" [Āli 'Imrān 3:185]
- o "Wherever you may be, death will overcome you - even if you were in fortified towers" [An-Nisā' 4:78]
- o "(It is) Allāh (Who) calls back the souls (of people) upon their death as well as (the souls) of the living during their sleep. Then He keeps those for whom He has ordained death, and releases the others until (their) appointed time. Surely in this are signs for people who reflect" [Az-Zumar 39:42]

The Prophet said:

- o "Remember (death) often, the terminator of pleasures" [At-Tirmidhī 2307, 2460]
- o "No one of you should die except thinking positively of Allāh" [Ṣaḥīḥ Muslim 2877:82]

When the Prophet lost his son Ibrāhīm, he wept but also praised Allāh, the source of life and death.

Ibn 'Umar used to say, "When you arrive at the evening do not expect to see the morning and when you arrive at the morning do not expect to see the evening. During health, prepare for illness and while you are alive, prepare for death." [Ṣaḥīḥ Al-Bukhārī 6416]

Imām Al-Ghazālī said "O disciple, your destination is the grave, and the people of the graves expect you at any moment to meet up with them. Beware, beware lest you meet up with them without provision!" [Letter to a Disciple/ Ayyuhāl Walad, p.16-17]

Antipathy Towards Death

Practical Treatment

Remembrance of Death, Pursuit of Good Deeds & Taking Oneself to Account

You remind yourself that achieving your goal without effort is just wishful thinking, so you work for what comes after death

When you speak about death, you speak about life and the urgency to live a faithful and wholesome life before death overtakes you

Your knowledge of death directs your heart's activities towards obedience

When you remember death, you promptly seek repentance to rectify your wrong action when you slip or err

When you remember death, you reflect, and as a result you are ennobled with contentment and a lack of greed

In an effort to eliminate love of this world from your heart, you remember death often and do not make extensive plans and preparations

You pass judgement on yourself on a frequent basis, paying close attention to your actions, and taking yourself to account for your 'deeds of the day'

Qur'ānic, Prophetic & Scholarly Evidence

Allāh ﷻ says:

- "Say, 'The death you are running away from will inevitably come to you. Then you will be returned to the Knower of the seen and unseen, and He will inform you of what you used to do'" [Al-Jumu'ah 62:8]
- "Wealth and children are the adornment of this worldly life, but the everlasting good deeds are far better with your Lord in reward and in hope" [Al-Kahf 18:46]

When the Prophet ﷺ lost his son Ibrāhīm, he wept but also praised Allāh ﷻ, the source of life and death.

A man said, "O Messenger of Allāh, which of the people are best?" The Prophet ﷺ said, "One whose life is long and his deeds are good." The man said, "Which of the people are worst?" The Prophet ﷺ said, "One whose life is long and his deeds are evil." [At-Tirmidhī 2330]

A man from the Anṣār asked, "O Prophet of Allāh! Who are the wisest and most honoured of people?" The Prophet ﷺ answered, "Those who remember death most and prepare for it before it arrives. They are the wise and pass away with the honour of this world and the dignity of the next." [Al-Mu'jam Aṣ-Ṣaghīr Aṭ-Ṭabarānī 1008]

The Prophet ﷺ described the world as follows: "What relationship with the world have I? My likeness is as a traveller on a mount, halting in the shade of a tree (for a short) while, only to leave it again and proceed along the way." [Musnad Aḥmad 3709]

The Prophet ﷺ said, "The astute man is the one who passes judgement on himself and works for what is after death, and the fool is the one who pursues vain pleasures and counts on Allāh the Exalted to realise his wishes." [At-Tirmidhī 2459, Ibn Mājah 4260]

Ibn 'Umar (رضي الله عنهما) related that the Prophet ﷺ took hold of his shoulders and said, "Be in the world as if you are a stranger or a traveller." [Ṣaḥīḥ Al-Bukhārī 6416]

Antipathy Towards Death

Exceptions	Qur'ānic, Prophetic & Scholarly Evidence
Fear of Not Being Prepared for the Day of Judgement	Allāh ﷻ says: o "O believers! Be mindful of Allāh and let every soul look to what (deeds) it has sent forth for tomorrow. And fear Allāh, (for) certainly Allāh is All-Aware of what you do" [Al-Ḥashr 59:18] o "And the record (of deeds) will be laid (open), and you will see the wicked in fear of what is (written) in it. They will cry, "Woe to us! What kind of record is this that does not leave any sin, small or large, unlisted?" They will find whatever they did present (before them). And your Lord will never wrong anyone" [Al-Kahf 18:49] o "This is the Hell you were warned of. Burn in it today for your disbelief" [Yā Sīn 36: 63-64]
Your fear of death is entirely influenced by a feeling of not being prepared to meet Allāh ﷻ with a book of good deeds that will tilt the scales in your soul's favour. This worry pushes and compels you to good actions, practically all of the time	
You are fearful of Allāh's ﷻ disapproval, and recall His warnings and punishments upon death, resulting in your turning towards virtue and steering yourself away from sin	

التَواضُعُ المَلْؤُوم

Blameworthy Modesty

SIGNS & SYMPTOMS

- Failure through Shyness
- Supporting the Oppressor

TREATMENTS

— Forthright & Courageous in Condemning Evil & Seeking Knowledge

NO EXCEPTIONS

— Ill-Timed or Ill-Conceived Modesty is always Blameworthy

CHAPTER 3

Blameworthy Modesty

[At-Tawāḍu' al-Malūm] التَواضُعُ المَلْوُوم

In general, modesty is something praised in Islām and is considered virtuous. The type of modesty that becomes blameworthy is that which prevents one from criticising clear brutality or corruption. This form of modesty results in shyness at an unsuitable time, when one instead needs to be direct and courageous. Something blameworthy (munkar) is wrong regardless of the status of the wrongdoer, whether he or she is a close relative or a person normally held in high regard.

Apart from preventing a person from avoiding munkar, unwarranted or blameworthy modesty is also the failure to seek sacred knowledge.

Blameworthy Modesty

Signs & Symptoms	Qur'ānic, Prophetic & Scholarly Evidence
Failure through Shyness	
You fail through shyness to denounce what is undeniably blameworthy	
You fail through hesitancy and awkwardness to ask about important matters from those who know	
Supporting the Oppressor	The Prophet ﷺ said, "When people see an oppressor but do not prevent him from (doing evil), it is likely that Allāh will punish them all." [Sunan Abī Dawūd 4338]
You support the oppressor by taking little or no action (either physically or verbally) to restrain or reprimand them	
You hesitate from supporting the oppressed for fear of negative consequences	

Blameworthy Modesty

Academic & Practical Treatment	Qur'ānic, Prophetic & Scholarly Evidence
Forthright & Courageous in Condemning Evil & Seeking Knowledge	
When you identify an evil, at the very least you denounce it in your heart. Indeed, you know that this action, whilst obligatory, is the weakest demonstration of faith	Allāh ﷻ says: o "And when you come across those who ridicule Our revelations, do not sit with them unless they engage in a different topic. Should Satan make you forget, then once you remember, do not (continue to) sit with the wrongdoing people" [Al An'ām 6:68] o "He has already revealed to you in the Book that when you hear Allāh's revelations being denied or ridiculed, then do not sit in that company unless they engage in a different topic, or else you will be like them. Surely Allāh will gather the hypocrites and disbelievers all together in Hell" [An-Nisā' 4:140]
Your modesty does not prevent you from seeking knowledge in religious affairs	The Prophet ﷺ said: o "Help your brother whether he is an oppressor or is being oppressed." It was said, "O Messenger of Allāh, we help the one being oppressed but how do we help an oppressor?" The Prophet said, "You can restrain him from committing oppression. That will be your help to him" [Ṣaḥīḥ Al-Bukhārī 6952]
You are forthright and courageous, yet manage to employ wisdom (ḥikmah) when condemning an obvious act of corruption or oppression, regardless of the status of the person who is engaged in it (possibly a person of status, wealth or authority)	o "Whosoever of you sees an evil, let him change it with his hand; and if he is not able to do so, then (let him change it) with his tongue; and if he is not able to do so, then with his heart – and that is the weakest of faith" [Ṣaḥīḥ Muslim 49:78]
You do not assist the oppressor (even if he is a relative or close companion): instead you take action to prevent or describe his or her wrong	Umm Sulaym came to the Prophet ﷺ and said, "Verily, Allāh is not shy of (telling you) the truth." She then asked the Prophet ﷺ a question regarding a personal matter. 'Āishah reprimanded Umm Sulaym for being so forthright. However the Prophet ﷺ dismissed 'Āishah's rebuke and praised Umm Sulaym for it. [Ṣaḥīḥ Al-Bukhārī 130, Ṣaḥīḥ Muslim 310:29]
You disengage from conversation by walking away from the gathering, only returning when the topic of discussion has changed	

Blameworthy Modesty

No Exceptions	Qur'ānic, Prophetic & Scholarly Evidence
Ill-Timed or Ill-Conceived Modesty is always Blameworthy	
You realise blameworthy modesty, through shyness, prevents you criticising what is clearly wrong, regardless of the status of the wrongdoer, whether he or she is a close relative or a person normally held in high regard.	Allāh ﷻ says, "You are the best community ever raised for humanity - you encourage good, forbid evil, and believe in Allāh." [Āli 'Imrān 3:110]
You also appreciate that unwarranted or blameworthy modesty is also the failure to seek sacred knowledge.	

BLAMEWORTHY MODESTY

التَّفَاخُر الكِبْر التَّكَبُّر

Boasting
Arrogance & Pride

TREATMENTS

- Remember Your Humble Origins
- Remember the Source of Your Blessings
- Follow the Prophetic Example & Approach to Social Media
- Follow the Honourable Actions of Our Pious Predecessors
- God-Consciousness is the True Criterion
- Reality of Your Lineage
- Avoid Your Own Vanity & Condescending or Belittling Others
- Humble Yourself & Strengthen Your Relationship with Allāh ﷻ
- Recognise that Beauty is Deceptive & Temporary
- Recognise the Consequences of Arrogance
- Silence on Social Media
- Avoiding People of Arrogance
- Showing Humility Towards Others

SIGNS & SYMPTOMS

- Self-Righteousness
- Bragging About Lineage
- Generally Boastful & Arrogant
- Boasting on Social Media
- Bragging About Knowledge
- Arrogance Because of Beauty
- Arrogance due to Wealth, Status & Position
- Arrogance due to Strength
- Arrogance due to Possessing a Lot of Something
- Arrogance due to a Dislike of Submitting to Allāh ﷻ

EXCEPTIONS

- When Not Belittling Others & Showing Gratefulness

CHAPTER 4

Boasting [Tafākhur] التفَاخُر

Arrogance [Kibr] الكِبْر & Pride [Takabbur] التَكَبُّر

In a nutshell, tafākhur (boasting) and kibr (arrogance) are to willingly and consciously regard oneself superior to others in religious or worldly matters in a way which creates contempt in the heart for others. What is suggested here is unhealthy glorification of the self.

For the person practising Islām, this 'I am better than you' mentality is forbidden. Ironically - and perhaps fittingly - the person who allows arrogance into their heart usually finds that other people come to dislike him or her.

There are many forms of pride, most being subtle and creeping. It works its way into the heart and influences the character of a believer when he or she fails to adequately check their intentions.

Allāh ﷻ says, "So do not (falsely) elevate yourselves. He knows best who is (truly) righteous." [An-Najm 53:32]

The Prophet ﷺ said, "Arrogance is refusing to admit the truth and considering people inferior." [Ṣaḥīḥ Muslim 91:147, Al-Ḥākim 7367]

The Prophet ﷺ warned against arrogance: "No one will enter Paradise who has an atom's weight of arrogance in his heart" [Ṣaḥīḥ Muslim 91:147, 91:149]. Similar to this is pride (or takabbur), which is to think of oneself as being closer to perfection in attributes than others.

Boasting, Arrogance & Pride

Signs & Symptoms	Qur'ānic, Prophetic & Scholarly Evidence
Self-Righteousness	
As a 'religious person' you start to believe that you are better than other people	
You become lofty or self-righteous particularly when you observe that other people are in the state of disobedience	
You show contempt and scorn for others, and act arrogantly because you hold the notion that there are very few who are your equal in the sight of Allāh ﷻ	Allāh ﷻ Himself reveals His dislike of bragging: "And do not turn your nose up to people, nor walk pridefully upon the earth. Surely Allāh does not like whoever is arrogant, boastful." [Luqmān 31:18]
You feel that it is necessary for people to respect and honour you, and you are therefore offended when people do not approach you with humility	The Arabs used to shout out, "I am the son of so and so!" claiming somehow that one's pedigree suffices as a mark of one's status and privilege, an ethic that loomed large in pre-Islāmic Arab social structure (e.g. if a man from the Arabs was born into a clan known for generosity, it was mandatory for him to be generous).
Bragging About Lineage	
You brag about your ancestry, 'borrowing' from some past nobility	
You regard yourself as one from a 'high birth' and therefore feel obliged to behave nobly; you feel and act superior simply because of your race or lineage	
You feel honoured by having lineage traceable to the Prophet ﷺ and his family, but you do not pay much heed to ensuring your actions are likewise honourable	

Boasting, Arrogance & Pride

Signs & Symptoms

Generally Boastful & Arrogant

You are very easily offended or annoyed when you perceive someone has scolded you

You take offence when others do not greet you first or offer you respect

You walk with a swank and swagger, and cannot be in the company of others without speaking about yourself or drawing attention to what you have done

Your boasting evokes objection and no one likes it

When you walk in public, you tend to step ahead of others, and when you sit in a gathering then you occupy the front or 'honourable' spot

You look at others condescendingly and with disdain (belittling others)

When you are advised then you usually draw offence from it

You do not accept even the truth when it is presented to you

You attempt to attain the mere appearance of humility

Boasting on Social Media

You use social media to 'post and boast' your latest achievement or experience

Bragging About Knowledge

You deem yourself superior to others for being blessed with knowledge and you seek adoration

Qur'ānic, Prophetic & Scholarly Evidence

Allāh ﷻ says:

- "Indeed, Korah was from the people of Moses, but he behaved arrogantly towards them. We had granted him such treasures that even their keys would burden a group of strong men. (Some of) his people advised him, "Do not be prideful! Surely Allāh does not like the prideful" [Al-Qaṣaṣ 28:76]
- "So enter the gates of Hell, to stay there forever. Indeed, what an evil home for the arrogant!" [An-Naḥl 16:29]
- "Know that this worldly life is no more than play, amusement, luxury, mutual boasting, and competition in wealth and children. This is like rain that causes plants to grow, to the delight of the planters. But later the plants dry up and you see them wither, then they are reduced to chaff. And in the Hereafter there will be either severe punishment or forgiveness and pleasure of Allāh, whereas the life of this world is no more than the delusion of enjoyment" [Al-Ḥadīd 57:20]
- "No calamity (or blessing) occurs on earth or in yourselves without being (written) in a Record before We bring it into being. This is certainly easy for Allāh. (We let you know this) so that you neither grieve over what you have missed nor boast over what He has granted you. For Allāh does not like whoever is arrogant, boastful" [Al-Ḥadīd 57: 22-23]
- The Qur'ān lays waste to false claims of superiority and states that the only rank that matters relates to one's relationship with Allāh; "Surely the most noble of you in the sight of Allāh is the most righteous among you. Allāh is truly All-Knowing, All-Aware" [Al-Ḥujurāt 49:13]

The Prophet ﷺ said:

- "Might is His garment (Allāh) and pride is His cloak; (Allāh says) whoever seeks to compete with Me concerning them, I will punish him" [Ṣaḥīḥ Muslim 2620:136]
- "On the Day of Resurrection, the arrogant will be gathered like ants in the form of men. Humiliation will overwhelm them from all sides. They will be driven to a prison in Hell called Buwlas, with the hottest fire rising over them, and they will be given to drink of the juice of the inhabitants of Hell, which is Tīnat al-Khabāl" [At-Tirmidhī 2492]. **In another ḥadīth we find the Prophet's** ﷺ **definition of** Tīnat al-Khabāl ... **It was said:** "O Allāh's Messenger! What is Tīnat al-Khabāl?" **He answered,** "It is the sweat that the people of the Hellfire ooze or their seepage (of flesh and bones)" [Ṣaḥīḥ Muslim 2002:72]

Imām Al-Ghazālī (raḥimahullāh) said, "People of knowledge are in greater danger of arrogance than anyone else" **because the knowledge they have attained may lead them to feelings of superiority.** [Iḥyā 'Ulūm Ad-Dīn 3:347]

Boasting, Arrogance & Pride

Signs & Symptoms	Qur'ānic, Prophetic & Scholarly Evidence
Arrogance Because of Beauty You display arrogance owing to your beauty	Allāh says, "(Imagine, O Prophet) how many peoples We have destroyed before them, who were far better in luxury and splendour!" [Maryam 19:74] The Messenger of Allāh said, "He who has a grain of pride in his heart will not enter Paradise." [Ṣaḥīḥ Muslim 91-148]
Arrogance due to Wealth, Status & Position You display arrogance due to wealth, status and/or position, and show contempt to those of lesser means	Allāh says, "So enter the gates of Hell, to stay there forever. Indeed, what an evil home for the arrogant!" [An-Naḥl 16:29]
Arrogance due to Strength You show arrogance because of your physical strength, which you think none can match	Until his conversion to Islām, the Quraysh's strongest man, Rukānah, was not fond of the Prophet. As is famously recorded in the books of ḥadīth, a wrestling challenge took place between the two men. While the story is most entertaining and remarkable for showing us the miraculous positive use of strength and wisdom on the part of the Prophet Muḥammad, it also recounts that, in the 7th and 21st Centuries alike, young men in particular tend to take pride in physical strength. It was arrogance and pride that prevented Rukānah from accepting defeat until he was body-slammed for the third time: "I've never been thrown to the ground," the challenger said. [Marāsīl of Abū Dawūd, 308]
Arrogance due to Possessing a Lot of Something You show arrogance because you have a lot of something You boast of having many friends, especially those in so-called 'high places' **Arrogance due to a Dislike of Submitting to Allāh** You find all good acts difficult because you feel your wealth, strength, and prestige are born out of your own devices, hence you don't 'see the need' You find the Muslim prayer objectionable because of its postures of humility and awe before Allāh Your struggle is not merely with the postures of the Muslim prayer but your aversion to being Allāh's servant and submission to Him, claiming that you are 'free' to pursue your own whims and passions	Allāh says: o "He certainly does not like those who are too proud" [An-Naḥl 16:23] o "When you see them, their appearance impresses you. And when they speak, you listen to their (impressive) speech. But they are (just) like (worthless) planks of wood leaned (against a wall). They think every cry is against them. They are the enemy, so beware of them. May Allāh condemn them! How can they be deluded (from the truth)?" [Al-Munāfiqūn 63:4] There are dire warnings with regard to pride. Allāh has warned that, "Enter the gates of Hell, to stay there forever. What an evil home for the arrogant!" [Ghāfir 40:76] People rejected the Prophet's message not because they were not convinced. They knew that what the Prophet brought was the truth from Allāh Himself, but they rejected him out of arrogance.

Boasting, Arrogance & Pride

Academic Treatment	Qur'ānic, Prophetic & Scholarly Evidence
Remember Your Humble Origins You remember your humble organic origins, that your beginning was from an impure drop of sperm and your end is a rotten corpse, which will be food for worms and other creatures	As the Qur'ān reminds us, we are created from a drop of semen "Were they not (once) a sperm-drop emitted?" [Al-Qiyāmah 75:37]
You remind yourself of times when you have been afflicted, and so you sit down feeling helpless You remind yourself that on the Day of Resurrection you will be gathered in a small form like an ant, with the potential to be trampled underfoot	Allāh says: o "Condemned are (disbelieving) humans! How ungrateful they are (to Allāh)! From what substance did He create them? He created them from a sperm-drop, and ordained their development" ['Abasa 80: 17-19] o "Let people then consider what they were created from! (They were) created from a spurting fluid, stemming from between the backbone and the ribcage" [At-Ṭāriq 86: 5-7] o "Is there not a period of time when each human is nothing yet worth mentioning? (For) indeed, We (alone) created humans from a drop of mixed fluids, (in order) to test them, so We made them hear and see" [Al-Insān 76: 1-2]
Remember the Source of Your Blessings You remind yourself not to forget that your wealth, strength, your intellect and capacity for insight and judgement are all blessings from Allāh and something you are responsible for You remind yourself that both wealth and health are unstable You remember that such blessings can be removed with one fell swoop and that Allāh can select any which way He chooses to restrict wealth and diminish health	Allāh says: o "(He is the One) Who created life and death in order to test which of you is best in deeds. And He is the Almighty, All-Forgiving" [Al-Mulk 67:2] o "Have We not given them two eyes, a tongue, and two lips; and shown them the two ways (of right and wrong)? If only they had attempted the challenging path (of goodness instead)!" [Al-Balad 90: 8-11]

Boasting, Arrogance & Pride

Academic Treatment	Qur'ānic, Prophetic & Scholarly Evidence

Follow the Prophetic Example & Approach to Social Media

- You remind yourself that the Prophet ﷺ himself, the best of creation, remained humble
- You remind yourself that the Prophet ﷺ was a true slave of Allāh ﷻ in each and every way, treating all people with the utmost kindness, and that his character was one of complete humility based on sincerity towards Allāh ﷻ and compassion towards the slaves of Allāh ﷻ
- You remind yourself that one of the greatest tricks of the internet, with its chat rooms and comment sections, is to make you feel accomplished and productive after giving your views in a debate and discrediting someone else
- You learn to be less concerned about being right, and more concerned about upholding good moral conduct no matter what the circumstance
- You remember that the most villainous beings in history were filled with arrogance and false pride: i.e. Satan, Fir'awn, the opponents of the Prophet ﷺ and many tyrants since

Allāh ﷻ:

- Says, "And you are truly (a man) of outstanding character" [Al-Qalam 68:4]
- Instructed His beloved Prophet ﷺ, "And be gracious to the believers who follow you" [As-Shu'arā' 26:215]

The Prophet ﷺ said:

- "And no one humbles himself before Allāh but Allāh will raise him (in status)" [Ṣaḥīḥ Muslim 2588:69]
- "I guarantee a house on the outskirts of Paradise for one who leaves arguments even if he is right, and a house in the middle of Paradise for one who abandons lies even when joking, and a house in the highest part of Paradise for one who makes his character excellent" [Sunan Abī Dawūd 4800]

Anas ؓ said, "I served the Prophet for ten years and he never told me, 'Uff!' Nor did he ever scold me by saying, 'Why did you do such and such a thing or why did you not do such a thing?'" [Ṣaḥīḥ Al-Bukhārī 6038]

Follow the Honourable Actions of Our Pious Predecessors

- You take time to study the personalities of the Companions of the Prophet ﷺ and reflect on how incredibly great and humble these people were

Muḥammad ibn Al-Ḥanafiyyah said, "I asked my father (ʿAlī ibn Abī Ṭālib ؓ), 'Who are the best people after Allāh's Messenger?' He said, 'Abū Bakr.' I asked, 'Who then?' He said, 'Then ʿUmar.' I was afraid he would say 'Uthmān (next), so I said, 'Then you?' He said, 'I am only a person from amongst the Muslims.'" [Ṣaḥīḥ Al-Bukhārī 3671]

- You feel honoured by having lineage traceable to the Prophet ﷺ and his family, and ensure that your actions are likewise honourable

Imām Al-Ghazālī ؒ said, "If one wishes to master calligraphy, then he must go to a master calligrapher and repeat what he does." [Iḥyā 'Ulūm Ad-Dīn 3:59]

- You realise that it is better to be humble, and even to simulate humility, than it is to be an outright arrogant person

The scholars say the following: "If you are not like the real people, at least mimic them."

Boasting, Arrogance & Pride

Academic Treatment	Qur'ānic, Prophetic & Scholarly Evidence
God-Consciousness is the True Criterion	
You understand that pompous actions will not enter you into Paradise, hence as a 'religious' person, you remind yourself that you have little to be boastful of	**Allāh ﷻ says,** "Surely the most noble of you in the sight of Allāh is the most righteous among you. Allāh is truly All-Knowing, All-Aware." [Al-Ḥujurāt 49:13]
You learn that taqwā or God-consciousness (piety, fear of Allāh ﷻ) is the true criterion of superiority	**The Prophet ﷺ said,** "Verily, none of you will enter Paradise by his deeds alone." [Ṣaḥīḥ Al-Bukhārī 5673, Ṣaḥīḥ Muslim 2816:71]
Reality of Your Lineage	**Allāh ﷻ says,** "Surely the most noble of you in the sight of Allāh is the most righteous among you. Allāh is truly All-Knowing, All-Aware." [Al-Ḥujurāt 49:13]"
You realise that only a foolish person struts around with pride because of the good name or notable qualities of someone else (e.g. the bravery, generosity or wealth of a father or grandfather)	**The Messenger of Allāh ﷺ addressed the people on the day of the conquest of Makkah and said,** "O people, verily Allāh has taken away from you the arrogance of Jāhiliyyah* (PTO) and its pride in forefathers. People are of two types: righteous and pious who are dear to Allāh and doomed evildoers who are insignificant before Allāh. People are the descendants of Ādam, and Allāh created Ādam from dust." [At-Tirmidhī 3270]
You appreciate that you do not know the final destination of that forefather upon whose reputation you rely, that it is instead possible that he became fuel for the Fire of Jahannam and yearns that he had rather been created a dog or pig, so that he could be saved from his present dilemma	
You understand that if your forefathers were around even they would express surprise at your behaviour, which is based wholly on their achievements	**Abū Naḍrah narrates,** "Someone who heard the khutbah of the Messenger of Allāh ﷺ on the second of the days of at-Tashrīq told me that he said: 'O people, verily your Lord is One and your father is one. Verily there is no superiority of an Arab over a non-Arab or of a non-Arab over an Arab, or of a red man over a black man, or of a black man over a red man, except in terms of taqwā. Have I conveyed the message?' They said: 'The Messenger of Allāh ﷺ has conveyed the message.'" [Musnad Aḥmad 23489]
You remind yourself that the Qur'ān lays waste to false claims of superiority and states that the only rank that matters relates to one's relationship with Allāh ﷻ	**The Prophet ﷺ said,** "He who is made slow by his actions will not be speeded by his genealogy." [Sunan Abī Dawūd 3643]

Boasting, Arrogance & Pride

Academic Treatment	Qur'ānic, Prophetic & Scholarly Evidence
Avoid Your Own Vanity & Condescending or Belittling Others	
You remind yourself that knowledge which gives rise to pride is worse than ignorance, and that true knowledge is such that the more you acquire, the greater the increase in your fear and awe of Allāh ﷻ	Allāh ﷻ says: o "I will turn away from My signs those who act unjustly with arrogance in the land" [Al-'A'rāf 7:146] In this we see that Allāh ﷻ recompenses the arrogant ones by turning them away from understanding His Book, His Prophets, and His signs o "This is how Allāh seals the heart of every arrogant tyrant" [Ghāfir 40:35] o "Without a doubt, Allāh knows what they conceal and what they reveal. He certainly does not like those who are too proud" [An-Naḥl 16:23]
You understand that Allāh ﷻ looks at the hearts of man and not their physical appearance	
You remind yourself that regardless of how much knowledge you may possess, there is no guarantee that your end will be good	One of the attributes of Allāh ﷻ is 'Al-Mutakabhir' (the Proud), which is reserved for Himself, hence it is not becoming for anyone to have such intense pride in his or her heart.
You remind yourself that, on the contrary, regardless of how ignorant another person may be, there is no guarantee that he will not meet a good end	The Prophet ﷺ said: o "O Allāh, I take refuge in Thee from knowledge which is not useful!" [Ṣaḥīḥ Muslim 2722, Sunan Abī Dawūd 1548, At-Tirmidhī 3482] o "No one will enter Paradise who has an atom's weight of arrogance in his heart" [Ṣaḥīḥ Muslim 91:148]
You recognise there may be vanity in your own heart, and therefore avoid any possibility of condescending others	
You are aware in yourself that when others indulge in wrongdoing you cannot afford to belittle them in your own heart. After all, they surely have the capacity to be overcome with feelings of shame, and therefore they can be inspired towards repentance	*Jāhiliyyah is the condition which the majority of Arabs were in prior to Islām, which manifest in their: ~ ignorance of Allāh ﷻ and His Messengers ~ boasting about lineage ~ general pride and haughtiness ~ insufficient knowledge of the revealed laws of religion

Boasting, Arrogance & Pride

Academic Treatment	Qur'ānic, Prophetic & Scholarly Evidence
Humble Yourself & Strengthen Your Relationship with Allāh ﷻ	
You reflect on the splendour, glory, and majesty of Allāh ﷻ, and therefore realise your own humble position You ponder over your limitations: without Allāh ﷻ you are unfortunate, weak and helpless You appreciate that you cannot be both arrogant and grateful at the same time, and that humility, by its nature, gives rise to gratitude You show humility (dhul) with respect to Allāh ﷻ You show no aversion to being Allāh's ﷻ servant, by submitting to Him rather than submitting to your whims and passions You make postures of humility and awe before Allāh ﷻ (i.e. the Muslim prayer) You get to know yourself, your origins, and your ultimate return, recognising that humbling yourself for the sake of Allāh ﷻ elevates you in rank You remind yourself that it was arrogance and pride that made Satan a deviant	The Qur'ān lays waste to false claims of superiority and states that the only rank that matters relates to one's relationship with Allāh ﷻ: "Surely the most noble of you in the sight of Allāh is the most righteous among you. Allāh is truly All-Knowing, All-Aware." [Al-Hujurāt 49:13] The Prophet ﷺ said, "I am the most noble of the children of Ādam with my Lord and I am not boasting" [At-Tirmidhī 3610]. His honour was entirely based on his servitude to Allāh ﷻ, not wealth, lineage, power, or authority.
Recognise that Beauty is Deceptive & Temporary	
You realise that beauty can be the most illusory of things You notice the impact that social conditioning (e.g. social media, advertising, social influences) has on you and the way you (feel you need to) present yourself You recognise that you actually have nothing to do with your beauty because Allāh ﷻ is Al-Muṣawwir (the Fashioner, the Shaper, the Designer); it is He who gives all things their shape and form You realise that beauty fades, as the pressures of age and stress wear out flesh and bones You remind yourself that a temporary quality like beauty can be totally transformed by just a single bout of fever or illness You focus on what really matters, which is the content of your character, your beliefs, and your deeds, and reflect on the importance of addressing your inner impurities and defects	Allāh ﷻ says, "Surely the most noble of you in the sight of Allāh is the most righteous among you. Allāh is truly All-Knowing, All-Aware." [Al-Hujurāt 49:13] The Prophet ﷺ said, "Allāh does not look at your outward appearance and your wealth, rather He looks at your hearts and deeds." [Sahīh Muslim 2564:34]

Boasting, Arrogance & Pride

Academic Treatment

Recognise the Consequences of Arrogance
You recognise that justice will always follow every vice, that the possessors of arrogance will end up being the most abject people in the Hereafter
You remind yourself that on the Day of Resurrection, the arrogant will envy those whom they once thought to be beneath them in honour and status (i.e. those who were patient, grateful, and humble in this life)
You allow the lessons from the Qur'ān to inform you of the dishonour that Allāh ﷻ inflicted upon past communities because of their barefaced rejection of Allāh ﷻ, their mocking of His apostles, and their mockery of His laws
You realise that boasting universally evokes objection, that typically no one likes a boaster, and that the station of arrogance invites only humiliation

Qur'ānic, Prophetic & Scholarly Evidence

The Prophet ﷺ said:

- "It is not for the believer to humiliate himself" [At-Tirmidhī 2254]; being humble is different from humiliation
- "On the Day of Resurrection, the arrogant will be gathered like ants in the form of men. Humiliation will overwhelm them from all sides. They will be driven to a prison in Hell called Buwlas, with the hottest fire rising over them, and they will be given to drink of the juice of the inhabitants of Hell, which is Tīnat al-Khabāl" [At-Tirmidhī 2492]. In another ḥadīth we find the Prophet's ﷺ definition of Tīnat al-Khabāl ... It was said: "O Allāh's Messenger! What is Tīnat al-Khabāl?" He answered, "It is the sweat that the people of the Hellfire ooze or their seepage (of flesh and bones)" [Ṣaḥīḥ Muslim 2002:72]

Boasting, Arrogance & Pride

Practical Treatment	Qur'ānic, Prophetic & Scholarly Evidence
Silence on Social Media	The Qur'ān teaches us to seek refuge in Allāh ﷻ: "Say (O Prophet), "I seek refuge in the Lord of the daybreak from the evil of whatever He has created, and from the evil of the night when it grows dark, and from the evil of those (witches casting spells by) blowing onto knots, and from the evil of an envier when they envy." [Al-Falaq 113: 1-5] The Prophet ﷺ said, "He who believes in Allāh and the Last Day must either speak good or remain silent." [Ṣaḥīḥ Muslim 47:74]
You remind yourself that these bounties you are tempted to flaunt via social media may prompt jealousy and envy among others, so you preserve and protect them	
Aside from their stimulating jealousy among others, you're well aware that the exploits of this world are temporary. For this reason, and because you realise that it is better to remain reserved, you shy from posting images of yourself, your experiences or your achievements	
You have come to appreciate the near meaninglessness of accumulating 'followers' on social media. Instead, you hope to communicate with any 'follower' in a beneficial way	
Avoiding People of Arrogance	Allāh ﷻ says: o "Worship Allāh (alone) and associate none with Him. And be kind to parents, relatives, orphans, the poor, near and distant neighbours, close friends, (needy) travellers, and those (bondspeople) in your possession. Surely Allāh does not like whoever is arrogant, boastful" [An-Nisā' 4:36] o "And do not turn your cheek away from people, and do not walk on the earth haughtily. Surely, Allāh does not like anyone who is arrogant, proud. And be moderate in your walk, and lower your voice. Surely, the ugliest of voices is the voice of the donkeys" [Luqmān 31: 18-19] o "And so We have made you (believers) an upright community so that you may be witnesses over humanity" [Al-Baqarah 2:143]
You realise that arrogant people are hated by other people just as they are hated by Allāh ﷻ; humble, tolerant and gentle people are much more beloved	
You avoid those who are harsh and cruel to people	
Showing Humility Towards Others	
As a wealthy person, you still adopt humility, humbling yourself in the presence of those whom you might be tempted to regard as your inferiors	
You learn that taqwā or God-consciousness (piety, fear of Allāh ﷻ) is the true criterion of superiority	
You balance the idea that humility is a praiseworthy virtue with the consciousness that excess can lead to dishonour. You stick to this code of uprightness (following the Islāmic ethic of wasaṭā)	
You recognise that abject humiliation is disapproved of even in the face of tribulation, so you face tests with dignity and patience	
To oppose any level of arrogance, you encourage and train yourself to spend on the orphan, relieve the distressed, and incline yourself to all good acts. You identify the acts that would be difficult on the 'arrogant' self, and work closely towards them	

Boasting, Arrogance & Pride

Exceptions

When Not Belittling Others & Showing Gratefulness

If you express your pride in something, it will not be forbidden if you do not intend to belittle another, and if you consider that thing to be a blessing of Allāh ﷻ

Qur'ānic, Prophetic & Scholarly Evidence

The Prophet ﷺ said, "No one will enter Paradise who has an atom's weight of arrogance in his heart." A person said: Verily a person loves that his dress should be fine, and his shoes should be fine. The Prophet replied "Verily, Allāh is Graceful and He loves Grace. Arrogance is disdaining the truth (out of self-conceit) and contempt for the people." [Ṣaḥīḥ Muslim 91:147]

كَرَاهِيَةُ الإِسْتِنْكَار

Displeasure with Blame or Disapproval

SIGNS & SYMPTOMS	TREATMENTS	EXCEPTIONS
Not Encouraging Right & Forbidding Wrong	Only Allāh ﷻ Benefits & Harms	When Allāh ﷻ or Someone Rightly Guided Disapproves
Social Media & Spoiling Your Intention	Self-Reflection	
Engaging in Forbidden Matters & Neglecting Obligations	Defend the Truth for the Sake of Allāh ﷻ	
	Use Wisdom to Inform the Truth	

CHAPTER 5

Displeasure with Blame or Disapproval

[Karāhiyat al-Istinkār] كَرَاهِيَةُ الإِسْتِنْكَار

This particular undesirable behaviour is so extremely efficient in steering a person towards a love of this world that it can come to form a considerable barrier between a person and the station of iḥsān (excellence in worship).

Being uneasy at the thought of blame or criticism, and searching for praise from Allāh's ﷻ creation, one forgets that true praise is for the Creator and the most deserving, Allāh ﷻ, the 'Ḥamīd'. This crucial understanding slips away, and takes with it the integrity of the individual who so panders to his or her own whims and yearns for the approval of others.

Displeasure with Blame or Disapproval

Signs & Symptoms

Not Encouraging Right & Forbidding Wrong

You give up encouraging what is right for fear of earning other people's displeasure

You deny the existence of divine values for the sake of gaining the praise and approval of people

To avoid other people's blame or disapproval, you fail to stand as a witness to the truth, irrespective of right or wrong

Social Media & Spoiling Your Intention

You demonstrate an addictive (repetitive) use of social media, which leads to disappointment, displeasure and in some cases depression

You experience annoyance when you do not receive the number of expected 'likes' having posted the latest 'selfie', or any visual shot that you consider worthy of the gaze of others (including your most recent plate of food!)

Your quest for pleasing people or seeking their favour interferes with your intention to do deeds for the sake of Allāh ﷻ

Engaging in Forbidden Matters & Neglecting Obligations

You possess an excessive fear of blame and criticism. This often centres on your worry of how people may perceive you when you practise your faith, which leads you to neglecting your obligations or engaging in prohibited matters

Qur'ānic, Prophetic & Scholarly Evidence

The Prophet ﷺ said:

- "Allāh does not send His punishment on all the people for the sins of a specific group until they see wrong around them ,and despite being capable of preventing it, they do not prevent it. If they do this, then Allāh will punish all the people and the specific group" [Musnad Aḥmad 17720]
- "I swear by Allāh, the One in whose hands my life is, continue to order and guide people towards virtuous deeds and prevent people from immoral acts and sins. Otherwise, Almighty Allāh will surely send His severe punishment upon you. Then you will call upon Him, but He will not respond to you" [At-Tirmidhī 2169]

Displeasure with Blame or Disapproval

Academic Treatment

Only Allāh ﷻ Benefits & Harms

You believe that if you are beloved in the eyes of Allāh ﷻ, then the criticism of people cannot harm you

You remind yourself that the criticism of the people is due to some imagined temporary factor, whereas displeasing Allāh ﷻ can cause disgrace and dishonour in this world and the next

You fulfil your obligations because you do not worry about how people will receive you when you practise your faith

You overcome a barrier by realising that there is no benefit or harm except by Allāh's ﷻ permission and plan, the Possessor of all dominion

Self-Reflection

You acknowledge your own wrongdoings, admitting to yourself your own weaknesses, and learn from them by correcting them

Qur'ānic, Prophetic & Scholarly Evidence

Two of Allāh's ﷻ most excellent names are An-Nāf'i and Aḍ-Ḍārr, the Giver of Benefit and the Bringer of Harm.

Allāh ﷻ says:

- "Whatever good befalls you is from Allāh and whatever evil befalls you is from yourself. We have sent you (O Prophet) as a messenger to (all) people. And Allāh is sufficient as a Witness" [An-Nisā' 4:79]
- "Indeed, Allāh does not wrong people in the least, but it is people who wrong themselves" [Yūnus 10:44]
- "Whatever affliction befalls you is because of what your own hands have committed. And He pardons much" [Ash-Shūrā 42:30]
- "Indeed, Allāh would never change a people's state (of favour) until they change their own state (of faith)" [Ar-Ra'ad 13:11]
- "Say, 'Nothing will ever befall us except what Allāh has destined for us. He is our Protector.' So in Allāh let the believers put their trust" [At-Tawbah 9:51]

Displeasure with Blame or Disapproval

Practical Treatment	Qur'ānic, Prophetic & Scholarly Evidence
Defend the Truth for the Sake of Allāh ﷻ In matters of truth, you react indifferently to praise or condemnation, because your heart is filled with those things in which the pleasure and happiness of Allāh ﷻ lie You are willing to defend the truth no matter how unpopular it may be, realising that truth has the power to penetrate the hearts of people You do something only for the sake of Allāh ﷻ, and remind yourself that your deeds cannot share other intentions, namely, pleasing people or seeking their favour (whether someone praises you or not is entirely inconsequential)	The Prophet ﷺ said: o "Whoever seeks to please Allāh with something displeasing to people, then Allāh will be sufficient for him. Whoever seeks to please people with something displeasing to Allāh, then Allāh will hand him over to the people" [Ibn Ḥibbān 277] o "Be mindful of Allāh, and Allāh will protect you. Be mindful of Allāh, and you will find Him in front of you. If you ask, ask of Allāh. If you seek help, seek help from Allāh. Know that if the whole nation were to gather together to benefit you with anything, it would benefit you only with something that Allāh had already prescribed for you. And if (the whole nation) were to gather together to harm you, it would harm you only with something that Allāh had already prescribed for you. The pens have been lifted and the ink has dried" [At-Tirmidhī 2516] o "The most valuable jihād is to advocate justice in the face of an unjust ruler" [Sunan Abī Dawūd 4344, At-Tirmidhī 2174, Ibn Mājah 4011] What we saw in the Companions of the Prophet ﷺ was complete loyalty to the ethics of Islām. Many times they were confronted with decisions that would evoke displeasure among the people and tribes around Madinah, but they still made them in accordance with the teachings of the Prophet ﷺ.
Use Wisdom to Inform the Truth You employ an eagle-eyed wisdom in selecting the best moment and manner in which to apply the truth. Tact and diplomacy are your abiding traits, but not because you fear blame of any kind	Allāh ﷻ says, "And so We have made you (believers) an upright community so that you may be witnesses over humanity." [Al-Baqarah 2:143] So it is that Allāh ﷻ calls the ummah to act collectively in enjoining both the rights of fellow humans and the rights owed to Allāh ﷻ.

Displeasure with Blame or Disapproval

Exceptions

When Allāh ﷻ or Someone Rightly Guided Disapproves

You feel displeasure when Allāh ﷻ or someone rightly guided disapproves or takes a dim view of your action or intention with respect to what is commanded or prohibited, motivating you to continually better yourself

Qur'ānic, Prophetic & Scholarly Evidence

Allāh ﷻ says:

- "O humanity! Indeed, there has come to you a warning from your Lord, a cure for what is in the hearts, a guide, and a mercy for the believers" [Yūnus 10:57]
- "As for those who repent afterwards and mend their ways, then surely Allāh is All-Forgiving, Most Merciful" [Āli 'Imrān 3:89]

The Prophet ﷺ said, "The superiority of the religious scholar ('Ālim) over the worshipper is like My superiority over the least of you." [At-Tirmidhī 2685]

كَرَاهِيَةُ القَدر

Displeasure with the Divine Decree

SIGNS & SYMPTOMS

- Perceived Injustices
- Abuse of Blessings
- Regret & Frustration
- Showing Contempt Towards Others

TREATMENTS

- Love for Allāh ﷻ
- Acknowledging the Prophet's ﷺ Tribulations
- Response to Afflictions & Trials
- Repentance to Allāh ﷻ for Disobedience
- Showing Gratitude
- Being Thankful by Fulfilling Obligatory Actions

EXCEPTIONS

- Displeased with Immorality

CHAPTER 6

Displeasure with the Divine Decree

[Karāhiyat al-Qadr] كَرَاهِيَةُ القَدر

It has been said that there is a quality in people of which most are unaware, yet it consumes good deeds: when one is displeased with what Allāh ﷻ has decreed (i.e. Allāh's ﷻ divine decree or qadr), resulting in plunging into heedlessness (ghaflah). This is usually because one holds an attitude that stems from a denial of His All-Powerful nature and that Allāh ﷻ alone decrees all things. Put simply, this can also be referred to as ingratitude.

Allāh ﷻ says, "Perhaps you dislike something which is good for you and like something which is bad for you. Allāh knows and you do not know." [Al-Baqarah 2:216]

There are four possible states in which the human being can live, according to revealed sources. A person is either receiving blessings (ni'mah) or tribulations (balā') from Allāh ﷻ, or is either living in obedience (ṭā'ah) to Allāh ﷻ or in disobedience (ma'ṣiyah). Each condition is purposefully exacted upon the individual, as part of the test of life from Allāh ﷻ, and is designed to elicit a response.

Displeasure with the Divine Decree

Signs & Symptoms

Perceived Injustices

You often grieve to yourself, "I do not deserve this!" or "Why me?" or "I did not warrant this happening to me!" or "What did I do to deserve this suffering?" or similar declarations

When you are afflicted with a calamity, you rankle with feelings of hostility, anxiety, and disbelief, and even complain and lose patience

You become so overwhelmed and depressed that you abandon your obligations and neglect your commitments

You live with bitter regret in your heart because of what you have been apportioned in life

You hold a belief that there is only this world, and this understanding creates a blind spot to the wondrousness of Allāh's creation and the signs strewn throughout

Abuse of Blessings

You abuse your material assets by hoarding them without consideration of the needy or by using them for forbidden matters (an obvious act of ingratitude)

Regret & Frustration

You are frustrated by a certain outcome and wish you had taken another course of action

Qur'ānic, Prophetic & Scholarly Evidence

Allāh says:

- "Perhaps you dislike something which is good for you and like something which is bad for you. Allāh knows and you do not know" [Al-Baqarah 2:216]
- "Do people think once they say, 'We believe', that they will be left without being put to the test?" [Al-'Ankabūt 29:2]

The Prophet said, "The strong believer is better and more beloved to Allāh than the weak believer, although both are good. Strive to do that which will benefit you and seek the help of Allāh, and do not feel helpless. If anything befalls you, do not say 'If only I had done (such and such), such and such would have happened,' rather say: 'Allāh has decreed and what He wills He does,' for 'if only' opens the door to the work of Satan." [Ṣaḥīḥ Muslim 2664:34]

Signs & Symptoms

Showing Contempt Towards Others

You look with ridicule at those in tribulation, exhibiting a mocking sarcasm towards 'those', the ones who seem (to you) unguided

For instance, you have this feeling towards the homeless, whom you believe have brought such circumstances upon themselves through laziness, for example

Qur'ānic, Prophetic & Scholarly Evidence

Allāh says, "As for those who abuse believing men and women unjustifiably, they will definitely bear the guilt of slander and blatant sin." [Al-Aḥzāb 33:58]

The Prophet said, "Whoever taunts a brother with a sin (which the brother has committed), will not die until he (the taunter) commits the same sin." [At-Tirmidhī 2505]

Displeasure with the Divine Decree

Academic Treatment	Qur'ānic, Prophetic & Scholarly Evidence
Love for Allāh	
You understand that to be content with Allāh's decree, you must love Him, and to love Him, you must know Him	Allāh says: o "O believers! When you are told to make room in gatherings, then do so. Allāh will make room for you (in His grace). And if you are told to rise, then do so. Allāh will elevate those of you who are faithful, and (raise) those gifted with knowledge in rank. And Allāh is All-Aware of what you do" [Al-Mujādilah 58:11] o "Say (O Prophet), 'Are those who know equal to those who do not know?' None will be mindful (of this) except people of reason" [Az-Zumar 39:9]
You remind yourself that the quickest route to accessing Allāh is through the pursuit of knowledge	The Prophet said: o "The person for whom Allāh intends good, He blesses him with the understanding of Dīn" [Ṣaḥīḥ Al-Bukhārī 71, 3116, 7312, Ṣaḥīḥ Muslim 1037:100] o "That person who treads the path towards acquiring knowledge, Allāh simplifies a path for him into Jannah" [Ṣaḥīḥ Muslim 2699:38]
Acknowledging the Prophet's Tribulations	The Prophet faced the following tribulations, however not once in a single ḥadīth is there a complaint from him, except when beseeching his Lord: o He lived to see all of his children buried, except for Fāṭimah o His father died before his birth o His mother died when he was just a boy
You are conscious of the fact that no one faced greater tribulation than the Prophet	o His guardian grandfather died at a time when his presence was invaluable o When he received his calling, he saw people turn against him with vehemence and brutality o People who had once honoured him now slandered him, calling him a madman, a liar, and a sorcerer o People stalked him and threw stones at him until he bled o People boycotted him and composed stinging and abusive language against him o He lost his closest friends and relatives, like Ḥamzah, who was killed on the battlefield o His beloved wife Khadījah, after 25 years of blissful marriage, died during the Prophet's most difficult moment o Abū Ṭālib, his protecting uncle, also died o He was the target of 13 assassination attempts
You realise that although you cannot choose what befalls you, you can choose your responses to the trials of life, which are inevitable	When the Prophet saw people severely tried, he made the supplication: "Praise be to Allāh who has saved me from what He has afflicted you with, and for honouring me over many of His creation" [At-Tirmidhī 3431, Ibn Mājah 3892]. The Prophet would say this du'ā without letting the afflicted person hear him, so as not to hurt him.

Displeasure with the Divine Decree

Practical Treatment

Response to Afflictions & Trials

Your knowledge of the nature of this world reminds you that it is a temporary testing ground of trial and purification, so you are more patient with afflictions and trials

You say, "Allāh ﷻ is testing me, but it is His will and there is wisdom in it". This is initially tiresome for you, but with time and regular reflection, it becomes an ingrained quality

You immediately engage in a prescribed remembrance (dhikr) at any time of difficulty and hardship

You meditate upon the fact that you are the exclusive property of Allāh ﷻ, you belong to Him, and He has the full right to utilise and dispose of His property as He sees fit; you are therefore content with His divine decree

You endeavour to apply either of two reactions to those things which you dislike:

1. You show contentment or happiness (riḍā)
2. You show patience (ṣabr, displaying perseverance and determination)

You understand that riḍā (contentment) is more virtuous and recommended (mustahab) whereas ṣabr is necessary (wājib)

You should be certain that difficulties will only affect you as much as you permit them to

You recognise that what Allāh ﷻ asks from people is simply to acknowledge that their obedience is a gift from Allāh ﷻ, that what comes to you in your life may help you move closer to Allāh ﷻ

Repentance to Allāh ﷻ for Disobedience

You repent to Allāh ﷻ (tawbah), seeking His forgiveness, pardon, and mercy, feeling remorse for the past, and resolving never to sink into disobedience again

Qur'ānic, Prophetic & Scholarly Evidence

Allāh ﷻ says:

- "Who, when faced with a disaster, say, 'Surely to Allāh we belong and to Him we will (all) return'" [Al-Baqarah 2:156]
- "So in Allāh let the believers put their trust" [Āli 'Imrān 3:160]
- "Perhaps you dislike something which is good for you and like something which is bad for you. Allāh knows and you do not know" [Al-Baqarah 2:216]

The Prophet ﷺ said:

- "No misfortune or disease befalls a Muslim, no worry or grief or harm or distress – not even a thorn that pricks him – but Allāh will expiate for some of his sins because of that" [Ṣaḥīḥ Al-Bukhārī 5641]
- "Indeed greater reward comes with greater trial. And indeed, when Allāh loves a people He subjects them to trials, so whoever is content, then for him is pleasure, and whoever is discontent, then for him is wrath" [At-Tirmidhī 2396]
- When the Prophet ﷺ saw people severely tried, he made the supplication: "Praise be to Allāh who has saved me from what He has afflicted you with, and for honouring me over many of His creation" [At-Tirmidhī 3432]

Abdullah Ibn 'Umar رضي الله عنه used to say, "When you arrive at the evening do not expect to see the morning and when you arrive at the morning do not expect to see the evening. During health, prepare for illness and while you are alive, prepare for death." [Ṣaḥīḥ Al-Bukhārī 6416]

Displeasure with the Divine Decree

Practical Treatment

Showing Gratitude

You internalise the concept of riḍā (contentment), which means that even though you experience pain and difficulty, you wholeheartedly accept this as the divine decree and you do not even hope for its elimination

When you are given blessings, your response is gratitude in all of its manifestations; there is an awakening of appreciation in your heart, acknowledging what you have received

When witnessing people in difficulty, you respond with compassion for those in tribulation and gratitude for your own well-being

You become more conscious of Allāh ﷻ when asked about what your Lord has given you, saying that all of it is good

Being Thankful by Fulfilling Obligatory Actions

Your expression of gratitude at an intellectual level (accepting that all benefit is from the True Benefactor) manifests in how you employ the use of your eyes, your ears, your tongue, and your limbs, ensuring that their utilisation conforms with the sharīʿah

Your gratitude is expressed first by performing what is obligatory (wājib), then going beyond that by performing virtuous, recommended acts (mandūb)

You develop an inherent trust in the Creator alone (called tawakkul), which means that you 'act in accordance with' Allāh's ﷻ plan, i.e. you adopt the principles and commands of the sharīʿah, and place trust in Allāh ﷻ

Qur'ānic, Prophetic & Scholarly Evidence

Allāh ﷻ says:

- "Their reward with their Lord will be Gardens of Eternity, under which rivers flow, to stay there for ever and ever. Allāh is pleased with them and they are pleased with Him. This is (only) for those in awe of their Lord" [Al-Bayyinah 98:8]
- "Say, 'Nothing will ever befall us except what Allāh has destined for us. He is our Protector.' So in Allāh let the believers put their trust" [At-Tawbah 9:51]
- "We have indeed established you on earth and provided you with a means of livelihood. (Yet) you seldom give any thanks" [Al-A'rāf 7:10]
- "If you tried to count Allāh's blessings, you would never be able to number them. Surely Allāh is All-Forgiving, Most Merciful" [An-Naḥl 16:18]
- "And know that your wealth and your children are only a test and that with Allāh is a great reward" [Al-'Anfāl 8:28]
- "Perhaps you dislike something which is good for you and like something which is bad for you. Allāh knows and you do not know" [Al-Baqarah 2:216]

The Prophet ﷺ said:

- "Of the good fortune of man is his contentment with what Allāh has decreed for him" [At-Tirmidhī 2151]
- "Whoever among you wakes up in the morning secured in his dwelling, healthy in his body, having his food for the day, then it is as if the world has been gathered for him" [At-Tirmidhī 2346]
- "Happiness is due to him who is guided to Islām and possesses provision that suffices him for his day and remains content" [At-Tirmidhī 2349]

Displeasure with the Divine Decree

Exceptions

Displeased with Immorality
When you see societies falling into the pit of sin, it is something you are displeased with
Indeed, you dislike it, however you also understand that the evil that Allāh ﷻ has decreed exists in the world as a test for mankind, and for reasons that accord with His ultimate wisdom

Qur'ānic, Prophetic & Scholarly Evidence

Allāh ﷻ says: "You are the best community ever raised for humanity - you encourage good, forbid evil, and believe in Allāh. Had the People of the Book believed, it would have been better for them. Some of them are faithful, but most are rebellious." [Āli 'Imrān 3:110]

كراهية القدر

DISPLEASURE WITH THE DIVINE DECREE

الحَسَد

Envy

SIGNS & SYMPTOMS

- Casting Criticism Towards Other Nations
- Envious of Others' Possessions
- Competing on Social Media
- Intention & Actions to Remove Blessings

TREATMENTS

- Content that Allāh ﷻ is All-Wise
- Shunning Envy & Avoiding Depression
- Knowing that Envy Consumes Good Deeds
- Acting Contrary to Caprice (Hawā)
- Supplicate for the One You Envy
- You Seek Your Own Provision
- Protecting Your Blessings (Social Media)

EXCEPTIONS

- Your Fear of Allāh ﷻ Prevents Harm
- Wealth for Righteous Deeds
- Righteous Wisdom
- Focused on the Hereafter

CHAPTER 7

Envy [Ḥasad] الحَسَد

Envy is when you identify a blessing (or perceived blessing) bestowed on someone else, and then desire, through some trick or deception, that the blessing be extinguished. It has 3 stages:

1. Envy as a human quality: in this degree of envy, man is excused and is not at fault
2. Acting according to the demands of envy: in this degree, man is a sinner
3. Opposing the demands of envy: in this degree, man deserves praise and will be rewarded

The Qur'ān therefore teaches us to seek refuge in Allāh ﷻ: "Say (O Prophet), 'I seek refuge in the Lord of the daybreak...and from the evil of an envier when they envy.'" [Al-Falaq 113: 1&5]

The Prophet ﷺ said, "Resort to secrecy for the fulfilment and success of your needs for, verily, everyone who has a blessing is envied" [Al-Mu'jam Aṣ-Ṣaghīr Aṭ-Ṭabarānī 1186, Al-Mu'jam Al-Kabīr Aṭ-Ṭabarānī 183, Al-Bayhaqī in Shu'ab Al-Īmān 6228]; that is to say that someone of means will invariably have someone who envies him for what he possesses.

Envy can be caused by a number of things: holding animosity towards others (enmity or 'adāwah, when someone is doing better than oneself), arrogance, pride (takabbur), deceit (gharūr), poor self-worth or low-esteem (ta'azzu), an inferiority complex, vanity, love for leadership and status, extreme greed for wealth, material gain, money or possessions.

Envy

Signs & Symptoms

Casting Criticism Towards Other Nations

You cast criticisms at wealthier nations, applying all kinds of exaggerated speech, which appears to be moral outrage but you are actually envious of their worldly possessions

You glance towards the Gulf nations and cannot resist but pass judgement about how they waste 'Muslim money'

Envious of Others' Possessions

You feel envious towards another person with respect to their worldly possessions, fame, or the like

You think or say that Allāh ﷻ should not have given another person a blessing or, that He was wrong to do so 'because you deserve it more' (you desire to have what is in possession of another person)

As a person in a position of leadership, you resent it when others achieve something significant, because you fear a change in the equilibrium; you desire that others are deprived of accomplishment and authority

You feel the harm of envy in terms of constant frustration and worry in your worldly life

Competing on Social Media

You feel jealous when you read someone's post with respect to their achievement, experience, or the like

You realise that the main reason you are posting an experience or achievement is because you are competing with someone else who has recently done something of similar nature, in order to match or exceed the other person's accomplishments

You begin to evoke envy for that person, preferring that they lose their blessing whilst at the same time feeling at a loss because you have 'less' than they do

Qur'ānic, Prophetic & Scholarly Evidence

The Prophet ﷺ said:

- "The effect of the evil eye is a fact" [Ṣaḥīḥ Al-Bukhārī 5740, 5944, Ṣaḥīḥ Muslim 2187:41]
- "Do not envy one another; do not hate one another; do not turn your back on one another (in discontent); (but) be slaves of Allāh as brothers" [Ṣaḥīḥ Al-Bukhārī 6066, Ṣaḥīḥ Muslim 2563:28]
- "Beware of envy, for it consumes good deeds just as fire consumes wood or grass" [Sunan Abī Dawūd 4903]
- "Beware of suspicion, for suspicion is the most false of speech" [Ṣaḥīḥ Al-Bukhārī 6066]

Allāh ﷻ says, "That one who harbours jealousy is an enemy to my blessings, (it is as though he is) angry with My judgement and displeased with my distribution (of My bounties) amongst My servants." [Al-Bayhaqī in Shu'ab al-Īmān 6213]

Envy

Signs & Symptoms

Intention & Actions to Remove Blessings

You desire something that is actually in the possession of someone else (specifically referred to as envy)

If you yourself were able, through some trick or deception, you would direct affairs in order to eliminate someone's blessing: this 'blessing' could range from the small or trivial such as an item of clothing or jewellery - to something more substantial, such as a house, car or job

You are severely occupied with your object of envy, consciously or sub-consciously desiring that just as you are the first to refrain from giving to others, Allāh ﷻ should withhold His bounties from others too

You see someone making headway and you feel that this person is not worthy of such advancement. As a straightforward example, you are envious that your co-worker has been promoted, to the point that you wish that this person loses their position

You envy another person because of their spouse, such that you hope that a marital crisis plagues the couple and ruins their relationship

Qur'ānic, Prophetic & Scholarly Evidence

In the days of the Prophet ﷺ, when the disbelievers of Quraysh protested aloud, they excalimed, "If only this Qur'ān was revealed to a great man from (one of) the two cities!" [Az-Zukhruf 43:31] This is like saying, "How can he be a Prophet, while he is like us and we are not Prophets?"

Fir'awn grew arrogant and envious when Mūsa (عليه السلام) came to him with Allāh's ﷻ message. Part of Fir'awn's problem was seeing a Prophet chosen from among those that he deemed to be common, lesser people.

Envy

Academic Treatment	Qur'ānic, Prophetic & Scholarly Evidence
Content that Allāh ﷻ is All-Wise	Allāh ﷻ says: o "The believers are but one brotherhood, so make peace between your brothers. And be mindful of Allāh so you may be shown mercy" [Hujurat 49:10] o "And hold firmly to the rope of Allāh and do not be divided. Remember Allāh's favour upon you when you were enemies, then He united your hearts, so you - by His grace - became brothers. And you were at the brink of a fiery pit and He saved you from it. This is how Allāh makes His revelations clear to you, so that you may be (rightly) guided" [Āli 'Imrān 3:103] o "And those who come after them will pray, 'Our Lord! Forgive us and our fellow believers who preceded us in faith, and do not allow bitterness into our hearts towards those who believe. Our Lord! Indeed, You are Ever Gracious, Most Merciful" [Al-Ḥashr 59:10]
You realise that Allāh ﷻ is all-Wise, fully-Aware and all-Knowing in what He gives to people, so you do not question the blessings a person has received	
You are in awe of Allāh ﷻ; you have an active awareness of Him as the ultimate power over all creation, so you do not question the Giver of material wealth and prestige	
You realise that what you perceive as a blessing could be based on a false notion; in reality it could very well be nothing but trouble and difficulty	
You also realise that there is hidden blessing in something difficult	
You pass only constructive criticism (of other nations, for instance) that leads to a positive impact	
You realise that from the point of view of Sacred Law, both the affluent and the needy have obligations: o As someone who is poor, you do not envy the rich or harbour resentment towards them o As someone who is rich, you do not belittle the needy, grow arrogant, hoard wealth, or work to keep others in a state of need	
Shunning Envy & Avoiding Depression	The Prophet ﷺ said, "People will remain in goodness as long as they do not harbour jealousy for each other." [At-Targhīb wa At-Tarhīb by Al-Mundhirī 4378]
You shun envy because you realise that envy requires negative thoughts to thrive, even when others around you seem to be passing you by, and this motivates you to excel	
You shun envy because by shunning it you shun insanity, depression and resentment	
Knowing that Envy Consumes Good Deeds	The Prophet ﷺ said that, "Beware of envy, for it consumes good deeds just as fire consumes wood or grass." [Sunan Abī Dawūd 4903]
You realise that envy neither benefits you, nor does it remove the blessing or honour from whom you envy	
You realise that envy is harmful to both your spiritual and worldly life, as it destroys both your Hereafter and your worldly comfort and peace of mind	
You realise in fact that the one of whom you are jealous stands to benefit because he or she acquires your virtuous deeds as compensation for your jealousy	

Envy

Practical Treatment

Acting Contrary to Caprice (Hawā)	Qur'ānic, Prophetic & Scholarly Evidence
You understand that your objective should be to transform these diseases into something beneficial; transforming a disability into an advantage, which is what successful people tend to do	
You act contrary to your impulse of greed, by being beneficent to a person when it seems appealing to harm him (there is no hypocrisy in this); this will incline that person towards you (when you show them good)	Allāh ﷻ praises those who resist the impulses of their souls and promises the Paradise: "And as for those who were in awe of standing before their Lord and restrained themselves from (evil) desires, Paradise will certainly be (their) home." [An-Nāzi'āt 79:40-41]
You defy the commands of your impulses (and gain the pleasure of Allāh ﷻ) by honouring this person and meeting them with respect and humility	Allāh ﷻ also says, "And whoever is saved from the selfishness of their own souls, it is they who are (truly) successful." [Al-Ḥashr 59:9]
You praise a person when you desire to find fault in them (or feel the urge to slander them), no matter how difficult this may seem	The Prophet ﷺ said: o "There is no Muslim servant who supplicates for his brother in his absence except that the angel says: 'For you the same!'" [Ṣaḥīḥ Muslim 2732:85] o "The one who loves for the sake of Allāh, hates for the sake of Allāh, gives for the sake of Allāh and withholds for the sake of Allāh has completed the faith" [Sunan Abī Dawūd 4681] o "The better of the two is the one who initiates the greeting to the other" [Ṣaḥīḥ Muslim 2560:25]
You give that person a gift (even just a simple greeting) or do them a favour such that love (muḥabbah) is created in their heart for you; they will then treat you likewise, which will result in you having love for them	
Supplicate for the One You Envy	
You supplicate for your brother or sister to be blessed instead of wishing that their blessing should cease to exist	Imām Al-Ghazālī says, "I understood that the distribution was from God the Exalted in eternity, so I did not envy anyone and I was content with the distribution of God the Exalted." [Letter To A Disciple/Ayyuhāl Walad, p32-33]
You remind yourself that this supplication will not harm you, rather it is something through which Allāh ﷻ will benefit you	

Envy

Practical Treatment

Qur'ānic, Prophetic & Scholarly Evidence

You Seek Your Own Provision

You realise that perhaps you are the one who has fallen short, that the fault lies with you, being the one with a self-inflicted laziness

You cultivate a drive within yourself to employ the means of earning your own livelihood, avoiding sitting about idly and being lazy

The Prophet ﷺ said:

- "Begging is allowable only to one of three classes: a man who has become a guarantor for a payment to whom begging is allowed till he gets it, after which he must stop (begging); a man who has been stricken by a calamity and it destroys his property to whom begging is allowed till he gets what will support life (or he said, what will provide a reasonable subsistence); and a man who has been smitten by poverty, about whom three intelligent members of his people confirm by saying: 'So-and-so has been smitten by poverty.' To such a person begging is allowed till he gets what will support life (or he said, what will provide a reasonable subsistence), after which he must stop (begging)" [Sunan Abī Dawūd 1640]
- "By Him in Whose Hand my life is, it is better for anyone of you to take a rope and cut the wood (from the forest) and carry it over his back and sell it (as a means of earning his living) rather than to ask a person for something and that person may give him or not" [Ṣaḥīḥ Al-Bukhārī 1470]
- The Prophet ﷺ used to constantly seek refuge with Allāh ﷻ from laziness: "O Allāh! I seek refuge in You from incapacity, from laziness, from cowardice, from miserliness, from ineptitude and from the torment of the grave" [Ṣaḥīḥ Muslim 2706:50]

Protecting Your Blessings (Social Media)

When you read someone's post which heralds some sort of achievement, experience, or the like, first and foremost you reflect on the untold bounties with which Allāh ﷻ has blessed you

You take the necessary steps to protect and preserve your untold bounties from the 'evil eye'

You remind yourself that you should only compete on two fronts:

- With a person to whom Allāh ﷻ has granted wisdom, and he rules by this and teaches it to the people
- With a person to whom Allāh ﷻ has granted wealth and property and along with this the power to spend it in the cause of truth

You unfollow a person if their social media comments upset you, whilst ensuring that this does not lead to further issue

The Qur'ān therefore teaches us to seek refuge in Allāh ﷻ: "Say (O Prophet), 'I seek refuge in the Lord of the daybreak...and from the evil of an envier when they envy.'" [Al-Falaq 113: 1&5]

And He says, "The Day when neither wealth nor children will be of any benefit. Only those who come before Allāh with a pure heart (will be saved)." [As-Shu'arā' 26: 88-89]

The Prophet ﷺ said:

- "There is no envy (ḥasad) except in two cases: a person to whom Allāh has granted wealth and property and along with this the power to spend it in the cause of truth and a person to whom Allāh has granted wisdom, and he rules by this and teaches it to the people." [Ṣaḥīḥ Al-Bukhārī 73, Ṣaḥīḥ Muslim 816:268] Competition is not considered blameworthy in general, rather it is considered to be praiseworthy when competing for righteousness
- "Resort to secrecy for the fulfilment and success of your needs for, verily, everyone who has a blessing is envied." [Al-Mu'jam Aṣ-Ṣaghīr Aṭ-Ṭabarānī 1186, Al-Mu'jam Al-Awsaṭ Aṭ-Ṭabarānī 2455] Someone of means will have someone who envies him for what he possesses

Envy

Exceptions

Your Fear of Allāh ﷻ Prevents Harm

Your sense of taqwā (an awareness of Allāh's ﷻ constant presence) drives you to decline the evil whisperings which call you to deception that would extinguish or diminish someone's blessing

You look desirously at the bounties of someone else, hoping that you also acquire the same without him losing what he has (called ghibtah or rashk, which is permissible because there is no desire for harm to anyone else)

Wealth for Righteous Deeds

You desire wealth in order to do the righteous deed of giving to the needy, and also envy such a person, but not in the sense of hoping that he might lose his wealth

Righteous Wisdom

You envy a person who has been given wisdom and teaches it to people, because you wish to be blessed with some of that wisdom in order to teach others (however you do not wish the other person to lose their blessing)

Focused on the Hereafter

You are envious but not for temporary things, like worldly assets that are usually hoarded and displayed for show; your desire is instead for what will serve your Hereafter (without wishing the other party to lose their blessing), and you therefore convert negative feelings into positive ones

Qur'ānic, Prophetic & Scholarly Evidence

The Prophet ﷺ said, "There is no envy (ḥasad) except in two cases: a person to whom Allāh has granted wealth and property and along with this the power to spend it in the cause of truth and a person to whom Allāh has granted wisdom, and he rules by this and teaches it to the people." [Ṣaḥīḥ Al-Bukhārī 73, Ṣaḥīḥ Muslim 816:268] Competition is not considered blameworthy in general, rather it is considered to be praiseworthy when competing for righteousness.

Imām Al-Ghazālī states that if one hates envy and is ashamed that he or she harbours it, the person is not essentially an envious person. [Iḥyā 'Ulūm Ad-Dīn 3:200]

الإِسْرَاف

Extravagance

SIGNS & SYMPTOMS

- Over-Eating: Going Beyond Moderation
- Wasting Water & Food
- Extravagant Purchases & Brand Flaunting
- Hoarding Unused Items
- Falling Short in Your Responsibilities
- Excessive Love & Attention

TREATMENTS

- Identify Your Extravagance
- Remove Unnecessary Purchases
- Control Your Food Purchases
- Control Your Eating Habits
- Managing Leftover Food
- Avoid Becoming a Shopaholic
- Control Your Brand Purchases

EXCEPTIONS

- Allāh ﷻ Loves Beauty
- Moderation, without Extravagance or Arrogance

CHAPTER 8

Extravagance [Isrāf] الإسْرَاف

Extravagance is demonstrated through a lack of restraint in spending money or using resources, and is also referred to as wastefulness (tabdhir) or lavishness. It is when one, for instance, oversteps the mark by spending or consuming more than is necessary or reasonable.

Allāh ﷻ has created a natural balance and harmony. He ﷻ says, "As for the sky, He raised it (high), and set the balance (of justice) so that you do not defraud the scales." [Ar-Raḥmān 55 :7-8]

The Prophet ﷺ said, "By Allāh, it is not poverty that I fear for you, rather what I fear for you is that worldly riches may be given to you as they were given to those who came before you, and you will compete for them with one another as they competed with one another, and it will destroy you as it destroyed them." [Ṣaḥīḥ Al-Bukhārī 3158]

'Āishah ﵂ is reported to have said, "The first calamity for this nation after the Prophet's ﷺ death is fullness of their stomachs; when their stomachs became full, they became obese: their hearts weakened and their desires became wild." [Al-Jū'u Ibn Abī Dunyā: 22]

Extravagance

Signs & Symptoms	Qur'ānic, Prophetic & Scholarly Evidence
Over-Eating: Going Beyond Moderation You eat beyond your point of fullness, including those food types that you are supposed to avoid, passing the bounds of moderation	The Prophet ﷺ said: o "It is extravagance that one eats whatever he desires" [Ibn Mājah 3352] o "A believer eats in one intestine (is satisfied with a little food), and a kāfir (unbeliever) or a hypocrite eats in seven intestines (eats too much)" [Ṣaḥīḥ Al-Bukhārī 5393, 5934] 'Āishah is reported to have said, "The first calamity for this nation after the Prophet's ﷺ death is fullness of their stomachs; when their stomachs became full, they became obese: their hearts weakened and their desires became wild." [Al-Jū'u Ibn Abī Dunyā: 22] A man burped in the presence of the Messenger of Allāh ﷺ and he said: "Keep your burps away from us, for the one who eats his fill the most in this world will be hungry for the longest time on the Day of Resurrection." [Al-Mu'jam Al-Awsaṭ Aṭ-Ṭabarānī 8929] Imām Abū Ḥāmid Al-Ghazālī said, "The one whose concern is with that which enters the belly will discover that his value is found in that which goes out of it." [Mīzān Al-'Amal, p.311]
Wasting Water & Food Your extravagance is related to the way you spend your money as well as your unnecessary waste of food and water: o Wasting water while performing ablution o Leaving food on your plate because you filled it beyond your appetite	Allāh says: o "Eat from the fruit they bear and pay the dues at harvest, but do not waste. Surely He does not like the wasteful" [Al-An'ām 6:141] o "Give to close relatives their due, as well as the poor and (needy) travellers. And do not spend wastefully. Surely the wasteful are (like) brothers to the devils. And the Devil is ever ungrateful to his Lord" [Al-'Isrā 17:26-27] The Prophet ﷺ said "Satan is present with any one of you in all his affairs, and he is even present with him when he eats. If one of you drops a morsel, let him remove any dirt that has gotten onto it, then eat it, and not leave it for Satan. And when he has finished let him lick his fingers, for he does not know in which part of his food the blessing is." [Ṣaḥīḥ Muslim 2033:135] The Prophet ﷺ said with regards to wasting food and throwing it away that it is wrong and is a transgression against the blessing of Allāh, and "not to leave it for the Satan." [Ṣaḥīḥ Muslim 2033:134] The Prophet ﷺ passed by Sa'd when he was doing wuḍ'ū, and he ﷺ said, "What is this extravagance, O Sa'd?" who replied, "Can there be any extravagance in wuḍ'ū?" He ﷺ said, "Yes, even if you are on the bank of a flowing river." [Musnad Aḥmad 7065, Ibn Mājah 425]

Extravagance

Signs & Symptoms

Extravagant Purchases & Brand Flaunting
You acquire or purchase what is surplus to your needs, bragging and boasting about it
You show off to attract the attentions of others, or for reasons of power, false pride, or to fulfil some (selfish) desires
You show-off so as to look down upon others because of the stylish design and/or value of your (new) worldly item
Your display of beauty is an end in itself for you and is all you care about
You buy and prominently display expensive name brand products in front of others under the belief that this will bring you prestige and admiration, regardless of the actual quality or value of the product
You purchase all variations of a product or service when one alone would suffice
You expose yourself to interest-based loans for the sake of competing with others in, for instance, building and decorating your home, and in making it spacious

Qur'ānic, Prophetic & Scholarly Evidence

Allāh ﷻ says:

- "And the transgressors will be the inmates of the Fire" [Ghāfir 40:43]
- "Give to close relatives their due, as well as the poor and (needy) travellers. And do not spend wastefully. Surely the wasteful are (like) brothers to the devils. And the Devil is ever ungrateful to his Lord" [Al-'Isrā' 17:26-27]
- "Do not be so tight-fisted, for you will be blameworthy; nor so open-handed, for you will end up in poverty" [Al-'Isrā' 17:29]
- "Eat and drink, but do not waste. Surely He does not like the wasteful" [Al-'A'rāf 7:31]
- "(Watch for) the Day (when) the disbelievers will be exposed to the Fire. (They will be told,) 'You (already) exhausted your (share of) pleasures during your worldly life, and (fully) enjoyed them. So today you will be rewarded with the torment of disgrace for your arrogance throughout the land with no right, and for your rebelliousness'" [Al-Aḥqāf 46:20]

The Prophet ﷺ said:

- "There is a bedding for a man, a bedding for his wife, the third bedding for his guest, and the fourth is for Satan" [Ṣaḥīḥ Muslim 2084:41]
- "He who wears a dress of high repute (to show-off or as a status symbol) in this world will be dressed in humiliating clothes on the Day of Judgement" [Musnad Aḥmad 5664, Sunan Abī Dawūd 4029]

"Allāh the Exalted says that He does not like those who trespass the limits on an allowed matter or a prohibited matter, those who go to the extreme over what He has allowed, allow what He has prohibited, or prohibit what He has allowed. But, He likes that what He has allowed be considered as such (without extravagance) and what He has prohibited be considered as such. This is the justice that He has commanded."
[Tafsīr Ibn Kathīr 3:408 under verse 7:31]

Extravagance

Signs & Symptoms	Qur'ānic, Prophetic & Scholarly Evidence
Hoarding Unused Items	
Your supply of food (e.g. in your pantry) is overflowing from the previous month as you unnecessarily collect and hoard unused items (which eventually expire)	The Prophet ﷺ said, "No one hoards but one who is in error." [Ṣaḥīḥ Muslim 1605:129]
You collect and begin to hoard unused trinkets over the years but can't convince yourself to let go of them	
Falling Short in Your Responsibilities	
Your excess and extravagant behaviour towards one thing leads to you falling short in others, such as your responsibilities towards parents, siblings, your spouse, children, religious duties, work, financial commitments, friends and your physical health	Allāh ﷻ says: o "And so We have made you (believers) an upright community so that you may be witnesses over humanity" [Al-Baqarah 2:143] o "O People of the Book! Do not go to extremes regarding your faith" [An-Nisā' 4:171]
Your excess results in you depriving others of their rights, which results in instability in your relationships with others	
Excessive Love & Attention	
You pay more attention to one child over another, leading to their resentment and sibling rivalry	Allāh ﷻ says: "Wealth and children are the adornment of this worldly life, but the everlasting good deeds are far better with your Lord in reward and in hope." [Al-Kahf 18:46]

Extravagance

Academic & Practical Treatment	Qur'ānic, Prophetic & Scholarly Evidence
Identify Your Extravagance	
You take steps to identify extravagance in your life: o Where your balance has been lost (e.g. areas of obsession or excess) o Where you are not doing enough, or indeed where you are doing too much	Allāh ﷻ says, "And all they said was, 'Our Lord! Forgive our sins and excesses, make our steps firm, and grant us victory over the disbelieving people.'" [Āli 'Imrān 3:147]
Remove Unnecessary Purchases	
You determine where you spend your money, and after making a list of all expenditures, you prioritise them, immediately removing unnecessary purchases	
Control Your Food Purchases	
You minimise food wastage by ensuring you take note of what you already have in stock before purchasing additional food	Allāh ﷻ says, "(They are) those who spend neither wastefully nor stingily, but moderately in between." [Al-Furqān 25:67]
You purchase only that which you require and can easily consume, taking note of the expiry date	
Control Your Eating Habits	
You take only what you are able to consume with ease	The Prophet ﷺ said: o "The son of Ādam does not fill any vessel worse than his stomach. It is sufficient for the son of Ādam to eat a few mouthfuls, that will support his back. If this is not possible, then let him fill one third with food, one third with drink and one third with air" [At-Tirmidhī 2380] o Ibn Abbās رضي الله عنه said: "Eat what you wish and wear what you wish, as long as you avoid two things: extravagance and arrogance" [Ṣaḥīḥ Al-Bukhārī Title of Chapter 1 of Book 77, Ibn Mājah 3605, Muṣannaf Ibn Abi Shaybah 25375]
You ensure you eat small amounts of food and are content with that which is enough to keep you going	
You remind yourself that what matters is: o Taking care of your body and not causing any harm to it, whether by overeating or deprivation o Having the strength to carry out acts of worship, which is achieved by eating moderate amounts, not by eating heavy amounts or going too hungry	
Managing Leftover Food	
You remind yourself that wasteful extravagance is forbidden, and wasting money is forbidden	
You keep leftover food for another time, or give it to the needy, and if there are no needy people then you give it to animals	

Extravagance

Academic & Practical Treatment	Qur'ānic, Prophetic & Scholarly Evidence
Avoid Becoming a Shopaholic You avoid becoming a 'shopaholic' by: o Altering your perspective of shopping by viewing it as a source of need or purpose rather than solely as a source of fun and enjoyment, 'killing' precious time o Keeping your expenditure under control o Not falling for every sale and discount o Avoiding making unnecessary purchases under the guise of 'buy 2 get 1 free' (when you only required 1 item)	Allāh says: o "(They are) those who spend neither wastefully nor stingily, but moderately in between" [Al-Furqān 25:67] o "Let the man of wealth provide according to his means. As for the one with limited resources, let him provide according to whatever Allāh has given him. Allāh does not require of any soul beyond what He has given it. After hardship, Allāh will bring about ease" [At-Ṭalāq 65:7] o "And give them a parable of this worldly life. (It is) like the plants of the earth, thriving when sustained by the rain We send down from the sky. Then they (soon) turn into chaff scattered by the wind. And Allāh is fully capable of (doing) all things" [Al-Kahf 18:45] Ibn Abbās said: "Eat what you wish and wear what you wish, as long as you avoid two things: extravagance and arrogance." [Ṣaḥīḥ Al-Bukhārī Title of Chapter 1 of Book 77, Ibn Mājah 3605, Muṣannaf Ibn Abi Shaybah 25375]
Control Your Brand Purchases You remind yourself of the negative consequences of the delights of this world and the evil of the temptation to compete with others You realise that you are simply a walking advertisement for a clothing store or brand You make the most of your existing clothes and other fashion accessories (before considering purchasing more) You keep in mind your modesty as well as affordability when making your next purchase	

Extravagance

Exceptions

Exceptions	Qur'ānic, Prophetic & Scholarly Evidence
Allāh ﷻ Loves Beauty	
Reflecting on Allāh's ﷻ love of beauty, you dress well and look presentable: o For His sake only o To help you to obey Allāh ﷻ o To fulfil His commands, such as when the Prophet ﷺ made himself look more handsome when meeting the delegations that came to him You remind yourself that Allāh ﷻ loves the effects of His blessings on His slave to be made clear (without extravagance), for this is part of the beauty that He loves, and that is part of the gratitude for His blessings which forms an inner beauty (beauty of character)	**Allāh ﷻ says,** "O children of Ādam! We have provided for you clothing to cover your nakedness and as an adornment. However, the best clothing is righteousness. This is one of Allāh's bounties, so perhaps you will be mindful." [Al-'A'rāf 7:26] **Mālik ibn Nadla ؓ narrates:** "The Prophet saw me wearing old, tattered clothes, and asked me, 'Do you have any wealth?' I said, 'Yes.' He said, 'What kind of wealth?' I said, 'All that Allāh has given me of camels and sheep.' He said, 'Then show the generous blessings that He has given you.'" [Musnad Aḥmad 15887]
Moderation, without Extravagance or Arrogance	
The permissibility in Allāh's ﷻ sight of eating, drinking and purchasing creature comforts for your family is tempered by your understanding that it should not be spoilt by extravagance or arrogance	**The Prophet ﷺ said,** "There are four things that are means of happiness: a righteous wife, a spacious home, a good neighbour and a sound means of transportation. And there are four things that make one miserable: a bad neighbour, a bad wife, a small house and a bad means of transportation." [Ibn Ḥibbān 4032] **Ibn Abbās ؓ said,** "Eat what you wish and wear what you wish, as long as you avoid two things: extravagance and arrogance." [Ṣaḥīḥ Al-Bukhārī Title of Chapter 1 of Book 77, Ibn Mājah 3605, Muṣannaf Ibn Abi Shaybah 25375]

EXTRAVAGANCE

الأَمَل

False Hope

SIGNS & SYMPTOMS

- Indifference, Laziness & Neglecting Obligatory Duties
- Superstitions

TREATMENTS

- Good Opinion of Allāh ﷻ
- Establishing a Balance Between Hope & Fear
- Contemplating the Hereafter
- Avoiding Superstitions
- Prioritising the Hereafter by Focusing on Action in Accordance with the Pillars

EXCEPTIONS

- Extended Hope is a Human Condition
- Preparing for the Hereafter
- Absolute Hope in Allāh ﷻ

CHAPTER 9

False Hope [Amal] الأمَل

Extended false hope (tatwīl al-amal) is a peculiar phenomenon. For many people it is an ever-present part of their psyche, a kind of everyday assurance that death for them is a long way away. At the same time however, in a heartbeat, it can act on an individual like a quick-acting poison to inspire immoral behaviour, or - at the very least - an inclination towards material possessions over and above any spiritual concerns. It is a mental environment that leads people to live their lives as if a long life is guaranteed. This delusion can generate hard-heartedness and inaction due to the heedlessness of the Hereafter.

Another kind of hope (umniyya) is having hope but neglecting the means to achieve what one hopes for, which is often referred to as an 'empty wish'. One hopes to become healthier, for example, but remains idle and is altogether careless about diet.

The cause of (extended) false hope may be due to:

- A heedlessness of the reality of death
- A lack of certainty (disbelief) in the Hereafter
- A negative understanding of the reality of Allāh ﷻ and His authority and presence
- Ignorance of the fact that the entire affair (of this life) is Allāh's ﷻ alone: that everything belongs to Allāh ﷻ

An enduring characteristic of the teachings of every Prophet and thus every revealed religion, is the idea that entry into Paradise is a matter of Allāh's ﷻ mercy. The reward of this eternal abode comes by combining faith with sincere deeds that confirm one's profession of faith. It is a misguided extension of false hope, however, that will exclude many from Paradise: many a soul that vouches for Islām will find itself cast into Hell on the Day of Judgement.

False Hope

Signs & Symptoms	Qur'ānic, Prophetic & Scholarly Evidence
Indifference, Laziness & Neglecting Obligatory Duties	
You show hard-heartedness and laziness or sloth (kasl) regarding matters of the Hereafter You believe that you will live for a long time, so you do not attach much (if any) importance to pondering over your mortality You demonstrate an indifference, reluctance or laziness towards fulfilling the obligatory acts of worship and other religious dictates	The Qur'ān states that there are people who desire to continue in their wrongdoing throughout the entirety of their lives. "asking (mockingly), 'When is this Day of Judgement?'" [Al-Qiyāmah 75:6]. One interpretation of this verse, according to scholars, is that although people may be aware of their ultimate accountability, they put off repentance as if they are guaranteed a long life. Imām Al-Ghazālī said "O disciple, be neither destitute of good deeds nor devoid of spiritual states, for you can be sure that mere knowledge will not help." [Letter to a Disciple/ Ayyuhāl Walad, p.8-9]
You find reservoirs of energy when it comes to worldly matters, but are overcome with sloth (laziness) when it comes to matters of the Hereafter You find excuses for neglecting prayer (ṣalāh), the foundation of spirituality, claiming that you are exhausted from the day's work You hope for the Hereafter but do nothing for it in terms of conduct and morality All you have to show for your religiosity is the mere declaration of faith, a testimony unconfirmed by deeds, especially the (obligatory) rites of worship and charitable acts towards others	Allāh says, "However, repentance is not accepted from those who knowingly persist in sin until they start dying, and then say, 'Now I repent!' nor those who die as disbelievers. For them We have prepared a painful punishment." [An-Nisā' 4:18] Imām Al-Ghazālī said "O disciple, knowledge without action is madness and action without knowledge is void. Know that the knowledge which does not remove you from sins today and does not convert you to obedience, will not remove you tomorrow from the Hellfire." [Letter to a Disciple/Ayyuhāl Walad, p.16-17]

False Hope

Signs & Symptoms

Superstitions

You have a near-paranoid concern with superstition (tatayyur, which means having the feeling that something bad will happen), exemplified by the following behaviour:

- o You avoid walking under any ladders
- o You stay clear of black cats
- o You associate the number 13 with bad luck
- o You support the stigma attached to breaking a mirror
- o You 'knock on wood' to avoid bad luck

You routinely read the astrology page of the newspaper before starting the day

You may even buy and sell stocks based on the advice of an astrologer

Qur'ānic, Prophetic & Scholarly Evidence

The Prophet ﷺ said:

- o "Whoever partakes in one part of astrology (the art of the stars), verily he has partaken in sorcery" [Sunan Abī Dawūd 3904]
- o "Whoever approaches a fortune-teller and inquires from him/her, his prayers will not be accepted for forty days" [Ṣaḥīḥ Muslim 2230:125]
- o "Whoever approaches a fortune-teller and acknowledges him/her, that person has nothing to do with what has been sent down to Muḥammad ﷺ" [Sunan Abī Dawūd 3904]

The Prophet ﷺ warned against superstition; no matter how widespread it may be in societies, while these practices take on an aura of innocence and light humour, they are nonetheless connected to their pagan and idolatrous ancestry.

False Hope

Academic Treatment	Qur'ānic, Prophetic & Scholarly Evidence
Good Opinion of Allāh ﷻ	The Prophet ﷺ said: o "Have taqwā (fear) of Allāh wherever you may be, and follow up a bad deed with a good deed which will wipe it out, and behave well towards the people" [At-Tirmidhī 1987] o "Verily, thinking well about Allāh is a part of the excellent worship of Allāh" [At-Tirmidhī 3604:5] o Allāh ﷻ says, "I am as My servant thinks (expects) I am. I am with him when he mentions Me. If he mentions Me to himself, I mention him to Myself; and if he mentions Me in an assembly, I mention him in an assembly greater than it. If he draws near to Me a hand's length, I draw near to him an arm's length. If he draws near to Me an arm's length, I draw near to him by the span of two outstetched arms. And if he comes to Me walking, I go to him at speed" [Ṣaḥīḥ Muslim 2675:2]
You recognise Allāh's ﷻ power and authority in the world, and do not attribute or equate any similar amount of power to any part of the creation	
You have much optimism and hope, in that where your past has been marred with evil, you strongly believe this is a new day and opportunity to turn things around	
You see your hope for a long life as a mercy from Allāh ﷻ, so that you have more opportunity to taste the sweetness of being a source of goodness and benefit to others	

False Hope

Academic Treatment

Establishing a Balance Between Hope & Fear

You establish in your mind and actions a balance between hope and fear, understanding that fear (khawf) treats or prevents two maladies: moral complacency and self-righteousness

You realise that faith must be coupled with good works for your religion to be complete

Contemplating the Hereafter

You meditate on death, its agonies and the various states after it

You imagine, while you have life and are safe, the trial of the 'Crossing of the Bridge' (Sirāt) which every soul must traverse in the Hereafter, and beneath which is an awesome inferno. The soul which is engaged in this gruelling crossing hears the screams and anguish of those evildoers who have already been cast therein

Athletes visualise going through all the steps required for success so as a believer you visualise what is more important and of great consequence: preparing yourself psychologically for the ultimate journey

Qur'ānic, Prophetic & Scholarly Evidence

Allāh ﷻ says,

- "Do not spread corruption in the land after it has been set in order. And call upon Him with hope and fear. Indeed, Allāh's mercy is always close to the good-doers" [Al-'A'rāf 7:56]
- "(It is) Allāh (Who) calls back the souls (of people) upon their death as well as (the souls) of the living during their sleep. Then He keeps those for whom He has ordained death, and releases the others until (their) appointed time. Surely in this are signs for people who reflect" [Az-Zumar 39:42]

The Prophet ﷺ said:

- "I forbade you to visit the graves then it appeared to me that they soften the heart, bring tears to the eyes, and remind one of the Hereafter, so now visit them" [Musnad Aḥmad 13487]
- "Visit graves, for it reminds one of death" [Ṣaḥīḥ Muslim 976:108]

Visiting graves is considered something highly recommended (mandūb), in the same way that the remembrance of Allāh ﷻ is recommended.

False Hope

Practical Treatment	Qur'ānic, Prophetic & Scholarly Evidence
Avoiding Superstitions	
You do not delve into superstitious practices, which are explicitly forbidden in Islām You say certain prayers, and read certain passages of the Qur'ān that ward off evil You give extra charity, and the like, as an act of worship To avoid the trap of superstition you simply persist in what you are doing when confronted with something viewed as a bad omen	The Messenger of Allāh ﷺ said, "Tiyarah (derived from the word tatayyur - superstitious belief in omens) is shirk." [At-Tirmidhī 1614, Sunan Abī Dawūd 3915, Ibn Mājah 3538]
Prioritising the Hereafter by Focusing on Actions in Accordance with the Pillars	
You understand that people die at all ages and that you may never get the chance to repent and make amends Regardless of your material accomplishments in this life, you live a life that prepares you for the Next World, which includes the enjoyment of Allāh's ﷻ blessings, such as your family, friends, and recreation, but not to the extent that you forget your purpose and ultimate destiny You realise that you do not have forever to take care of your worldly affairs, so you do not waste your time, instead tending to the Hereafter as if death awaits tomorrow	Allāh ﷻ says: o "Did you then think that We had created you without purpose, and that you would never be returned to Us? Exalted is Allāh, the True King! There is no god (worthy of worship) except Him, the Lord of the Honourable Throne" [Al-Mu'minūn 23: 115-116] o "We did not create the heavens and the earth and everything in between for sport. We only created them for a purpose, but most of these (pagans) do not know" [Ad-Dukhān 44: 38-39] o "And that each person will only have what they endeavoured towards" [An-Najm 53:39] o "So whoever hopes for the meeting with their Lord, let them do good deeds and associate none in the worship of their Lord" [Al-Kahf 18:110] o "Indeed, those who believe and do good will have the Gardens of Paradise as an accommodation, where they will be forever, never desiring anywhere else" [Al-Kahf 18: 107-108] Thomas Jefferson added "the pursuit of happiness" in the Declaration of Independence, which implied leisure, however what was originally meant by leisure was to study and meditate on life, the pursuit of 'true' happiness.
You do not neglect your work in this life, rather, you direct your intentions such that your work in the world does not detract from the Hereafter Your ultimate focus on and prioritisation of the Hereafter means that you do not neglect prayer (ṣalāh, the foundation of spirituality) during work	Allāh ﷻ says: o "Rather, seek the (reward) of the Hereafter by means of what Allāh has granted you, without forgetting your share of this world" [Al-Qaṣaṣ 28:77] o "But they were succeeded by generations who neglected prayer and followed their lusts and so will soon face the evil consequences" [Maryam 19:59] The Messenger of Allāh ﷺ said, "Act for your world as if you will live forever, and act for your Hereafter as if you are going to die tomorrow" [Al-Jāmi' Aṣ-Ṣaghīr 1201]. People frequently misunderstand this saying and use it as a justification for working very hard for the world only.

False Hope

Exceptions

Extended Hope is a Human Condition

You understand that extended hope is a necessary human condition that gives you the opportunity to change things for the better

Preparing for the Hereafter

It is not blameworthy when you are engaged in preparing for tomorrow or writing works of knowledge from which many people may benefit, because you seek to strive in ways that serve Allāh ﷻ, His religion and humanity

You give perpetual charity (ṣadaqah jāriyah) whose reward accumulates in your favour even after you have died (e.g. establishing a water well, building a masjid)

Absolute Hope in Allāh ﷻ

When you reach your deathbed, you have absolute hope in Allāh ﷻ, be certain that Allāh ﷻ will offer forgiveness and entry into Paradise (having a good opinion of Allāh ﷻ)

Qur'ānic, Prophetic & Scholarly Evidence

Allāh ﷻ says, "So whoever hopes for the meeting with their Lord, let them do good deeds and associate none in the worship of their Lord." [Al-Kahf 18:110]

The Prophet ﷺ warned that no one should die except with a "good opinion of Allāh." [Ṣaḥīḥ Muslim 2877]

A famous ḥadīth narrated by 'Āishah رضي الله عنها relates that the Prophet ﷺ said "Whoever loves to meet Allāh, then Allāh loves to meet him. And whoever dislikes meeting Allāh, then Allāh dislikes meeting him." And 'Āishah asked, "O Messenger of Allāh! All of us dislike death." He ﷺ said: "It is not like that. But when the believer is given the good news of Allāh's mercy, His pleasure, and His Paradise, then he loves to meet Allāh and Allāh loves to meet him." [At-Tirmidhī 1067]. This kind of hope is known as 'rajā'. It is hope coupled with sincere effort to achieve what one hopes for.

A famous Persian story speaks of a Shah who asked, "Do you believe this tree will be of any benefit to you, old man? You will die before it bears fruit." The old man replied, "Those before me planted and we benefitted. We should plant so that others after us might benefit." The Shah was so impressed that he rewarded the old man with money (i.e. the tree had started to bring benefit already).

A similar Arab proverb states, "Before us they planted, and now we eat what they have planted. We too must plant, so that those after us will likewise eat."

التَخَيُّل

Fantasizing

SIGNS & SYMPTOMS

- Reflecting on What is Prohibited

TREATMENTS

- Repenting to Allāh ﷻ & Doing Good Deeds
- Being Conscious of Allāh ﷻ
- Better Use of Time & Moderation in Friendship (Social Media)
- Cutting off Thoughts & Lowering Your Gaze (Social Media)

EXCEPTIONS

- Not Dwelling on What Crosses One's Mind

CHAPTER 10

Fantasizing [Takhayyul] التَخَيُّل

Extensive reflection, and working a prohibited action through one's mind, perhaps picturing the fantasy or describing it in detail to others is reaching the brink of active engagement: be it robbing a bank, winning at roulette or committing adultery. 'Fantasizing' is when the heart dwells on forbidden or prohibited matters and those inspirations that do not concern it. Included in this is thinking about the weaknesses or faults of others, whether they are present or not.

Fantasizing

Signs & Symptoms

Reflecting on What is Prohibited

You reflect on things that are prohibited, such as lustful fantasizing about the beauty of a person one is not married to (for instance by way of day-dreaming, gazing, glancing)

The result of your (excessive) gazing and glancing gives rise to beauty-worship and infatuations, etching in your heart the impression of the 'beloved' or 'admired'

As a consequence of your evil gazes, you find that your heart and mind are always scattered and in disarray, to such an extent that you forget your own well-being and welfare, an obstruction to your functioning and duties, making you heedless and rendering you a slave to your base desires

You think or talk about the weaknesses and faults of others

Qur'ānic, Prophetic & Scholarly Evidence

Allāh ﷻ says, "And do not obey those whose hearts We have made heedless of Our remembrance, who follow (only) their desires and whose state is (total) loss." [Al-Kahf 18:28]

The Prophet ﷺ said:

- "The furtive (secretive) glance is one of the poisoned arrows of Satan" [Al-Ḥākim 7875]
- "The adultery of the eyes is by looking" [Ṣaḥīḥ Al-Bukhārī 6243] (i.e. by looking at what Allāh ﷻ has forbidden)
- "I fear for you the carnal desires of your bellies and private parts" [Musnad Aḥmad 19772]
- "If any person peeps at you without your permission and you poke him with a stick and injure his eye, you will not be blamed" [Ṣaḥīḥ Al-Bukharī 6902]
- "Whoever eavesdrops on the conversation of other people when they do not want him to listen, or they move away from him, molten lead will be poured into his ears on the Day of Resurrection" [Ṣaḥīḥ Al-Bukhārī 7042]

Fantasizing

Academic Treatment	Qur'ānic, Prophetic & Scholarly Evidence
Repenting to Allāh ﷻ & Doing Good Deeds	The Prophet ﷺ said: o "Indeed every host loves that people come to his table spread, and indeed the table spread of Allāh is the Qur'ān, so do not abandon it" [Al-Bayhaqī in Shu'ab Al-Īmān 1857] o "Allāh decreed good deeds and bad deeds, then He explained that. Whoever thinks of doing a good deed then does not do it, Allāh will write it down as one complete good deed. If he thinks of doing a good deed and then does it, Allāh will write it down between ten and seven hundred-fold, or many more. If he thinks of doing a bad deed then he does not do it, Allāh will write it down as one complete good deed, and if he thinks of it then does it, Allāh will write it down as one bad deed" [Ṣaḥīḥ Al-Bukhārī 6491, Ṣaḥīḥ Muslim 131:207]
You repent to Allāh ﷻ and increase your love for Him, for indeed you understand that this is more satisfying and purer than anything else	
You reflect on His attributes revealed in the Qur'ān, about Himself (His awesome majesty, knowledge, and power) in order to deepen your love for Him and your desire to follow His commandments, and thus prepare for the Hereafter	
You fear Allāh ﷻ and the occurrence of a harm as a consequence of your fantasies, which is more hateful to you than leaving your fantasy	
You realise that each time you obey Allāh ﷻ out of love and fear, and leave a prohibited action out of love and fear, your love and fear become stronger, and any love or fear of anything else besides Allāh ﷻ begins to disappear from your heart	
Being Conscious of Allāh ﷻ	The Prophet ﷺ said, "Have taqwā (fear) of Allāh wherever you may be, and follow up a bad deed with a good deed which will wipe it out, and behave well towards the people." [At-Tirmidhī 1987]
You realise that modern technology has made it easy for you to commit practically any evil or sinful act behind the privacy (and anonymity) of your laptop or phone screen	
You remind yourself that Allāh ﷻ is watching you, and therefore make sure that your private persona is 'in sync' with your public one	

Fantasizing

<table>
<tr><th>Practical Treatment</th><th>Qur'ānic, Prophetic & Scholarly Evidence</th></tr>
<tr><td>Better Use of Time & Moderation in Friendship (Social Media)</td><td rowspan="5">Allāh ﷻ says, "Successful indeed is the one who purifies their soul." [As-Shams 91:9]

The Prophet ﷺ said:
o "A person is upon the religion of his close friend, so beware whom you befriend" [Sunan Abī Dawūd 4833]
o "Love whom you love moderately, perhaps he will become hated to you someday. And hate the one for whom you have hatred moderately, perhaps he will become beloved to you someday" [At-Tirmidhī 1997]</td></tr>
<tr><td>You realise that spending time thinking or talking about other people's faults is foolish</td></tr>
<tr><td>You try to limit friendships, relationships or interactions online to people you have met in real life, because you have a better understanding of their value system, ethics, morals, and character</td></tr>
<tr><td>You realise that time is short and is better invested in contemplating what is permissible, and recognising one's own shortcomings and then working consistently to eradicate them</td></tr>
<tr><td>You adopt moderation in friendship and with the information you share with others, particularly sensitive family issues, because what you share could be used against you later</td></tr>
</table>

Fantasizing

Practical Treatment	Qur'ānic, Prophetic & Scholarly Evidence
Cutting off Thoughts & Lowering Your Gaze (Social Media) You realise that harbouring thoughts and fantasies about another person whilst with your partner is a kind of adultery (zina) You refrain from such thinking by reducing usage of everything that may provoke such fantasies, such as TV and social media, and instead regularly recite prescribed words of remembrance (adhkār), and focus on the present enjoyment instead of that which is absent You imagine your partner having fantasies like you do, and that this would therefore not be acceptable, and hence you try to use this thought to get rid of what you are feeling You realise that it is better to block or remove someone on social media who may be the cause of such fantasies You remind yourself that not everyone knows how to properly appreciate the value of personal privacy and modesty, therefore you deem it your responsibility to respect others. You steer clear of posting pictures without a person's permission, and also avoid stalking someone's profile You remind yourself that your heart darkens with evil glancing and unrestrained gazes, and in the same way, your heart gains illumination with the lowering of your gaze You lower your gaze for the pleasure of Allāh ﷻ, and as a recompense, you feel a sweetness and a sense of harmony in your heart, which will also be felt in your worship	Allāh ﷻ says: o "(O Prophet!) Tell the believing men to lower their gaze and guard their chastity. That is purer for them. Surely Allāh is All-Aware of what they do. And tell the believing women to lower their gaze and guard their chastity, and not to reveal their adornments except what normally appears" [An-Nūr 24:30] o And as for those who were in awe of standing before their Lord and restrained themselves from (evil) desires, Paradise will certainly be (their) home" [An-Nāzi'āt 79:40-41] o "Surely whoever is mindful (of Allāh) and patient, then certainly Allāh never discounts the reward of the good-doers" [Yūsuf 12:90] The Prophet ﷺ said: o "A man shall not look at the nakedness of (another) man, nor shall a woman look at the nakedness of (another) woman" [Ṣaḥīḥ Muslim 338:74] o "Beware of sitting in the roads." They said, "O Messenger of Allāh, we have nowhere else to sit and talk." The Prophet ﷺ said, "If you insist, then give the road its right." They said, "What is its right, O Messenger of Allāh?" The Prophet ﷺ said, "Lower the gaze, refrain from harming others, return greetings of peace, enjoin good and forbid evil" [Ṣaḥīḥ Al-Bukhārī 2465, Ṣaḥīḥ Muslim 2121:114] Imām Al-Ghazālī ﷺ writes: "The way to ward off distracting thoughts is to cut off their source, i.e. avoid the means that could create these thoughts; if the source of such thoughts is not stopped, it will keep generating them." [Iḥyā 'Ulūm Ad-Dīn 1:162]

FANTASIZING

Fantasizing

Exceptions	Qur'ānic, Prophetic & Scholarly Evidence
Not Dwelling on What Crosses One's Mind You remind yourself that whatever forbidden activity crosses your mind, so long as you do not dwell on it or continue to think of it, you are forgiven for it	Allāh ﷻ says, "Allāh does not require of any soul more than what it can afford." [Al-Baqarah 2:286] The Prophet ﷺ said: o "Allāh has forgiven my ummah for whatever crosses their mind so long as they do not speak of it nor act upon it" [Ṣaḥīḥ Al-Bukhārī 5269, Ṣaḥīḥ Muslim 127:201] o (To another Companion,) not to follow the first (unintentional) look with a second (deliberate) look, for the first one is excused, but the second is not. If one's eyes unintentionally fall on a member of the opposite gender, one should stop looking as soon as one realises it, and should neither continue looking nor look again deliberately, for the gaze is one of the poisoned arrows of Satan: "The furtive glance is one of the poisoned arrows of Satan, on him be God's curse. Whoever forsakes it for the fear of Allāh, will receive from Him faith, the sweetness of which he will find within his heart" [Al-Ḥākim 7875] Imam An-Nawawī says "As for thoughts, when a person does not dwell on them or continue to think about them, they are forgiven according to the consensus of the scholars. This is because one does not have a choice in their occurrence nor does one have a way to avoid it." [Al-Adhkār by Imām An-Nawawī, p.535] Jarīr ibn Abdullāh رضي الله عنه said, "I asked the Messenger of Allāh ﷺ about (the Islāmic ruling on) anaccidental glance and he ordered me to turn my eyes away." [At-Tirmidhī 2776]

خَوْفُ الفَقْر

Fear of Poverty

SIGNS & SYMPTOMS

- Preoccupied with Loss of Wealth
- Constant Worry
- Keeping Bad Company

TREATMENTS

- Good Opinion of Allāh ﷻ
- Trusting in Allāh ﷻ & Severing Hope in Others
- Contentment
- Recognising & Deflecting Whisperings
- Spending on the Poor & Needy
- Seeking Forgiveness Abundantly
- Keeping Transactions Free from Sin
- Constantly Worshipping & Making Du'ā (Supplicating) to Allāh ﷻ
- Establishing Ties of Kinship

EXCEPTIONS

- Inability to Support the Needy

CHAPTER 11

Fear of Poverty

[Khawf al-Faqr] خَوْفُ الفَقْر

When the heart is not correctly aligned to the decree of the Almighty, then dissatisfaction will always arise. Dislike of poverty can sit with a person when they are poor, but by far the more widespread disease is the fear of poverty when wealth is in place.

The general characteristic of this fear is that one's cash, capital, estates or resources will be destroyed or diminished, thus impacting on lifestyle and esteem. When this fear is placed in the heart of a person, the clinging greed intensifies, and they redouble their efforts to accumulate more wealth.

Without doubt, dissatisfaction with one's allotted portion goes hand in hand with spending little or no time in worshipping Allāh ﷻ or performing genuine acts of charity. The pursuit of worldly riches and comforts becomes the sufferer's goal in life.

The Prophet ﷺ said, "Whoever makes the Hereafter his goal, Allāh ﷻ makes his heart rich, and organizes his affairs, and the world comes to him whether it wants to or not. And whoever makes the world his goal, Allāh ﷻ puts his poverty right before his eyes, and disorganises his affairs, and the world does not come to him, except what has been decreed for him." [At-Tirmidhī 2465]

Fear of Poverty

Signs & Symptoms

Preoccupied with Loss of Wealth

You are preoccupied with the fear of losing wealth, and as a result you desperately cling to your money and deprive the needy, and yourself, of the goodness of giving for the sake of Allāh ﷻ

You are vulnerable to violating laws, even to the point of indulging in indecency, for the purpose of gaining or protecting personal or family profit and wealth

You compromise your religion (e.g. you delay in giving charity) in order to achieve worldly gain, often out of the fear of poverty or plain greed

Constant Worry

You grieve over an abundance of concerns and problems, which are controlling you, however none have yet materialised

You are constantly worried about your estate and its potential loss

You enjoy no peace of mind and your life is rife with conflict, contention and treachery

Qur'ānic, Prophetic & Scholarly Evidence

Allāh ﷻ says:

- "The Devil threatens you with (the prospect of) poverty and bids you to the shameful deed (of stinginess), while Allāh promises you forgiveness and (great) bounties from Him. And Allāh is All-Bountiful, All-Knowing" [Al-Baqarah 2:268]
- "Know that this worldly life is no more than play, amusement, luxury, mutual boasting, and competition in wealth and children. This is like rain that causes plants to grow, to the delight of the planters. But later the plants dry up and you see them wither, then they are reduced to chaff. And in the Hereafter there will be either severe punishment or forgiveness and pleasure of Allāh, whereas the life of this world is no more than the delusion of enjoyment" [Al-Ḥadīd 57:20]

The Prophet ﷺ said:

- "Whoever makes the Hereafter his goal, Allāh makes his heart rich, and organizes his affairs, and the world comes to him whether it wants to or not. And whoever makes the world his goal, Allāh puts his poverty right before his eyes, and disorganises his affairs, and the world does not come to him, except what has been decreed for him" [At-Tirmidhī 2465]
- "The likeness of the one who frees a slave (or gives charity) at the time of his death is that of the one who gives his food away only after he has eaten his fill" [At-Tirmidhī 2123, Sunan Abī Dawūd 3968]
  This type of charity is not the ideal. A person should give charity when he is fit and healthy

Fear of Poverty

Signs & Symptoms

Qur'ānic, Prophetic & Scholarly Evidence

Keeping Bad Company	
You keep the company of people of disobedience for fear of loss of wealth, by praising their actions and displaying pleasure at their condition without condemnation (i.e. you seek some material benefit)	The Prophet ﷺ said: o "When you see those who shower (undue) praise (upon others), throw dust upon their faces" [Ṣaḥīḥ Muslim 3002:69, At-Tirmidhī 2393, Sunan Abī Dawūd 4804] o "A good friend and a bad friend are like a perfume-seller and a blacksmith: The perfume-seller might give you some perfume as a gift, or you might buy some from him, or at least you might smell its fragrance. As for the blacksmith, he might singe your clothes, and at the very least you will breathe in the fumes of the furnace" [Ṣaḥīḥ Al-Bukhārī 2101, 5534, Ṣaḥīḥ Muslim 2628:146]

Fear of Poverty

Academic Treatment

Good Opinion of Allāh ﷻ

You have a good opinion of Allāh ﷻ

You realise that Allāh ﷻ is the Provider and source of wealth and comfort

You are content to do good and trust in Allāh ﷻ

You realise that His dominion is never diminished in the least when He gives to His creation all that they need

Trusting in Allāh ﷻ & Severing Hope in Others

You establish an absolute trust in Allāh ﷻ, and this means that you become completely independent of other things

You begin to sever all hope in what others have

You understand that your provision depends on Allāh ﷻ and that He has guaranteed it, so you instead occupy yourself with worshipping Him

Contentment

You do not harbour bad thoughts towards someone who is given more than you

You understand that your share of life is there waiting for you and your sustenance has been preordained even before the creation of humankind

Your wholesome thoughts are expressed by your contentment with what you have, and because you do not stretch your eyes towards the assets of others

You remind yourself that the great bounty of 'ilm (knowledge) is true wealth, that nothing can be compared to the great bounty of knowledge and intelligence (particularly material wealth)

Qur'ānic, Prophetic & Scholarly Evidence

Allāh ﷻ has revealed:

- o "The Devil threatens you with (the prospect of) poverty and bids you to the shameful deed (of stinginess), while Allāh promises you forgiveness and (great) bounties from Him. And Allāh is All-Bountiful, All-Knowing" [Al-Baqarah 2:268]
- o "And whoever is mindful of Allāh, He will make a way out for them, and provide for them from sources they could never imagine. And whoever puts their trust in Allāh, then He (alone) is sufficient for them" [At-Ṭalāq 65: 2-3]
- o "Is Allāh not sufficient for His servant? Yet they threaten you with other (powerless) gods besides Him! Whoever Allāh leaves to stray will be left with no guide" [Az-Zumar 39:36]
- o "I seek no provision from them, nor do I need them to feed Me" [Ad-Dhāriyāt 51:57]
- o "Perhaps you dislike something which is good for you and like something which is bad for you. Allāh knows and you do not know" [Al-Baqarah 2:216]
- o "Had Allāh given abundant provisions to (all) His servants, they would have certainly transgressed throughout the land. But He sends down whatever He wills in perfect measure. He is truly All-Aware, All-Seeing of His servants" [Ash-Shūrā 42:27]
- o "If you tried to count Allāh's blessings, you would never be able to number them. Surely Allāh is All-Forgiving, Most Merciful" [An-Naḥl 16:18]
- o "There is no moving creature on earth whose provision is not guaranteed by Allāh. And He knows where it lives and where it is laid to rest. All is (written) in a perfect Record" [Hūd 11:6]

The Prophet ﷺ has said:

- o "Contentment is a treasure that is never exhausted" [Al-Mu'jam Al-Awsaṭ At-Ṭabarānī 6922]
- o "When you wake up either in the morning or in the evening, say: 'O Allāh, I take refuge in You from anxiety and sorrow, weakness and laziness, miserliness and cowardice, the burden of debts and being overpowered by men" [Sunan Abī Dawūd 1555]

Fear of Poverty

Academic Treatment	Qur'ānic, Prophetic & Scholarly Evidence
Recognising & Deflecting Whisperings	
You understand that Satan attempts to inspire you to be penny-pinching and narrow-minded, preventing you from giving generously	**Allāh ﷻ has revealed,** "The Devil threatens you with (the prospect of) poverty and bids you to the shameful deed (of stinginess), while Allāh promises you forgiveness and (great) bounties from Him. And Allāh is All-Bountiful, All-Knowing." [Al-Baqarah 2:268]
You deflect his insidious whisperings and subtle provocations that create irrational fear in yourself	**The Messenger of Allāh ﷺ said,** "When a man decides to give something in charity, a group of seventy devils clings to him and tries to put him off it." [Musnad Aḥmad 22962]
You realise that you may never have to face the mountain of concerns and problems over which you grieve	"I've had a lot of worries in my life, most of which never happened." [Mark Twain, an American writer, humourist, etc.]

Fear of Poverty

Parctical Treatment	Qur'ānic, Prophetic & Scholarly Evidence
Spending on the Poor & Needy	
You remind yourself that the heaviest blow to Satan and the most successful method to counter his tricks is to spend your money in the cause of Allāh ﷻ You love for others what you love for yourself You expend on behalf of the needy because you realise that you shall receive a far more valuable return than the measure of what you spend	Allāh ﷻ says: o "And whoever puts their trust in Allāh, then He (alone) is sufficient for them" [At-Ṭalāq 65:3] o "So be mindful of Allāh to the best of your ability, hear and obey, and spend in charity - that will be best for you. And whoever is saved from the selfishness of their own souls, it is they who are (truly) successful. If you lend to Allāh a good loan, He will multiply it for you and forgive you. For Allāh is Most Appreciative, Most Forbearing. (He is the) Knower of the seen and unseen - the Almighty, All-Wise" [At-Taghābun 64: 16-18] The Prophet ﷺ said: o "The upper hand is superior to the lower hand, the upper hand is the one which spends and the lower hand is the one that asks" [Ṣaḥīḥ Muslim 1033:94] o "Love for others what you love for yourself, you will be a true believer" [Ibn Mājah 4217] o "None of you are true believers until you love for your brother what you love for yourself" [Ṣaḥīḥ Al-Bukhārī 13, Ṣaḥīḥ Muslim 45:71]

Fear of Poverty

Practical Treatment	Qur'ānic, Prophetic & Scholarly Evidence
Seeking Forgiveness Abundantly	
You look towards your own misdeeds and take them to be the reason for finding yourself in the predicament you are in, appreciating that sometimes, such circumstances are caused by Allāh ﷻ in order to make His servant turn towards Him	Allāh ﷻ says: o "Saying, 'Seek your Lord's forgiveness, (for) He is truly Most Forgiving. He will shower you with abundant rain, supply you with wealth and children, and give you gardens as well as rivers'" [Nūḥ 71: 10-12] o "And O my people! Seek your Lord's forgiveness and turn to Him in repentance. He will shower you with rain in abundance, and add strength to your strength. So do not turn away, persisting in wickedness" [Hūd 11:52]
You turn to Allāh ﷻ and repent	The Prophet ﷺ said, "If anyone continually asks pardon, Allāh will appoint for him a way out of every distress, and a relief from every anxiety, and will provide for him from where he did not reckon." [Sunan Abī Dawūd 1518]

Fear of Poverty

Practical Treatment	Qur'ānic, Prophetic & Scholarly Evidence
Keeping Transactions Free from Sin	
You learn in regards to what is permissible (halāl) and what is impermissible (harām), ensuring that any sustenance is both earned and used in a halāl manner	The Prophet ﷺ said: o "The two parties to a transaction have the option (of cancelling it) until they part. If they are honest and disclose any defects, their transaction will be blessed, but if they lie and conceal defects the blessing will be erased" [Ṣaḥīḥ Al-Bukhārī 2079, Ṣaḥīḥ Muslim 1532:47] o "Taking (false) oaths improves the sales, but it eradicates the blessings" [Ṣaḥīḥ Al-Bukhārī 2087, Ṣaḥīḥ Muslim 1606:131]
You ensure that all of your transactions are aligned with the teachings of Allāh ﷻ and His Messenger ﷺ because any that are not will be devoid of barakah (blessing), no matter how great the profit or benefit seems (i.e. this will soon disappear)	
Constantly Worshipping & Making Du'ā (Supplicating) to Allāh ﷻ	The Prophet ﷺ said, "Allāh says, 'O son of Ādam! Devote yourself to My worship, I will fill your chest with riches and alleviate your poverty. And if you do not do so, then I will fill your hands with problems and not alleviate your poverty'" [At-Tirmidhī 2466, Ibn Mājah 4107]
You worship and remember Allāh ﷻ always, striving to please Him by obeying His commandments and staying away from his prohibitions	
You remind yourself that in du'ā (supplication) lies the solution to all our problems	The Prophet ﷺ said, "Indeed, du'ā is of benefit for those things that have descended and (also) for those things that have not yet descended. O servants of Allāh, hold fast to du'ā." [At-Tirmidhī 3548]
Establishing Ties of Kinship	The Prophet ﷺ said: o "Whoever is pleased that he be granted more wealth and his life-span be extended, then let him establish the ties of kinship" [Ṣaḥīḥ Al-Bukhārī 5985] o "Learn (enough) of your lineage, so that you can establish the ties of kinship, for establishing the ties of kinship increases the love amongst families, and multiplies wealth, and extends age" [At-Tirmidhī 1979, Musnad Aḥmad 8868] o "Whoever is pleased to have his life extended, and that he be increased in his sustenance, and an evil death be averted from him, then let him be conscious of Allāh, and let him fulfil the ties of kinship!" [Musnad Aḥmad 1213]
You realise the importance of showing relatives kindness, compassion and mercy, by keeping in touch with them, paying them visits, and inquiring about their health and welfare	

Fear of Poverty

Exceptions

Inability to Support the Needy

There will be occasions when you cannot provide for the needy, however, you know and remind yourself that:

- This should encourage you to work hard so that you can fulfil both your own needs and also spend in the way of Allāh ﷻ
- There are a great variety of virtues and good deeds that fall within the category of ṣadaqah

Qur'ānic, Prophetic & Scholarly Evidence

The Prophet ﷺ said:

- "Giving in charity is an obligation upon every Muslim." **It was said (to him),** "What about one who does not find (the means) to do so?" **He said,** "Let him work with his hands, thus doing benefit to himself, and give in charity." **It was said to him,** "What if he does not have (the means) to do so?" **He said,** "Then let him assist the needy, the aggrieved." **It was said,** "What about if he cannot even do this?" **He said,** "Then he should enjoin good." **He was asked:** "What if he cannot do that?" **He said,** "He should then abstain from evil, for verily, that is a charity from him" [Ṣaḥīḥ Al-Bukhārī 6022, Ṣaḥīḥ Muslim 1008:55]
- "Every good deed (ma'rūf) is charity" [Ṣaḥīḥ Al-Bukhārī 6021]
- "Take advantage of five matters before five other matters: your youth before you become old; your health, before you fall sick; your wealth, before you become poor; your free time before you become preoccupied, and your life, before your death" [Al-Bayhaqī in Shu'ab Al-Īmān 9767]

الغِشّ

Fraud

TREATMENTS

- Being Conscious of Deceit & Corruption
- Honesty & Trustworthiness in Social Life & in Business
- Avoiding Deceit
- Acknowledging Wrongful Doing & Rectifying Your Affairs
- Keeping Good Company
- Consistency in Honesty & Forgiveness
- Honesty in Speech
- Intention & Verification (Social Media)
- Asking for Proof

SIGNS & SYMPTOMS

- Rumouring & Social Media
- Fake Persona on Social Media
- Concealing the Truth (e.g. Product or Service Defects)
- Breaking Promises
- Excessive use of Ambiguity or Indirectness in Speech

EXCEPTIONS

- In Reconciliation
- Concealing Sins for Fear of Admonishment
- Ambiguity or Indirectness in Speech

CHAPTER 12

Fraud [Ghish] الغِشّ

The next disease is fraud or 'ghish'. It isn't wholly confined to deceiving customers or the tax man: it might involve concealment of any worldly or religious fault, blemish, or harm, possibly due to greed or love of wealth.

For some people, the definition of fraud (whether related to a product or a service) is the act of deceit in making something useless or defective seem useful and beneficial.

The Prophet ﷺ happened to pass by a heap of eatables (corn). He thrust his hand in that (heap) and his fingers were moistened. He said to the owner of that heap of eatables (corn): "What is this?" He replied: "O Messenger of Allāh, these have been drenched by rainfall." He (the Prophet ﷺ) remarked: "Why did you not place this (the drenched part of the heap) over other eatables so that the people could see it? He who deceives is not of me (is not my follower)." [Ṣaḥīḥ Muslim 102:164]

Falsehood or lying (kidhb) is similar to fraud, in that it is when one speaks contrary to fact.

The Prophet ﷺ said:

- "Every ummah has a fitnah (means of testing). The fitnah of my ummah is wealth" [At-Tirmidhī 2336]
- "A time will come when one will not care how he gains his money: legally or illegally" [Ṣaḥīḥ Al-Bukhārī 2059]

Fraud

Signs & Symptoms	Qur'ānic, Prophetic & Scholarly Evidence
Rumouring & Social Media	
You love to show others that you care about causes, or that you are socially / politically / religiously active by commenting on anything and everything	Allāh ﷻ warns every Muslim against speaking without knowledge, as He says: o "Do not follow what you have no (sure) knowledge of. Indeed, all will be called to account for (their) hearing, sight, and intellect" [Al-'Isrā 17:36] o "O believers, if an evildoer brings you any news, verify (it) so you do not harm people unknowingly, becoming regretful for what you have done" [Al-Hujurāt 49:6]
You report every rumour or forward every post of the latest news story, gossip, or alleged 'major incident' without investigating whether it is factual or not	The Prophet ﷺ also warned us: o "It is enough lying for a man to speak of everything that he hears" [Ṣaḥīḥ Muslim 5:5] o "A man might speak a word (without thinking about its implications), but because of it, he will plunge into the Hellfire further than the distance between the East and West" [Ṣaḥīḥ Al-Bukhārī 6477, Ṣaḥīḥ Muslim 2988:49] o "The worst type of lie is for a man to claim that he saw something which his eyes did not see" [Sunan Abī Dawūd] o "And He dislikes gossip for you" [Ṣaḥīḥ Muslim 1715:10]
You share information via social media without verification, checking your sources, or ensuring that what you're sharing is actually true; your information has no basis in fact, but is presented as being factually accurate: it qualifies as 'fake news'	o "There will come to the people years of treachery, when the liar will be regarded as honest, and the honest man will be regarded as a liar. The traitor will be regarded as loyal, and the loyal will be regarded as a traitor. And the 'Ruwaybiḍah' will decide matters" It was said, "Who are the 'Ruwaybiḍah'?" He ﷺ said, "Ignorant people who comment on public affairs" [Ibn Mājah 4036] Qatādah said, "Do not say, 'I saw' when you did not see, or 'I heard' when you did not hear, or 'I know' when you do not know, for Allāh will ask you about all of that." [Tafsīr Ibn Kathīr 5:75 under verse 17:36]
Fake Persona on Social Media	
You project one thing (e.g. piety) online and something completely different in person	The Prophet ﷺ said: "From the most evil of people on the Day of Judgement is the two-faced person who shows one face to one group of people and a different face to another." [Ṣaḥīḥ Al-Bukhārī 6058]

Fraud

Signs & Symptoms

Concealing the Truth (e.g. Product or Service Defects)

As a business person, you conceal product or service defects - or at least fail to disclose them - intentionally

You convince yourself that whoever makes the most skilled and persuasive argument is right, that the most important thing is to be convincing, whether you are telling the truth or lying, whether you are defending corruption or upholding justice

You have developed the skill of embellishing the truth and presenting it persuasively

Qur'ānic, Prophetic & Scholarly Evidence

Abdullah ibn Amir narrates, "My mother called me one day when the Messenger of Allāh ﷺ was sitting in our house. She said: 'Come here and I shall give you something.' The Messenger of Allāh ﷺ asked her: 'What did you intend to give him?' She replied, 'I intended to give him some dates.' The Messenger of Allāh ﷺ said: 'If you were not to give him anything, a lie would be recorded against you.'" [Sunan Abī Dawūd 4991]

The Prophet ﷺ also said:

- o "Taking (false) oaths will hasten the sale of the commodity but will destroy the barakah (blessings)" [Ṣaḥīḥ Al-Bukhārī 2087, Ṣaḥīḥ Muslim 1606:131]
- o "A man speaks lies and becomes habituated to it, such that he is recorded as a liar by Allāh" [Ṣaḥīḥ Al-Bukhārī 6094]
- o "Three types of people Allāh will not speak to on the Day of Qiyāmah, nor will He look at them with the sight of mercy nor purify and cleanse them of their sins, and a severe punishment awaits them. (one of them is:) A man who takes an oath falsely that he has been offered for his goods so much more than what he is given" (i.e. he lies about the quality of the merchandise etc. to people with false oaths) [Ṣaḥīḥ Al-Bukhārī 2369]
- o "Beware of lying, for lying leads to transgression and transgression leads to the Fire" [Sunan Abī Dawūd 4989]
- o "He who deceives (cheats) is not of me" [Ṣaḥīḥ Muslim 102:164]

Fraud

Signs & Symptoms

Breaking Promises

You make promises of two kinds:

- o A promise made with no intention of being kept, by saying something akin to: 'I will do such-and-such in sha' Allāh'. In other words, you simultaneously tell a lie and break your promise
- o A promise made with the intention of keeping it, but then later broken by your own choice

As a result of your deception, you devour the rights of the needy, homeless, widows and orphans. You don't channel any of your surplus wealth their way in the form of zakāh or ṣadaqah

Excessive use of Ambiguity or Indirectness in Speech

You find yourself excessively using indirectness in speech, which places your friendship(s) at risk because your friends are always in doubt as to what you mean

Your friends or acquaintances come to know that the reality is different from what you have told; they were also not aware that you were actually engaging in deliberate ambiguity, so they start to consider you a liar

As a result of using such a technique frequently (i.e. deception) you become proud of your ability to take advantage of people

Qur'ānic, Prophetic & Scholarly Evidence

And regarding the one who breaks an agreement and is guilty of treachery, Allāh ﷻ says: "Surely Allāh does not like those who betray." [Al-'Anfāl 8:58]

The Prophet ﷺ said:

- o "The signs of a hypocrite are three: when he speaks he lies, when he promises he breaks it, and when entrusted he betrays his trust (he defrauds)" [Ṣaḥīḥ Al-Bukhārī 33, 2682, 2749, 60955]
- o "Falsehood leads to al-fajūr (i.e. wickedness, evil-doing), and al-fajūr (wickedness) leads to the (Hell) Fire, and a man may keep on telling lies till he is written before Allāh, as a liar" [Ṣaḥīḥ Al-Bukhārī 6094]
- o "Woe to the one who talks about something to make the people laugh, in which he lies. Woe to him! Woe to him!" [At-Tirmidhī 2315]
- o "There are four things that whoever has them, then he is a hypocrite. Whoever has one attribute from among them, then he has an attribute of hypocrisy until he leaves it. (1) When he speaks, he lies, (2) he does not fulfill whenever he promises, (3) he is vulgar whenever he argues, and (4) whenever he makes an agreement he proves to be treacherous" [At-Tirmidhī 2632]
- o "Whoever does not give up false statements (i.e. telling lies), and evil deeds, and speaking bad words to others, Allāh is not in need of his (fasting) leaving his food and drink" [Ṣaḥīḥ Al-Bukhārī 6057]

Fraud

Academic Treatment	Qur'ānic, Prophetic & Scholarly Evidence
Being Conscious of Deceit & Corruption	
You remind yourself that there are many people who have no hesitation in deceiving and cheating people, adorning their faces with smiles and appearing as wonderful people, but that they will cheat a person whenever the opportunity arises	**The Prophet ﷺ said,** "There will come to the people years of treachery, when the liar will be regarded as honest, and the honest man will be regarded as a liar. The traitor will be regarded as loyal, and the loyal will be regarded as a traitor. And the 'Ruwaybiḍah' will decide matters" **It was said,** "Who are the 'Ruwaybiḍah'?" **He ﷺ said,** "Ignorant people who comment on public affairs." [Ibn Mājah 4036]
You understand that it is regarded as ghabn (deception) to benefit from someone else's ignorance, lack of experience and gullibility	
You remind yourself that each lie, each untruth, each moment of dishonesty, marks your heart with a black dot, and if this does not cease, you will move steadily towards the point of no return, when the heart is irreversibly blackened: at this juncture your name joins the list of habitual liars	

Fraud

Academic Treatment	Qur'ānic, Prophetic & Scholarly Evidence
Honesty & Trustworthiness in Social Life & in Business You remind yourself that if you speak or trade with honesty and integrity, you will be honoured with the company of the Prophets, other honest men, the martyrs and the righteous on the Day of Resurrection	Allāh says: o "And whoever obeys Allāh and the Messenger will be in the company of those blessed by Allāh: the Prophets, the people of truth, the martyrs, and the righteous - what honourable company! This is Allāh's favour, and Allāh fully knows (who deserves it)" [An-Nisā' 4: 69-70] o "Honour (your) pledges, for you will surely be accountable for them" [Al-'Isrā 17:34] o "Honour Allāh's covenant when you make a pledge, and do not break your oaths after confirming them, having made Allāh your guarantor. Surely Allāh knows all you do" [An-Naḥl 16:91] o "The (true) believers are only those who believe in Allāh and His Messenger – never doubting – and strive with their wealth and their lives in the cause of Allāh. They are the ones true in faith" [Al-Hujurāt 49:15]
You understand that the foundation of honesty and trustworthiness in business is simply keeping your word and fulfilling your promises	The Prophet said: o "The trustworthy, honest merchant will be with the Prophets, the honest men, and martyrs (on the Day of Resurrection)" [At-Tirmidhī 1209] o "Indeed the merchants will be resurrected on the Day of Judgement with the wicked, except the one who has taqwā of Allāh, who behaves charitably and is truthful" [At-Tirmidhī 1210] o "An honest merchant (businessman) is in the shade of the Throne on the Day of Judgement" [At-Targhīb wa At-Tarhīb Al-Asbahani 794]

Fraud

Practical Treatment	Qur'ānic, Prophetic & Scholarly Evidence
Avoiding Deceit You avoid deceit by explaining about any defects or imperfections of the products or services you are trading	The Prophet ﷺ said, "The two parties to a transaction have the option (of cancelling it) until they part. If they are honest and disclose any defects, their transaction will be blessed, but if they lie and conceal defects the blessing will be erased." [Ṣaḥīḥ Al-Bukhārī 2079, Ṣaḥīḥ Muslim 1532:47]
Acknowledging Wrongful Doing & Rectifying Your Affairs Where you have seized anything unlawfully and/or have taken part in wrongful legal action (known as ghasb), you repent to Allāh ﷻ and return the seized property to its owner and ask him for forgiveness (or replace it if it no longer exists)	Allāh ﷻ says: o "Do not consume one another's wealth unjustly, nor deliberately bribe authorities in order to devour a portion of others' property, knowing that it is a sin" [Al-Baqarah 2:188] o "O believers! Do not devour one another's wealth illegally, but rather trade by mutual consent. And do not kill (each other or) yourselves. Surely Allāh is ever Merciful to you" [An-Nisā' 4:29] The Prophet ﷺ said: o "Your blood, your property and your honour are sacred to you" [Ṣaḥīḥ Al-Bukhārī 67, 105, Ṣaḥīḥ Muslim 1679:29] o "The property of one's fellow is not permissible for a person unless he gives his consent" [Al-Ḥākim 318] o "Whoever seizes a handspan of land unlawfully, it will surround him to the depth of seven earths on the Day of Judgement" [Ṣaḥīḥ Muslim 1610:137] o "Whoever has oppressed another person concerning his reputation or anything else, he should beg him to forgive him today (before the Day of Resurrection) when there will be no dīnār or dirham (to compensate for wrong deeds), but if he has good deeds, those good deeds will be taken from him according to his oppression which he has done, and if he has no good deeds, the sins of the oppressed person will be loaded on him" [Ṣaḥīḥ Al-Bukhārī 2449] The Prophet of Allāh ﷺ cursed the one giving a bribe and the one receiving a bribe as well as the go between. [Musnad Aḥmad 22399]

Fraud

Practical Treatment	Qur'ānic, Prophetic & Scholarly Evidence
Keeping Good Company	
You understand that you will be influenced by your friends and acquaintances, so you look carefully for those who guide and encourage you towards what is good and help you in accomplishing that which Allāh ﷻ has ordered	Allāh ﷻ said: o "O believers! Be mindful of Allāh and be with the truthful" [At-Tawbah 9:119] o "And (beware of) the Day the wrongdoer will bite his nails (in regret) and say, 'Oh! I wish I had followed the Way along with the Messenger! Woe to me! I wish I had never taken so-and-so as a close friend. It was he who truly made me stray from the Reminder after it had reached me'" [Al-Furqān 25: 27-29] o "Close friends will be enemies to one another on that Day, except the righteous" [Al-Anbiyā' 43:67] The Prophet ﷺ said, "A person is upon the religion of his close friend, so beware whom you befriend." [Sunan Abī Dawūd 4833, At-Tirmidhī 2378]
Consistency in Honesty & Forgiveness	
You ensure your state of truthfulness (ṣidq) is lasting and dominant (there is no alternation or wavering between ṣidq and ghish from one day to the next)	Allāh ﷻ says, "O believers! Be mindful of Allāh, and say what is right. He will bless your deeds for you, and forgive your sins. And whoever obeys Allāh and His Messenger, has truly achieved a great triumph." [Al-Aḥzāb, 33: 70-71]
You realise that the only way to wash away the dots already present on your heart is to sincerely repent for your misdeeds, including an honest vow to yourself and Allāh ﷻ not to repeat the evil deeds you have committed	
You are alert at all times and compensate for any shortcomings, ensuring that you constantly improve and perfect the truthfulness of your acts	

Fraud

Practical Treatment

Honesty in Speech

When speaking, you are cautious and do not speak without thinking

You remind yourself that telling, retelling and spreading untruths kills the heart, hence you avoid it as you would poison

You are firm in confronting and restricting the urge to speak what is false, and check yourself first as to whether it will anger Allāh ﷻ

You make sure you do not use indirect speech with any regularity: on the contrary, your use of ambiguity is restricted only to situations of great difficulty

You protect your honour by not giving people cause to doubt your integrity

If you speak falsehood, you make up for this error by seeking forgiveness

Intention & Verification (Social Media)

You verify any news before taking any action, because you realise that just as viruses developed to infect computers can damage hardware and infrastructure, fake news, alternative facts or just plain lies also act like viruses that can damage your mind and can corrupt you and your family in a diabolical way

Where you have shared false information, you make sure that you delete what you have posted as soon as possible, and try your utmost to rectify what you have done by letting people know of your error, because you remind yourself that the hallmark of a Muslim should be his honesty and dependability

You make an intention to use social networks (X, Facebook, Instagram, WhatsApp, Skype, etc) only to spread goodness and peace: to maintain family ties, to check on friends, to spread the message of goodness whenever you can, and endeavour to choose the best approach using wisdom and clarity of thought

Qur'ānic, Prophetic & Scholarly Evidence

Allāh ﷻ says:

- "So shun the impurity of idolatry, and shun words of falsehood" [Al-Haj 22:30]
- "Invite (all) to the Way of your Lord with wisdom and kind advice, and only debate with them in the best manner. Surely your Lord (alone) knows best who has strayed from His Way and who is (rightly) guided" [An-Naḥl 16:125]
- "Successful indeed are the believers: Those who avoid idle talk" [Al-Mu'minūn 23: 1&3]
- "Not a word does a person utter without having a (vigilant) observer ready (to write it down)" [Qāf 50:18]
- "O believers, if an evildoer brings you any news, verify (it) so you do not harm people unknowingly, becoming regretful for what you have done" [Al-Hujurāt 49:6]

The Prophet ﷺ said:

- "He who remains silent is successful" [At-Tirmidhī 2501]
- "Anyone who believes in Allāh and the Last Day should either utter good words or stay silent" [Ṣaḥīḥ Al-Bukhārī 6018, Ṣaḥīḥ Muslim 47:74]
- "You must be truthful, for truthfulness leads to righteousness and righteousness leads to Paradise. A man will keep speaking the truth and striving to speak the truth until he will be recorded with Allāh as a ṣiddīq (speaker of the truth). Beware of telling lies, for lying leads to immorality and immorality leads to Hellfire. A man will keep telling lies and striving to tell lies until he is recorded with Allāh as a liar" [Ṣaḥīḥ Muslim 2607:105]
- "Actions are judged by their intentions, so each man will have what he intended. Therefore, he whose migration was for Allāh and His Messenger, his migration is for Allāh and His Messenger. But he whose migration was for some worldly benefit, or for a wife he might marry, his migration is to that for which he migrated" [Ṣaḥīḥ Al-Bukhārī 1]

Fraud

<table>
<tr><th>Practical Treatment</th><th>Qur'ānic, Prophetic & Scholarly Evidence</th></tr>
<tr><td>Asking for Proof</td><td rowspan="6">Allāh says, "O believers, if an evildoer brings you any news, verify (it) so you do not harm people unknowingly, becoming regretful for what you have done. And keep in mind that Allāh's Messenger is (still) in your midst. If he were to yield to you in many matters, you would surely suffer (the consequences). But Allāh has endeared faith to you, making it appealing in your hearts. And He has made disbelief, rebelliousness, and disobedience detestable to you. Those are the ones rightly guided. (This is) a bounty and a blessing from Allāh. And Allāh is All-Knowing, All-Wise." [Al-Hujurāt 49: 6-8]</td></tr>
<tr><td>Assuming a matter concerns you, you ensure you ask for proof if someone says to you that a given person is bad because you know that without proof, what has been said is bordering on a lie</td></tr>
<tr><td>Because corruption and fraud are widespread, you are rigorous in your investigation because some people often present themselves as mired in poverty, though they are well-off</td></tr>
<tr><td>You do not accept the news, without forethought, of someone known to openly indulge in major sins</td></tr>
<tr><td>You always test someone's sincerity and trustworthiness before entrusting him with anything significant (until their goodness becomes manifest), especially where there is much corruption in a given generation</td></tr>
<tr><td>You are careful with your distribution of charity (zakāh) because charity is considered a trust from Allāh, and it must be given with care</td></tr>
</table>

Fraud

Exceptions

In Reconciliation

In reconciliation, when you want to unify two Muslims

You can go to one party and say, 'so-and-so says these good things about you, or really respects you', etc.

Concealing Sins for Fear of Admonishment

Where someone is outwardly and 'normally' righteous, your concealment of their sins is permissible if an error has been made:

- In this case, it is regarded as 'ḥayā' (modesty) to conceal sins and to be grieved at their being exposed, because Allāh ﷻ prefers sins to be concealed and He dislikes sins to be exposed and advertised
- When sins become exposed, this serves no interest and carries only negative consequences, such as immediate and widespread blame and scolding

Qur'ānic, Prophetic & Scholarly Evidence

The Prophet ﷺ said, "A liar is not one who tries to bring reconciliation amongst people and speaks good (in order to avert dispute), or he conveys good." Ibn Shihāb said he did not hear that exemption was granted in anything where the people speak a lie but in three cases: in battle, for bringing reconciliation amongst persons and the narration of the words of the husband to his wife, and the narration of the words of a wife to her husband (in a twisted form in order to bring reconciliation between them). [Ṣaḥīḥ Muslim 2605:101]

The Prophet ﷺ said:

- "Whoever removes a worldly hardship from a believer, Allāh ﷻ will remove one of the hardships of the Day of Resurrection from him. Whoever grants respite to (a debtor) who is in difficulty, Allāh will grant him relief in this world and in the Hereafter. Whoever conceals (the fault of) a Muslim in this world, Allāh will conceal him (his faults) in this world and in the Hereafter. Allāh will help a person so long as he is helping his brother" [Ṣaḥīḥ Muslim 2699:38]
- "Forgive the mistakes of people of good qualities, but not faults to which prescribed penalties apply" [Sunan Abī Dawūd 4375]

Fraud

Exceptions	Qur'ānic, Prophetic & Scholarly Evidence
Ambiguity or Indirectness in Speech	
In a troublesome or dangerous situation where you need to say what is against the truth in order to protect yourself or an innocent party, there is no sin	The Prophet ﷺ said, "Indirect speech is a safe way to avoid a lie." [Ṣaḥīḥ Al-Bukhārī Title of Chapter 116 Book 78, Al-Adab Al-Mufrad 885]
You say something which has a closer meaning that the hearer will understand, but it also has a remote meaning and is linguistically correct	A certain old woman came to the Prophet ﷺ and requested him to pray to Allāh ﷻ to make her enter Paradise. The Prophet said, "O mother of so and so! No old woman shall enter into Paradise." On hearing this the old woman went back weeping. The Prophet ﷺ said to the people around him to go and tell the old woman that she would not enter into Paradise as an old woman (but rather as a young woman) [Shamāil Al-Muḥammadiyyah by At-Tirmidhī 230]. Then he recited the verse: "Surely We have made up those females in a special creation, and have made them virgins, amorous to their husbands, matching them in age." [Al-Wāqi'ah 56: 35-37]
Whatever you say does not present a truth as falsehood and vice versa (i.e. when you say something it is not what is meant in your heart)	
You ensure that your use of ambiguity is restricted only to situations of great difficulty	It is known that people used to come frequently to the houses of certain scholars. These scholars liked to study and preferred not to be bothered by people, so they would tell their wives not to tell people where they were. When people came to their door asking where they were, the wives would reply, "Go and look for him in the masjid" (their wives did not lie and say they were not there, but rather suggested a place to look for him).

FRAUD

قَسْوَةُ الْقَلْبِ

Hard-Heartedness

SIGNS & SYMPTOMS

- No Care for Your Relationship with Allāh ﷻ
- Unaffected by the Words of the Qur'ān
- Indifferent to what is Permissible or Impermissible
- Indifferent to Actions of Worship
- Avoid Religious Gatherings & Advice
- Indifferent to the Difficulties of the Ummah
- Stubbornness in Times of Hardship
- Consumed by the Life of this World & Material Desires
- Unmoved by Funerals
- Persistent Harshness with Children

TREATMENTS

- Importance of the Condition of Your Heart & its Spiritual Health
- Re-Connecting with Allāh ﷻ
- Reflect on the Qur'ān & Remembrance of Allāh ﷻ
- Remembrance of Death
- Righteous Deeds
- Keeping Righteous Company
- Showing Compassion
- Forgiveness

NO EXCEPTIONS

- Any Level of Hard-Heartedness is Blameworthy

CHAPTER 13

Hard-Heartedness

[Qaswat al-Qalb] قَسْوَةُ القَلْب

The hard heart is that which contains a mixture of harshness and toughness, a heart that is continually void of submission and a sense of turning to Allāh ﷻ in repentance. Possessing a hard heart is in fact the severest of punishments because one is oblivious to the consequences of committing sins, and therefore neither repents nor experiences an ounce of guilt. His immune system, so to speak, shuts down to all other diseases of the heart. This is why the disbelievers are punished with having a hard and harsh heart.

The Prophet ﷺ said, "When a slave (a person) commits a sin (an evil deed) a black dot appears on his heart. Then if that person gives up that evil deed (sin), begs Allāh to forgive him, and repents, then his heart is cleared (from that heart-covering dot); but if he repeats the evil deed (sin), then that covering is increased till his heart is completely covered with it. And this is ar-rān that Allāh mentioned (in the Qur'ān), 'But no! In fact, their hearts have been stained by all (the evil) they used to commit!' [Al-Muṭaffifīn 83:14]" [At-Tirmidhī 3334]

Hard-Heartedness

Signs & Symptoms

No Care for Your Relationship with Allāh ﷻ

You have no care about establishing or revitalising a relationship with Allāh ﷻ

Unaffected by the Words of the Qur'ān

You listen to the Qur'ān and are reminded of the words of Allāh ﷻ, however you do not become fearful and humbled as a result

Indifferent to what is Permissible or Impermissible

You neither follow nor care about the laws of Islām; the issue of committing sins is not important to you

You are indifferent to whether something is permissible (halāl) or impermissible (harām), feeling little or no guilt

Indifferent to Actions of Worship

You do not enjoy actions of worship, such as praying, reading the Qur'ān, or attending religious gatherings; indeed you remain unconcerned when you do not perform some good deeds and miss prescribed times of worship

Avoid Religious Gatherings & Advice

When you do attend religious gatherings, you 'zone out', not taking any pleasure from them because you find them uninteresting or tedious

Indeed, you feel that you have no need of benefiting from 'spiritual' or 'religious' advice because your definition of 'goodness' is centred around being a 'good human being' and you therefore feel that this is sufficient

You avoid, ignore or discourage attending gatherings that involve the remembrance (dhikr) of Allāh ﷻ

Qur'ānic, Prophetic & Scholarly Evidence

Allāh ﷻ says:

- "So woe to those whose hearts are hardened at the remembrance of Allāh!" [Az-Zumar 39:22]
- "Has the time not yet come for believers' hearts to be humbled at the remembrance of Allāh and what has been revealed of the truth, and not be like those given the Scripture before - (those) who were spoiled for so long that their hearts became hardened. And many of them are (still) rebellious" [Al-Ḥadīd 57:16]
- "But they broke their covenant, so We condemned them and hardened their hearts" [Al-Mā'idah 5:13]
- "But no! In fact, their hearts have been stained by all (the evil) they used to commit!" [Al-Muṭaffifīn 83:14]
- "But whoever turns away from My Reminder will certainly have a miserable life, then We will raise them up blind on the Day of Judgement" [Tāhā 20:124]

Hard-Heartedness

Signs & Symptoms	Qur'ānic, Prophetic & Scholarly Evidence
Indifferent to the Difficulties of the Ummah	
You do not react to the needs of Muslims by making supplications, giving charity, or offering assistance	The Prophet ﷺ said: o "There are two blessings which many people do not make the best use of: good health and free time" [Ṣaḥīḥ Al-Bukhārī 6412] o "Do not laugh too much, for laughing deadens the heart" [At-Tirmidhī 2305, Ibn Mājah 4193]
You do not care if your brothers and sisters are afflicted by a hardship in any part of the world such as being overwhelmed and persecuted by oppressors, or being stricken by disasters	
You go to sleep at night thinking little of the difficulties that have been placed upon the Ummah and without thanking Allāh ﷻ for the blessings you have	
Stubbornness in Times of Hardship	
Even in times of hardship, you do not revert to humbleness and humility to Allāh ﷻ	Allāh ﷻ says, "Why did they not humble themselves when We made them suffer? Instead, their hearts were hardened, and Satan made their misdeeds appealing to them." [Al An'ām 6:43]

Hard-Heartedness

Signs & Symptoms	Qur'ānic, Prophetic & Scholarly Evidence
Consumed by the Life of this World & Material Desires	
You are consumed with the life of this world to the extent that you have forgotten or have become heedless and oblivious of the life to come	
You have become so attached to and pleased with material pleasures that your only concern is for the items that you do not have and with those you are so desperate to become	The Prophet ﷺ said: o "There are two blessings which many people do not make the best use of: good health and free time" [Ṣaḥīḥ Al-Bukhārī 6412] o "Do not laugh too much, for laughing deadens the heart" [At-Tirmidhī 2305, Ibn Mājah 4193]
You follow and fulfil your every single whim, desire and urge, paying little if any attention to your spirituality	
Your free time is centred around entertainment and wasting time, absorbing hours of TV, the internet and social media, as well as arranging and attending playful gatherings, one after the other	
Unmoved by Funerals	
You watch people die and attend funerals however you are not moved by this; you may even carry a corpse and bury it, yet you walk in the graveyard as if you are strolling between pine trees!	Allāh ﷻ says, "Even then your hearts became hardened like a rock or even harder." [Al-Baqarah 2:74]

Hard-Heartedness

Signs & Symptoms	Qur'ānic, Prophetic & Scholarly Evidence
Persistent Harshness with Children	
You consistently display unfair harshness towards your children	'Āishah (raḍiy Allāhu ʿanhā) said that a Bedouin man came to the Prophet (ṣallAllāhu ʿalayhi wa sallam) and said, "Indeed I have ten children and I have never kissed any of them." The Messenger of Allāh (ṣallAllāhu ʿalayhi wa sallam) looked at him and said, "Whoever does not show mercy will not be shown mercy." [Ṣaḥīḥ Al-Bukhārī 5997]
Your interactions with your children are largely based upon cold and hard rules, with an obvious lack of love, warmth and reassurance	

Hard-Heartedness

Academic Treatment	Qur'ānic, Prophetic & Scholarly Evidence
Importance of the Condition of Your Heart & its Spiritual Health	
You understand that the essential quality of a believer is that they are soft-hearted	Allāh ﷻ says, "It is out of Allāh's mercy that you (O Prophet) have been lenient with them. Had you been cruel or hard-hearted, they would have certainly abandoned you." [Āli 'Imrān 3:159]
You remind yourself that Allāh ﷻ cares about your deeds and the condition of your heart, not your appearance or wealth	The Prophet ﷺ said, "Allāh does not look at your outward appearance and your wealth, rather He looks at your hearts and deeds." [Ṣaḥīḥ Muslim 2564:33]
As you are vigilant over your physical health, whether that is monitoring your blood pressure or glucose levels, you also take steps to monitor the state of your 'spiritual' heart, ensuring that it remains or becomes soft	Allāh ﷻ says: o "Has the time not yet come for believers' hearts to be humbled at the remembrance of Allāh and what has been revealed of the truth?" [Al-Ḥadīd 57:16] o "Surely in the remembrance of Allāh do hearts find comfort" [Ar-Ra'ad 13:28] o "The remembrance of Allāh is (an) even greater (deterrent)" [Al-'Ankabūt 29:45] o "O believers! Remember Allāh often, and glorify Him morning and evening" [Al-Ahzāb 33: 41-42] o "Do they not ever reflect on camels – how they were (masterfully) created; and the sky – how it was raised (high); and the mountains – how they were firmly set up; and the earth – how it was levelled out?" [Al-Ghāshiyah 88: 17-20] o "We will show them Our signs in the universe and within themselves until it becomes clear to them that this (Qur'ān) is the truth. Is it not enough that your Lord is a Witness over all things?" [Al-Fuṣṣilat 41:53]
Re-Connecting with Allāh ﷻ	
You reflect on the creation of Allāh ﷻ, on natural phenomena, from the vastness of the sea to the watching of the sunset, all of which are truly mesmerising	
You monitor your relationship with Allāh ﷻ, and how often you remember and connect with Him	
You make du'ā to Allāh ﷻ, to re-establish your relationship and remain steadfast in your faith and soundness of heart	The Prophet ﷺ said: o "O Allāh! The turner of the hearts, turn our hearts towards Your obedience" [Ṣaḥīḥ Muslim 2654:17] o "Call upon Allāh with certainty that He will answer you. Know that Allāh will not answer the supplication of a heart that is negligent and distracted" [At-Tirmidhī 3479] o "When the believer commits sin, a black spot appears on his heart. If he repents and gives up that sin and seeks forgiveness, his heart will be polished" [Ibn Mājah 4244]

Hard-Heartedness

Academic Treatment	Qur'ānic, Prophetic & Scholarly Evidence
Reflect on the Qur'ān & Remembrance of Allāh ﷻ	
You remind yourself that dhikr or remembrance is the primary food of the soul, and that you should not deprive your soul of its core nourishment	Allāh ﷻ says: o "(It is) Allāh (Who) has sent down the best message – a Book of perfect consistency and repeated lessons – which causes the skin (and hearts) of those who fear their Lord to tremble, then their skin and hearts soften at the mention of (the mercy of) Allāh" [Az-Zumar 39:23] o "Has the time not yet come for believers' hearts to be humbled at the remembrance of Allāh and what has been revealed of the truth, and not be like those given the Scripture before – (those) who were spoiled for so long that their hearts became hardened? And many of them are (still) rebellious" [Al-Ḥadīd, 57:16] o (The Jinn said,) "Indeed, we have heard a wondrous recitation. It leads to right guidance so we believed in it, and we will never associate anyone with our Lord (in worship)" [Al-Jinn 72: 1-2]
You establish a routine whereby you are doing a certain amount of dhikr or remembrance every day and at certain times (e.g. before sleeping, upon awaking, after obligatory prayer), including recital of the Glorious Qur'ān, reminding yourself that remembrance of Allāh ﷻ is the spiritual food of your heart	The Prophet ﷺ said: "Allāh says, 'And My servant continues to draw near to me with nawāfil (supererogatory) deeds until I love him. When I love him, I am his hearing with which he hears, and his sight with which he sees, and his hand with which he feels, and his feet with which he walks. Were he to ask (something) of Me, I would surely give it to him; and were he to seek refuge with Me, I would surely grant him refuge.'" [Ṣaḥīḥ Al-Bukhārī 6502]

Hard-Heartedness

<table>
<tr><th>Practical Treatment</th><th>Qur'ānic, Prophetic
& Scholarly Evidence</th></tr>
<tr><td>Remembrance of Death</td><td rowspan="3">Allāh says, "You are distracted by mutual competition in amassing (worldly benefits), until you reach the graves. No! (This is not a correct attitude). You will soon know (the reality)." [At-Takāthur 102: 1-3]

The Prophet said:
o "I (once) had forbidden you from visiting graves, (and I now enjoin) you to do so, for in visiting them is a beneficial reminder" [Sunan Abī Dawūd 3235]
o "... for (such visits) soften the heart, bring tears to the eyes, and serve as a reminder of the Hereafter, (but be careful) not to speak forbidden expressions (i.e. while visiting)" [Al-Ḥākim 1393]</td></tr>
<tr><td>You treat your heart by constantly thinking of the Next World and the life to come, including those that were once close and dear to you that are now no longer here with you</td></tr>
<tr><td>You attend righteous gatherings, where you are happily reminded of the life to come</td></tr>
<tr><td>Righteous Deeds</td><td rowspan="2">The Prophet said, "Wondrous is the affair of the believer for there is good for him in every matter and this is not the case with anyone except the believer. If happiness reaches him, he is grateful (to Allāh) and thus there is good for him. If he is harmed, then he shows patience and thus there is good for him." [Ṣaḥīḥ Muslim 2999:64]</td></tr>
<tr><td>You are alerted at times of trial and calamity, by returning to Allāh, realising that indeed you are not perfect</td></tr>
<tr><td>You perform righteous deeds sincerely for the sake of Allāh only because you know that a slave of Allāh does not come closer to Him except by doing the deeds that He has made compulsory for him</td><td rowspan="2">The Prophet said:
o "Allāh will give shade, to seven, on the Day when there will be no shade but His. (These seven persons are) a just ruler, a youth who has been brought up in the worship of Allāh (i.e. worships Allāh sincerely from childhood), a man whose heart is attached to the mosques (i.e. to pray the compulsory prayers in the mosque in congregation), two persons who love each other only for Allāh's sake and they meet and part in Allāh's cause only, a man who refuses the call of a charming woman of noble birth for illicit intercourse with her and says: 'I am afraid of Allāh', a man who gives charitable gifts so secretly that his left hand does not know what his right hand has given (i.e. nobody knows how much he has given in charity), and a person who remembers Allāh in seclusion and his eyes are then flooded with tears" [Ṣaḥīḥ Al-Bukhārī 1423]
o "The Hell Fire is veiled by the things that are pleasing to us and Paradise is veiled by the things that we do not like" [Ṣaḥīḥ Al-Bukhārī 6487]</td></tr>
<tr><td>You therefore perform both the obligatory and supererogatory (nawāfil) deeds in order to become closer to Allāh</td></tr>
</table>

Hard-Heartedness

Practical Treatment	Qur'ānic, Prophetic & Scholarly Evidence
Keeping Righteous Company	
You are careful with respect to your circle of friends, ensuring you keep the company of persons who bring you closer to Allāh ﷻ	The Prophet ﷺ said, "A person is upon the religion of his close friend, so beware whom you befriend." [Sunan Abī Dawūd 4833, At-Tirmidhī 2378]
Showing Compassion	
You involve yourself in the trials and calamities of others, in order to appreciate the blessings that Allāh ﷻ has bestowed upon you alone, and so as to soften your heart (by shedding tears of gratefulness and also sorrow)	A man came to the Messenger of Allāh ﷺ, and he complained about the hardness of his heart. The Prophet ﷺ said, "If you want to soften your heart, feed the poor and pat the head of the orphan." [Musnad Aḥmad 7576, 9018] The Prophet ﷺ said: o "There is nothing that befalls a believer, not even a thorn that pricks him, but Allāh will record one good deed for him or will remove one bad deed from him" [Ṣaḥīḥ Muslim 2572:51] o "The likeness of the believers in their mutual love, mercy and compassion is that of the body; when one part of it suffers, the rest of the body joins it in staying awake and suffering fever" [Ṣaḥīḥ Al-Bukhārī 6011, Ṣaḥīḥ Muslim 2586:66]
You show kindness and compassion to your children, as you realise that a home that contains these qualities is a home that is full of happiness and joy	

Hard-Heartedness

Practical Treatment	Qur'ānic, Prophetic & Scholarly Evidence
Forgiveness	
You realise that there is no one who does not make mistakes and fall short, and who does not wrong other people or transgress their rights to some extent You come to understand that if you do not pardon another mortal like yourself, how can you hope for the pardon of Allāh ﷻ? You therefore let go of the pain you are feeling for the sake of Allāh ﷻ due to someone else's slip, mistake, or misunderstanding because this will free your heart of ill will and bitterness	Allāh ﷻ says: o "Let them pardon and forgive. Do you not love to be forgiven by Allāh? And Allāh is All-Forgiving, Most Merciful" [An-Nūr 24:22] o "But if you pardon, overlook, and forgive (their faults), then Allāh is truly All-Forgiving, Most Merciful" [At-Taghābun 64:14] o "But whoever pardons and seeks reconciliation, then their reward is with Allāh" [Ash-Shūrā 42:40] The Prophet ﷺ said: o "Be merciful to others and you will receive mercy. Forgive others and Allāh will forgive you" [Musnad Aḥmad 6541, 7041] o "If you hear something from your brother that you reject, make an excuse for him up to seventy excuses. If you cannot do it, then say: 'Perhaps he has an excuse I do not know'" [Al-Bayhaqī in Shu'ab Al-Īmān 7991]

Hard-Heartedness

NO Exceptions

Any Level of Hard-Heartedness is Blameworthy
You understand that a hard heart is that which contains a mixture of harshness and toughness
You understand that a heart that is void of submission and that does not turn to Allāh ﷻ in repentance will suffer the severest punishment
You remind yourself that this is why a stock punishment of the disbelievers is to be given a hard and harsh heart

Qur'ānic, Prophetic & Scholarly Evidence

The Prophet ﷺ said, "Do not talk for long without remembering Allāh, for talking much without remembering Allāh hardens the heart. The most distant of people from Allāh is one with a hardened heart." [At-Tirmidhī 2411]

البُغْض

Hatred

SIGNS & SYMPTOMS

- Illegitimate Hate
- Preventing you from Allāh's ﷻ Remembrance & Prayer
- Desiring Harm

TREATMENTS

- Accepting Allāh's ﷻ Decree
- Adopting Universal Brotherhood
- Understanding the Deceptions of Satan
- Adopting Moderation (Social Media)
- Suppressing the Ego & Reconciliation with Others

EXCEPTIONS

- Hating Corruption
- Mere Dislike, with No Intent or Desire to Harm

CHAPTER 14

Hatred [Bughd] البُغْض

Allāh ﷻ permits certain types of hatred: indeed, through revelation and the actions of the Noble Prophet ﷺ, we see that there are certain conditions whereby hatred can be deserving of merit. However, the hatred that is misguided and falls outside of the bounds of religion has no justification. Here, we are concerned with the hatred for other than that which Allāh ﷻ has decreed despicable.

Something similar to hatred is malice (hiqd), which asserts itself as repressed and frustrated anger when one lacks the power to take revenge or retribution. A more extreme form of anger is rancour (ghill), a despicable emotion that is rooted in being extremely angry at a person to the point that one wishes harm upon him.

The Prophet ﷺ once said to his Companions, "Do you want to see a man of Paradise?" A man then passed by and the Prophet ﷺ said, "That man is one of the people of Paradise." One Companion of the Prophet ﷺ took it upon himself to learn what it was about this man that earned him such a commendation from the Messenger of Allāh ﷺ. He spent time with this man and observed him closely: He noticed that he did not perform the night prayer vigil (tahajjud) or anything extraordinary; he appeared to be an average man of Madinah. The Companion finally confronted the man and told him what the Prophet ﷺ had said about him and asked if he did anything special. The man gave it some thought, and eventually replied, "The only thing that I can think of, other than what you have seen, is that I make sure that I never sleep with any rancour in my heart towards any believer, nor do I envy anyone for any goodness that Allāh has given them." That was his secret. [Musnad Aḥmad 12697]

Hatred

HATRED

Signs & Symptoms	Qur'ānic, Prophetic & Scholarly Evidence
Illegitimate Hate	
You hate or have a strong dislike for someone for no legitimate reason	The ultimate victim of rancour is its carrier. For this reason believers pray, "Our Lord! Forgive us and our fellow believers who preceded us in faith, and do not allow bitterness into our hearts towards those who believe. Our Lord! Indeed, You are Ever Gracious, Most Merciful." [Al-Ḥashr 59:10] Allāh ﷻ says, "Satan's plan is to stir up hostility and hatred between you with intoxicants and gambling and to prevent you from remembering Allāh and praying. Will you not then abstain?" [Al-Mā'idah 5:91] The Prophet ﷺ said: o "The deeds are presented on every Thursday and Monday and Allāh, the Exalted and Glorious, grants pardon to every person who does not associate anything with Allāh except the person in whose (heart) there is rancour against his brother. It would be said: Put both of them off until they are reconciled" [Ṣaḥīḥ Muslim 2565:35] o "Do not cut another off, nor desert one another, nor hate one another, nor envy one another. O worshippers of Allāh, be brothers. It is not lawful for the Muslim to shun his brother for more than three days" [At-Tirmidhī 1935]
You realise that when your anger has not been satisfied, its vapours engulf the heart, producing a raging effect that boils the heart	
Your heart contains evil for another by being busy with schemes to harm the one at whom your malice is directed	
You at times sleep with a grudge in your heart towards another	
You cut people off or boycott another over something quite petty or personal	
Preventing you from Allāh's ﷻ Remembrance & Prayer	
Your feelings of hatred distract you from the remembrance of Allāh ﷻ and prayer	
Desiring Harm	
You desire harm to befall the person you hate and discriminate against them because they are unlike you (in creed, colour or character)	

Hatred

Academic Treatment	Qur'ānic, Prophetic & Scholarly Evidence
Accepting Allāh's ﷻ Decree You realise that whenever you do not desire good for others, this is from envy, and envy is a rejection of Allāh's ﷻ decreed share for the creation in the world	Allāh ﷻ says, "And whoever puts their trust in Allāh, then He (alone) is sufficient for them. Certainly Allāh achieves His Will. Allāh has already set a destiny for everything." [At-Ṭalāq 65:3]
Adopting Universal Brotherhood You interpret 'brother' or 'sister' as universal brotherhood, which includes Muslims and non-Muslims alike You desire for your brother or sister that they enter into a state of submission (Islām) with their Lord and you therefore pray for their guidance You dislike things because of their potential outcome rather than focusing on the perpetrator of the act You understand that: o Love is an attribute of Allāh ﷻ, while hate is not o A name of Allāh ﷻ mentioned in the Qur'ān is Al-Wadūd, the Loving one o Hate is the absence of love, and only through love can hatred be removed from the heart	One of the great blessings of Paradise is that Allāh ﷻ will completely remove any semblance of rancour from one's heart. Allāh ﷻ says: o "We will remove whatever bitterness they had in their hearts. Rivers will flow under their feet. And they will say, 'Praise be to Allāh for guiding us to this. We would have never been guided if Allāh had not guided us. The messengers of our Lord had certainly come with the truth.' It will be announced to them, 'This is Paradise awarded to you for what you used to do'" [Al-'A'rāf 7:43] o "We will remove whatever bitterness they had in their hearts. In a friendly manner, they will be on thrones, facing one another" [Al-Ḥijr 15:47] The Prophet ﷺ taught us: o "Do not harbour mutual hatred" [Ṣaḥīḥ Al-Bukhārī 5143, 6064, 6065, 6066, Ṣaḥīḥ Muslim 2563:28] o "A believing man should not hate a believing woman. If he dislikes one characteristic in her, he is pleased with another" [Ṣaḥīḥ Muslim 1469:61] o "Do not have malice against a Muslim; do not be envious of other Muslims; do not go against a Muslim and forsake him. Be like brothers with each other. It is not permissible for a Muslim to desert his brother for over three days" [Ṣaḥīḥ Muslim 2559:23] o "Whoever desires an increase in their sustenance and age, should keep good relations with their kith and kin" [Ṣaḥīḥ Al-Bukhārī 2067, 5985] o "That the best form of faith is "that you love for the sake of Allāh and that you hate for the sake of Allāh" [Musnad Aḥmad 22130] Umar ibn Al-Khattāb رضي الله عنه said "Whoever does not show mercy will not receive mercy. Whoever does not forgive others will not be forgiven. Whoever does not pardon others will not be pardoned. Whoever does not protect others will not be protected." [Al-Adab Al-Mufrad 371] A man once asked the Prophet ﷺ, "O Messenger of Allāh, how many times do I forgive my servant?" The Prophet ﷺ said, "Seventy times in a day." [At-Tirmidhī 1949]

Hatred

Practical Treatment	Qur'ānic, Prophetic & Scholarly Evidence
Understanding the Deceptions of Satan	
You understand the deceptions of Satan and his evil whisperings that can eventually take full control of all your thoughts and actions (i.e. taking revenge is from the Devil's path)	Allāh says, "Indeed, Allāh commands justice, grace, as well as courtesy to close relatives. He forbids indecency, wickedness, and aggression. He instructs you so perhaps you will be mindful." [An-Naḥl 16:90]
You realise the heavy burden that hatred carries, which neither benefits you nor harms your offender in any way	The Prophet said: o "O My servants, I have made oppression unlawful for Me and unlawful for you, so do not commit oppression against one another" [Ṣaḥīḥ Muslim 2577:55] o "Mūsa asked Allāh "Who is the most honourable of your servants. Allāh said: "He who forgives having the power to release (his anger and take revenge)" [Al-Bayhaqī in Shu'ab Al-Īmān 7974]

HATRED

Hatred

Practical Treatment	Qur'ānic, Prophetic & Scholarly Evidence
Adopt Moderation (Social Media)	
You adopt moderation in friendship and with the information you share with others, particularly sensitive family issues, because what you share could be used against you later	The Prophet ﷺ said, "Love whom you love moderately, perhaps he will become hated to you someday. And hate the one for whom you have hatred moderately, perhaps he will become beloved to you someday." [At-Tirmidhī 1997]
You realise that it is better to block or remove someone on social media than to openly display hostility towards them	
Suppressing the Ego & Reconciliation with Others	
You are the first to exchange greetings, followed by forgiving the other person and dealing with him normally, even if it is difficult or exaggerated (at first)	Allāh ﷻ says, "Be gracious, enjoin what is right, and turn away from those who act ignorantly." [Al-'A'rāf 7:199] The Prophet ﷺ taught us: o "Young man, if you are able every morning and evening to remove any rancour from your heart towards anyone, then do so. Young man, that is my sunnah. Whoever revives my sunnah has loved me, and whoever loves me will be with me in Paradise" [At-Tirmidhī 2678] o "It is not lawful for anyone to abandon his brother in Islām for more than three nights, that when they meet they ignore one another, and the best of them is the one who greets the other first" [Ṣaḥīḥ Al-Bukhārī 6077, Ṣaḥīḥ Muslim 2560:25, Sunan Abī Dawūd 4911] o "Everything good is charity. And indeed among the good is to meet your brother with a smiling face" [At-Tirmidhī 1970] o "None of you has achieved faith until he loves for his brother what he loves for himself" [Ṣaḥīḥ Al-Bukhārī 13, Ṣaḥīḥ Muslim 45:71]
You remind yourself that, by nature, people are naturally inclined to love those who do good to them, so after a short while the malice or feelings of bitterness begin to fall to the wayside	
In your supplications, you call on Almighty Allāh ﷻ to bless and forgive the person for whom you feel hatred. You mention them by name, with total sincerity and conviction, in a way that suppresses your ego (nafs), asking Allāh ﷻ to give this person good things in this life and the next	
You desire for good and benefit to come to another, irrespective of the difficulty you may be experiencing	
You realise that bearing a grudge is a serious affliction that festers in your heart and blocks the path to good things	
Even when others sever contact with you, you maintain contact with them	

Hatred

Exceptions

Qur'ānic, Prophetic & Scholarly Evidence

Hating Corruption

It is commendable to hate corruption, evil, disbelief, murder, indecency, and anything else that Allāh ﷻ has exposed as despicable

Mere Dislike, with No Intent or Desire to Harm

When you experience a feeling of mere dislike, which arises against your will, (where you have no intention nor desire to harm), then this is regarded as a 'natural' state, and is known as downheartedness or inqibāḍ

The Prophet ﷺ was asked regarding the best form of faith. He ﷺ said, "It is that you love for the sake of Allāh and that you hate for the sake of Allāh." [Musnad Aḥmad 22130]

HATRED

البُغض

الغَفْلَة

Heedlessness

SIGNS & SYMPTOMS

- Heedless of Accountability
- Keeping Bad Company & Not Defending the Truth
- Enslaved by Technology & Social Media

TREATMENTS

- Fulfilling Allāh's ﷻ Rights
- Reflecting on the Value of Time
- The Value of Keeping Good Company
- Reality of Death
- Counsel Children at a Young Age (Social Media)
- Valuing Time & Your Environment (Social Media)
- Seeking Good Company & Using Social Media to Encourage Good
- Limiting Your Laughter
- Accounting for One's Deeds & Seeking Allāh's ﷻ Forgiveness
- Honouring Righteous People
- Invoking Salutations on the Prophet ﷺ
- Recitation & Contemplation of the Qur'ān

EXCEPTIONS

- Humankind is Forgetful

CHAPTER 15

Heedlessness

[Ghaflah] الغَفْلَة

Heedlessness or ghaflah is being careless (paying a lack of attention) to what is infinitely more important in one's life (than material goods), i.e. what Allāh ﷻ has commanded us to do and what has been prohibited. The heedlessness referenced here is the most menacing form: being heedless of divine purpose, accountability, the resurrection, the ultimate standing, and judgement in the Hereafter.

Scholars have said that heedlessness is the one pathogen that breeds all the diseases of the heart. A mughaffal (a simpleton) is a person who is easily fooled, i.e. one who is diverted away from what is essential and consequential, yet inclined towards what is temporary and ultimately pointless.

Heedlessness

Signs & Symptoms

Heedless of Accountability

You possess the bounties of intellect, talent and capability, but do not contemplate properly

You are heedless - or at least pay little attention - to divine purpose, to your accountability, to the resurrection, to the ultimate standing, and to your judgement in the Hereafter

You do not see things the way they truly are, choosing a way of living that allows divine signs to pass you by without notice or much attention

You are heedless of what Allāh ﷻ has commanded and what He has prohibited, or you see the difference between the two as irrelevant

Qur'ānic, Prophetic & Scholarly Evidence

Allāh ﷻ:

- Says, "And do not obey those whose hearts We have made heedless of Our remembrance, who follow (only) their desires and whose state is (total) loss" [Al-Kahf 18:28]. He warns the Prophet ﷺ himself from conforming to the will of those whose hearts are in the state of heedlessness: for the people who turn away from the truth, Allāh ﷻ increases their heedlessness
- Says, "And do not be like those who forgot Allāh, so He made them forget themselves. It is they who are (truly) rebellious" [Al-Ḥashr 59:19]
- Speaks of the disbelievers unaffected by the message of the Prophets as having a veil (ghishāwah) over their eyes: "Allāh has sealed their hearts and their hearing, and their sight is covered. They will suffer a tremendous punishment" [Al-Baqarah 2:7]

The Qur'ān uses other words to refer to unmindfulness: those who laugh at the Qur'ān are 'As-sāmidūn' [An-Najm 53:61], ones who are so immersed in amusement that they are oblivious to reality.

Imām Al-Ghazālī says: "O disciple, if you do not act according to your knowledge today, and you do not make amends for days gone-by, you will say tomorrow on the Day of Resurrection, 'Our Lord, we have now seen and heard, so send us back, and we will do righteous deeds.' [As-Sajdah 32:12] And it will be replied, 'Fool! You have just come from there!'" [Letter to a Disciple/Ayyuhāl Walad, p.16-17]

Heedlessness

Signs & Symptoms	Qur'ānic, Prophetic & Scholarly Evidence
Keeping Bad Company & Not Defending the Truth	
You sit with people of disobedience, keep their company, praise their actions and display pleasure at their condition without disapproval	Allāh ﷻ says: o "And leave those who take this faith (of Islām) as mere play and amusement and are deluded by (their) worldly life" [Al-'A'rāf 6:70] o "He has already revealed to you in the Book that when you hear Allāh's revelations being denied or ridiculed, then do not sit in that company unless they engage in a different topic, or else you will be like them. Surely Allāh will gather the hypocrites and disbelievers all together in Hell" [An-Nisā' 4:140] o "And (beware of) the Day the wrongdoer will bite his nails (in regret) and say, 'Oh! I wish I had followed the Way along with the Messenger! Woe to me! I wish I had never taken so-and-so as a close friend. It was he who truly made me stray from the Reminder after it had reached me.' And Satan has always betrayed humanity" [Al-Furqān 25: 27-29] o "But when such a person comes to Us, one will say (to their associate), 'I wish you were as distant from me as the east is from the west! What an evil associate (you were)!' (It will be said to both,) 'Since you all did wrong, sharing in the punishment will be of no benefit to you this Day'" [Az-Zukhruf 43: 38-39] o "Indeed, the worst of all beings in the sight of Allāh are the (wilfully) deaf and dumb, who do not understand" [Al-'Anfāl 8:22] The Prophet ﷺ said, "Do not talk for long without remembering Allāh, for talking much without remembering Allāh hardens the heart. The most distant of people from Allāh is one with a hardened heart." [At-Tirmidhī 2411]
You keep silent when you should defend the truth	
You neither struggle against injustice and mischief, nor do you enjoin what is right nor forbid what is wrong	
You do not invite others to the way of truth, but instead apply your intellect and time in the way of idle talks, backbiting, and flatteries before the possessors of wealth and power	

HEEDLESSNESS

Heedlessness

Signs & Symptoms

Enslaved by Technology & Social Media

You panic or feel at a loss when you do not have your mobile phone

You are addicted to entertaining yourself, to instant pleasure; you become lost in the endlessness of the internet, video games, mobile phone games etc

You mindlessly check your feed (Facebook, Instagram, X, Tumblr, email, text, WhatsApp, etc) dozens of times a day while walking, running, eating, relaxing, waiting in line, using the bathroom, at red lights (and even driving), to see how many likes and comments you have

You voluntarily allow your feed into your personal space, which has a negative effect on you and your personal well-being

You have become heedless of what constitutes good manners, particularly when you are with your parents, spouse, and children:

- You converse with one person while simultaneously texting someone else
- You constantly glance at your phone while speaking to someone, giving the impression that you have something better to do than speak to this person

You largely rely on 'religious' status updates rather than developing your personal connection with Allāh ﷻ

Qur'ānic, Prophetic & Scholarly Evidence

Allāh ﷻ says:

- "They (only) know the worldly affairs of this life, but are (totally) oblivious to the Hereafter" [Ar-Rūm 30:7]
- "Indeed, We have destined many jinn and humans for Hell. They have hearts they do not understand with, eyes they do not see with, and ears they do not hear with. They are like cattle. In fact, they are even less guided! Such (people) are (entirely) heedless" [Al-'A'rāf 7:179]

The Prophet ﷺ said:

- "Do not talk for long without remembering Allāh, for talking much without remembering Allāh hardens the heart. The most distant of people from Allāh is one with a hardened heart" [At-Tirmidhī 2411]
- "There are two blessings which many people do not make the best use of: good health and free time" [Ṣaḥīḥ Al-Bukhārī 6412]

"As of 2017, the average daily social media usage of global internet users amounted to 135 minutes per day, up from 126 minutes in the previous year." [Statista 2018]

"Teens are spending more than one-third of their days using media such as online video or music – nearly nine hours on average, according to a new study from the family technology education non-profit group, Common Sense Media. For tweens, those between the ages of 8 and 12, the average is nearly six hours per day." [The Washington Post, 2015]

Accumulatively therefore, the average person may end up spending between 4 and 5 years of his/her life using media.

Heedlessness

Academic Treatment	Qur'ānic, Prophetic & Scholarly Evidence
Fulfilling Allāh's ﷻ Rights	
You give Allāh ﷻ His due right, by recognising the importance of fulfilling His commandments and avoiding what is prohibited (known as Huquq Allāh or Allāh's ﷻ right to be worshipped)	Allāh ﷻ says, "O believers! Obey Allāh and His Messenger and do not turn away from him while you hear (his call)." [Al-'Anfāl 8:20]
Reflecting on the Value of Time	
You are conscious of the value of time, that it is a blessing from Allāh ﷻ, and that life in this world is but temporary because you do not know your appointed time of death	The Prophet ﷺ said: o "There are two blessings which many people do not make the best use of: good health and free time" [Ṣaḥīḥ Al-Bukhārī 6412] o "Take advantage of five matters before five other matters: your youth before you become old; your health, before you fall sick; your wealth, before you become poor; your free time before you become preoccupied, and your life, before your death" [Al-Bayhaqī in Shu'ab Al-Īmān 9767]
You understand that wasting even a single moment is an opportunity gone, never to return	

Heedlessness

Academic Treatment	Qur'ānic, Prophetic & Scholarly Evidence
The Value of Keeping Good Company	
You realise that the company you keep has inroads to your heart and your morality (as recognised in virtually all traditions and cultures)	Allāh ﷻ says, "And patiently stick with those who call upon their Lord morning and evening, seeking His pleasure. Do not let your eyes look beyond them, desiring the luxuries of this worldly life. And do not obey those whose hearts We have made heedless of Our remembrance, who follow (only) their desires and whose state is (total) loss." [Al-Kahf 18:28]
You realise that by being surrounded by people who are sincere and trustworthy, you will only stand to benefit from them, and even when you err, good companions will remind you and set you aright	The Prophet ﷺ said: o "A person is upon the religion of his close friend, so beware whom you befriend" [At-Tirmidhī 2378] o "A good friend and a bad friend are like a perfume-seller and a blacksmith: The perfume-seller might give you some perfume as a gift, or you might buy some from him, or at least you might smell its fragrance. As for the blacksmith, he might singe your clothes, and at the very least you will breathe in the fumes of the furnace" [Ṣaḥīḥ Al-Bukhārī 2101, Ṣaḥīḥ Muslim 2628:146]

Heedlessness

Academic Treatment	Qur'ānic, Prophetic & Scholarly Evidence
Reality of Death	
You remind yourself of what Allāh ﷻ has warned you about in the Qur'ān by letting you have a peek at the Day of Judgement You are reminded about what the wrongdoers will say and how exactly they will feel when they are called for His meeting You realise that as soon as you die, the veils are lifted and you will no longer live in heedlessness	When death comes to one of them, Allāh ﷻ says they will yearn to return, and regret the wasted time: o "When death approaches any of them, they cry, 'My Lord! Let me go back, so I may do good in what I left behind.' Never! It is only a (useless) appeal they make. And there is a barrier behind them until the Day they are resurrected" [Al-Mu'minūn 23: 99-100] o "If only you could see the wicked hanging their heads (in shame) before their Lord, (crying:) "Our Lord! We have now seen and heard, so send us back and we will do good. We truly have sure faith (now)!" [As-Sajdah 32:12] o "Losers indeed are those who deny the meeting with Allāh until the Hour takes them by surprise, then they will cry, "Woe to us for having ignored this!" They will bear (the burden of) their sins on their backs. Evil indeed is their burden!" [Al-An'ām 6:31] o "On the Day He will call you, you will (instantly) respond by praising Him, thinking you had remained (in the world) only for a little while" [Al-'Isrā 17:52]
You were created to remember Allāh ﷻ, so would rather be cured of heedlessness in this life, where it counts, when your obedience in this arena of tests and trials yields fruits	On the Day of Reckoning, the heedless will be driven to their chastisement and be told along the way, "(It will be said to the denier,) You were totally heedless of this. Now We have lifted this veil of yours, so Today your sight is sharp!" [Qāf 50:22]
Counsel Children at a Young Age (Social Media)	
As a responsible parent, you teach your children how to utilise social media responsibly You come together as a family and set appropriate guidelines, by having open and honest conversations, and establishing firm principles that hold true regardless of technological changes (e.g. strict usage limits)	The Prophet ﷺ said, "Each of you is a shepherd and each of you is responsible for his flock. The ruler who is over the people is a shepherd and is responsible for his flock; a man is a shepherd in charge of the inhabitants of his household and he is responsible for his flock; a woman is a shepherdess in charge of her husband's house and children and she is responsible for them; and a man's slave is a shepherd in charge of his master's property and he is responsible for it. So each of you is a shepherd and each of you is responsible for his flock." [Sunan Abī Dawūd 2928]

Heedlessness

Practical Treatment	Qur'ānic, Prophetic & Scholarly Evidence
Valuing Time & Your Environment (Social Media)	
You remain mindful of the amount of time you are spending on technology	Allāh ﷻ says: o "By the (passage of) time! Surely humanity is in (grave) loss, except those who have faith, do good, and urge each other to the truth, and urge each other to perseverance" [Al-'Aṣr 103: 1-3] o "O believers! Obey Allāh and obey the Messenger, and do not let your deeds be in vain" [Muḥammad 47:33]
You give preference to those around you instead of those you are chatting to via WhatsApp and other social media tools	The Prophet ﷺ said, " Race to do good deeds before seven things. Are you waiting but for overwhelming poverty, or distracting richness, or debilitating illness, or babbling senility, or sudden death, or the Dajjal, the worst hidden thing that is being awaited, or the Hour? The Hour is more calamitous and more bitter." [At-Tirmidhī 2306]
Seeking Good Company & Using Social Media to Encourage Good	
You are vigilant about protecting your environment and who you allow to influence you (including on social media)	The Prophet ﷺ said, "A good friend and a bad friend are like a perfume-seller and a blacksmith: The perfume-seller might give you some perfume as a gift, or you might buy some from him, or at least you might smell its fragrance. As for the blacksmith, he might singe your clothes, and at the very least you will breathe in the fumes of the furnace." [Ṣaḥīḥ Muslim 2628]
You keep (or seek out) good and sincere company: righteous people who do not cheat or lie	The Prophet ﷺ was reportedly asked: "Which of our companions are best?" He replied, "One whose appearance reminds you of Allāh, and whose speech increases you in knowledge, and whose actions remind you of the Hereafter." [Al-Bayhaqī in Shu'ab Al-Īmān 9000]
You utilise social media to try to encourage others to do good, and use it as a motivation for yourself as well	The Prophet ﷺ said: o "Whoever directs someone to do good will be rewarded equivalent to him who practises that good action" [Ṣaḥīḥ Muslim 1893:133] o "Convey from me, even if it is one āyah of the Qur'ān" [Ṣaḥīḥ Al-Bukhārī 3461] o "Let those who are present convey to those who are absent. For perhaps the one to whom it is conveyed will understand it better than the one who first heard it" [Ṣaḥīḥ Al-Bukhārī 67, 1741, 4406 Ṣaḥīḥ Muslim 1679:29]

Heedlessness

Practical Treatment	Qur'ānic, Prophetic & Scholarly Evidence
Limiting Your Laughter	
You realise that although there is no prohibition against laughter, prolonged amusement has the capacity to anaesthetise your soul, which can lead to foolishness	The Prophet ﷺ said o "Remember often the destroyer of pleasures (death)" [At-Tirmidhī 2307, Ibn Mājah 4258] o "Do not laugh too much, for verily excessive laughter kills the heart" [At-Tirmidhī 2305, Ibn Mājah 4193, 4217]
You control your moments of laughter and triviality by remembering death frequently	
Accounting for One's Deeds & Seeking Allāh's ﷻ Forgiveness	Istighfār (seeking forgiveness) at least a hundred times a day was one of the Prophet's ﷺ practices [Ṣaḥīḥ Muslim 2702:41, Sunan Abī Dawūd 1515, 1516], and closely followed by our righteous forebears (salaf). The Prophet ﷺ supplicated that Allāh ﷻ show him things in their reality, distinguished and clear: "Show me the truth as truth and give me the ability to follow it; and show me falsehood as falsehood and give me the ability to avoid it." [Tafsir Ibn Kathir 1:571 under verse 2:213]
You look at your 'moral book of accounts' at the end of each day to calculate your earnings with regard to what you have lost or gained with respect to Allāh's ﷻ pleasure (i.e. good deeds versus bad deeds)	
When you incur a loss (which you admit is a frequent occurrence), you seek Allāh's ﷻ forgiveness to balance things out	
You repent and seek forgiveness as a matter of regular worship	
Honouring Righteous People	Allāh ﷻ says, "Then We granted the Book to those We have chosen from Our servants." [Fāṭir 35:32]
You understand the spiritual status of righteous and knowledgeable people and you therefore honour and respect them	The Prophet ﷺ said: o "Scholars are the inheritors of the Prophets" [At-Tirmidhī 2682] o "Visit graves, for it reminds one of death" [Ṣaḥīḥ Muslim 976:108] o "Peace be upon you, dwellings of the believing people. There has come to you that which you were promised, and if Allāh wills we will follow you soon. O Allāh, forgive the people of Baqī' Al-Gharqad" [Ṣaḥīḥ Muslim 974:102]
You visit both the living as well as the dead as a sad reminder of death and the Hereafter	
You visit the graves of the great Muslims in Madinah, and you convey salutations of peace upon them, as the Prophet ﷺ visited the grave sites of his fallen Companions	Classically, the ranking of humanity proceeds as follows, as evidenced in the Qur'ān: "And whoever obeys Allāh and the Messenger will be in the company of those blessed by Allāh: the Prophets, the people of truth, the martyrs, and the righteous – what honourable company!" [An-Nisā' 4:69]

Heedlessness

Practical Treatment	Qur'ānic, Prophetic & Scholarly Evidence
Invoking Salutations on the Prophet ﷺ	
You realise that there is great light associated with invoking prayers of blessing upon the Prophet ﷺ	This is, in fact, a command from Allāh ﷻ Himself: "Indeed, Allāh showers His blessings upon the Prophet, and His angels pray for him. O believers! Invoke Allāh's blessings upon him, and salute him with worthy greetings of peace." [Al-Aḥzāb 33:56]
You understand that the muḥaddithīn (scholars of Prophetic traditions) are well known for this practice, and that many scholars have attested to the purifying effect that these prayers of blessings upon the Prophet ﷺ have upon the soul	The Companion Ubay ibn Ka'b ﵁ once asked the Prophet ﷺ how much of his litany of remembering Allāh ﷻ (dhikr) should be benedictions on the Prophet ﷺ. He said that a quarter would be good, and "If you add more, it is better." Ubay then asked, "And if I were to make it half?" The Prophet ﷺ said it was good, and "If you add more, it would be better." Ubay then asked, "And if I were to make it three-quarters?" The Prophet ﷺ said it was good, and "If you add more, it is better." Ubay ﵁ then declared that he would make all of his dhikr this way; the Prophet ﷺ said, "Then your problems would be solved and your sins would be forgiven." [At-Tirmidhī 2457]
You remind yourself that some scholars recommend that you repeat benedictions upon the Prophet ﷺ at least 500 times a day, and that others themselves would repeat it 5,000 times a day	
Recitation & Contemplation of the Qur'ān	
You remind yourself of the importance of establishing a daily connection with the Qur'ān by regularly reciting the Qur'ān and engaging with the Book of Allāh ﷻ, with tadabbur (reflection) to awaken your heart (noting that plain recitation is beneficial as well)	Allāh ﷻ says: o "O humanity! Indeed, there has come to you a warning from your Lord, a cure for what is in the hearts, a guide, and a mercy for the believers" [Yūnus 10:57] o "This is the Book! There is no doubt about it - a guide for those mindful (of Allāh)" [Al-Baqarah 2:2] o "(This is) a blessed Book which We have revealed to you (O Prophet) so that they may contemplate its verses, and people of reason may be mindful" [Ṣād 38:29]
You understand that it is important to know that the beauty of the Qur'ān comprises the meanings as well as the sound	The Prophet ﷺ said: o "Whoever recites ten ayahs (verses) in qiyām will not be recorded as one of the forgetful. Whoever recites a hundred ayahs in qiyām will be recorded as of the devout, and whoever prays a thousand ayahs in qiyām will be recorded as of one of the muqanṭarīn (those who pile up good deeds)" [Sunan Abī Dawūd 1398] o "Such a person who recites the Qur'ān and masters it by heart, will be with the noble righteous scribes (in Heaven). And such a person who exerts himself to learn the Qur'ān by heart, and recites it with great difficulty, will have a double reward" [Ṣaḥīḥ Al-Bukhārī 4937]
As a new Muslim, you strive with your utmost to learn how to read the text of the Qur'ān, and in the meantime, listen to well-known Qur'ān reciters or read a good English translation until you are able to read the Arabic	

Heedlessness

Exceptions

Humankind is Forgetful
You understand that some linguists believe the Arabic word for human being, 'insān', comes from the Arabic word 'nasya', which means 'to forget', implying that one of the characteristics of human beings is forgetfulness, which further implies that we need to be reminded often, hence the centrality of repetition in spiritual practices
You remind yourself that most verses containing forgetfulness in the Qur'ān attribute it and its results to Satan, as well as lack of concentration

Qur'ānic, Prophetic & Scholarly Evidence

Allāh ﷻ says, "And when you come across those who ridicule Our revelations, do not sit with them unless they engage in a different topic. Should Satan make you forget, then once you remember, do not (continue to) sit with the wrongdoing people." [Al An'ām 6:68]

The adolescent who was with Mūsa ﷺ said, "Do you remember when we rested by the rock? (That is when) I forgot the fish. None made me forget to mention this except Satan. And the fish made its way into the sea miraculously." [Al-Kahf: 18:63]

Abdullāh ibn Mas'ūd ﷺ reported: "The Messenger of Allāh prayed with us five units of prayer (raka'āt). We said, 'O Messenger of Allāh, you added something to the prayer.' The Prophet ﷺ said, 'What is that?' They said, 'You have prayed five raka'at.' The Prophet ﷺ said, 'Verily, I am only a human being like you. I remember as you remember and I forget as you forget.' Then the Prophet performed two prostrations for forgetfulness." [Ṣaḥīḥ Al-Bukhārī 401, Ṣaḥīḥ Muslim 572:93]

البَغْي

Iniquity

SIGNS & SYMPTOMS

- Oppressing Others for Authority or Position
- Committing Injustices (including Social Media)
- Turning Away from Allāh ﷻ Towards Others

TREATMENTS

- Certainty of Death
- Treat Others Fairly (& Yourself)
- Satan Creates Dissension in the Hearts of People
- Being Patient & Remaking Bonds, Seeking the Pleasure of Allāh ﷻ Only

NO EXCEPTIONS

- All Iniquity is Blameworthy

CHAPTER 16

Iniquity [Baghi] البَغْي

Iniquity or baghi is when one harms anything in creation without right or just cause, usually because one is entrapped and infatuated by the love of this world and of worldly position. With this hard crust over the heart, there is no moral barrier preventing one from wronging others. However, as Allāh ﷻ promises in His Qur'ān, the iniquity and injustice that people aim at others ultimately works its way back to them:

Allāh ﷻ says, "O humanity! Your transgression is only against your own souls." [Yūnus 10:23]

The Prophet ﷺ said, "After I am gone you will experience discrimination and will observe things that you will disapprove of." **Someone asked,** "O Messenger of Allāh, what do you command us to do then?" **He ﷺ said,** "Discharge your obligations and supplicate to Allāh for your rights." [Ṣaḥīḥ Al-Bukhārī 7052]

Iniquity

Signs & Symptoms	Qur'ānic, Prophetic & Scholarly Evidence
Oppressing Others for Authority or Position	
Violating the rights of others to get what you feel you 'deserve' seems to be part of your very nature You oppress your subordinates in the office for the purpose of defining territory and securing a permanent sense of 'superior' position You're looking to pull off 'power plays' at board level within the corporation in order to acquire more authority You plot the downfall or removal of those whom you perceive to be potential challengers You protect your illusory possessions and authority like a miser	The Prophet ﷺ said: o "Beware, if anyone oppresses (or wrongs) the one with whom one has an agreement (mu'āhid), or diminishes his right, or forces him to work beyond his capacity, or takes from him anything without his consent, I shall plead for him on the Day of Judgement" [Sunan Abī Dawūd 3052] o "The one who severs his family ties will not enter Paradise" [Ṣaḥīḥ Al-Bukhārī 5984, Ṣaḥīḥ Muslim 2556:18] o "Those who abuse their slaves cannot enter Paradise" [At-Tirmidhī 1946, Ibn Mājah 3691, Musnad Aḥmad 31]
Committing Injustices (including Social Media)	
You commit major injustices such as: o Devouring the property of orphans o Procrastination in repaying debts despite your ability to repay at the due time o Denying your spouse their rights such as dowry, clothing and provision o Denying your employee his wage or salary o Inaccurate divisions and valuations (e.g. inheritance) o Over-exerting yourself on social networks, resulting in you neglecting your family, missing opportunities to spend quality time with them because you are engaged with others online	Allāh ﷻ says: o "Allāh does not like the wrongdoers" [Āli 'Imrān 3:57] o "Blame is only on those who wrong people and transgress in the land unjustly. It is they who will suffer a painful punishment" [Ash-Shūrā 42:42] The Prophet ﷺ said: o "Protect yourselves against doing injustice, for injustice will be darkness on the Day of Resurrection" [Ṣaḥīḥ Al-Bukhārī 2447 Ṣaḥīḥ Muslim 2578:56] o "Whoever seizes unlawfully a hand-span of land, a collar of seven lands will be around his neck (in the Hereafter)" [Ṣaḥīḥ Al-Bukhārī 2453, Ṣaḥīḥ Muslim 1612:142]

Iniquity

Signs & Symptoms

Qur'ānic, Prophetic & Scholarly Evidence

Turning Away from Allāh ﷻ Towards Others	
You turn away from your Master towards His desperate and miserly servants	
Your concern with the affections of others is exhausting, and though you please some, others flee from you filled with anger, displeasure and resentfulness	
You do whatever you can in order to move closer to people of authority (illusory power)	The Prophet ﷺ said, "There is no obedience of the creation wherein there is disobedience to the Creator." [Al-Mu'jam Al-Kabīr Aṭ-Ṭabarānī 381 18/170]
You endeavour to please people and gain their love, admiration, or approval through trickery, ostentatious display of religiosity, or hypocritical flattery	
Your pursuit leaves some people pleased and happy, but others displeased and resentful	

Academic & Practical Treatment

Qur'ānic, Prophetic & Scholarly Evidence

Certainty of Death	
You have certainty of your morality by keeping death constantly before your eyes, realising that even the most powerful leaders and 'successful' greedy materialists ultimately tasted death	Allāh ﷻ says, "On the Day He will call you, you will (instantly) respond by praising Him, thinking you had remained (in the world) only for a little while." [Al-'Isrā 17:52]
When alone, in close company or large gatherings, you stress on the importance of remembering the reality of death, the destroyer of pleasure	The Prophet ﷺ said, "Remember often the destroyer of pleasures (death)." [At-Tirmidhī 2307]

Iniquity

Academic & Practical Treatment	Qur'ānic, Prophetic & Scholarly Evidence
Treating Others Fairly (& Yourself)	
You understand that the principle of justice in Islām applies to everyone, regardless of race, ethnicity, age, gender, or status	Allāh ﷻ states: o "Indeed, Allāh commands you to return trusts to their rightful owners; and when you judge between people, judge with fairness. What a noble commandment from Allāh to you! Surely Allāh is All-Hearing, All-Seeing" [An-Nisā' 4:58] o "Surely Allāh loves those who are just" [Al Ma'idah 5:42]
You are therefore selfless, compassionate and sensitive to the rights of others, so you do not wrong them	The Prophet ﷺ said: o "The most beloved of you all to me is the one who has the best of manners" [Ṣaḥīḥ Al-Bukhārī 3759] o "The Muslim has six rights that other Muslims must fulfil: if you meet him, salute him (with the greeting of peace, saying 'salam'); if he calls you, answer his call; if he asks for advice, give him your advice; if he sneezes and thanks Allāh, ask Allāh to bless him; if he is sick, visit him; and when he dies, attend his funeral" [Ṣaḥīḥ Muslim 2162:5]
You do not neglect yourself either, and remind yourself that your mind has a right upon you and needs time to rest and reflect as well	o "The word 'raḥm' (womb) is derived from the name 'Ar-Raḥmān' (Most Gracious, one of Allāh's names), and Allāh said: 'I will keep good relations with the one who keeps good relations with you (the womb, meaning kith and kin) and sever relations with him who severs relations with you'" [Ṣaḥīḥ Al-Bukhārī 5988] o "Fear Allāh and treat your children equally" [Ṣaḥīḥ Al-Bukhārī 2587]
You know to treat others as you would like to be treated	o "O Abdullāh! I have been informed that you fast all day and stand in prayer all night?" **I said**, "Yes, O Allāh's Messenger!" **He said**, "Do not do that! Fast some days, and leave it off on other days. Stand for prayer at night and also sleep some nights. Your body has a right over you, your eyes have a right over you and your wife has a right over you" [Ṣaḥīḥ Al-Bukhārī 5199]
You ensure that you do not speak or even text secretly to another while in a group of three because you know that this makes the other persons feel excluded	o "When three people are sitting together, then two of them should not hold a secret conversation excluding the third person. Wait to be in a larger group so as not to upset the other person" [Ṣaḥīḥ Al-Bukhārī 6288, Ṣaḥīḥ Muslim 2184:37] Imām Al-Ghazālī رحمه الله **said**, "Whenever you interact with people, deal with them as you would wish to be dealt with by them, for a worshipper's faith is incomplete until he wants for other people what he wants for himself." [Letter to a Disciple/Ayyuhāl Walad, p.56-57]

Iniquity

Academic & Practical Treatment	Qur'ānic, Prophetic & Scholarly Evidence
Satan Creates Dissension in the Hearts of People	Allāh ﷻ says, "Obey Allāh and His Messenger and do not dispute with one another, or you would be discouraged and weakened. Persevere! Surely Allāh is with those who persevere." [Al-'Anfāl 8:46]
You remind yourself that it is Satan who sows seeds of discord or disagreement between people You are patient and make a concerted effort to cease quarrelling (whatever the reason may be)	The Prophet ﷺ said: o "Iblīs (Satan) places his throne upon water; he then sends detachments (for creating dissension between people); the nearer to him in rank are those who are most notorious in creating dissension. One of them comes and says: 'I did such and such'. And he (Iblīs) says: 'You have done nothing.' Then one amongst them comes and says: 'I did not spare so-and-so, until I sowed the seed of discord between a husband and a wife'. Satan goes near him and says: 'You have done well.' He then embraces him" [Ṣaḥīḥ Muslim 2813:67] o "It is sin enough for you not to cease quarrelling" [At-Tirmidhī 1994]
Being Patient & Remaking Bonds, Seeking the Pleasure of Allāh ﷻ Only You reconcile with the person who has harmed you, or whom you have harmed without just cause You place your hopes for reconciliation in Allāh ﷻ, and not in people, because He is All-Seeing and All-Hearing, and He will reward you for your patience and sincerity You realise that honour and fame are forever linked with the status one has with Allāh ﷻ You seek the pleasure of Allāh ﷻ only, and you have no concern with the commentary (e.g. discouragement) of the corrupt, the miserly, the power-hungry, the proud, the self-centred, and their like	Allāh ﷻ says: o "The believers are but one brotherhood, so make peace between your brothers. And be mindful of Allāh so you may be shown mercy" [Al-Hujurāt 49:10] o "Is it not enough that your Lord is a Witness over all things?" [Al-Fuṣṣilat 41:53] o "Be gracious, enjoin what is right, and turn away from those who act ignorantly" [A'raf 7:199] The Prophet ﷺ said: o "Remake the bond with one who severs it from you, give charity to the one who deprives you and forgive the one who oppresses you" [Musnad Aḥmad 17452] o "The Muslim who mixes with the people and bears patiently their hurtful words is better than one who does not mix with people and does not show patience under their abuse" [At-Tirmidhī 2507, Ibn Mājah 4032, Musnad Aḥmad 5022] o "Do not be of those who do to others as the others do to them, and say that we will do them a favour if they do us a favour, and if they will be mean and unjust to us then we, too, will be mean and unjust to them. On the contrary, resolve that you will do good if the others do good, and if they do a wrong and act unjustly, even then you will not be unfair to them" [At-Tirmidhī 2007]

Iniquity

NO Exceptions

All Iniquity is Blameworthy

You understand that Allāh ﷻ enjoins justice and the worship of none but Allāh ﷻ alone (Al-Adl), and the correct action is to be patient in performing your duties to Allāh ﷻ (Al-Iḥsān), totally for Allāh's ﷻ sake and in perfect accord with the Sunnah (legal ways) of the Prophet ﷺ

Qur'ānic, Prophetic & Scholarly Evidence

Allāh ﷻ says, "Indeed, Allāh commands justice, grace, as well as courtesy to close relatives. He forbids indecency, wickedness, and aggression. He instructs you so perhaps you will be mindful." [An-Naḥl 16:90]

The Prophet ﷺ said, "O My servants, I have made oppression unlawful for Me and unlawful for you, so do not commit oppression against one another." [Ṣaḥīḥ Muslim 2577:55]

البَغْي

حُبُّ الدُّنيا

Love of the World

SIGNS & SYMPTOMS

- Forgetfulness
- Disingenuousness
- Prying & Eavesdropping
- Vain & Sinful Pursuits (including Social Media)

TREATMENTS

- Seeking the Hereafter
- Using the World as a Means to Spiritual Elevation
- Valuing Your Time (Social Media)
- Seeking Moderation
- Expressing & Receiving Thanks

EXCEPTIONS

- Physical Needs
- Attaining the Best of the Hereafter
- Benefiting the Needy

CHAPTER 17

Love of the World

[Ḥubb ad-Dunyā] حُبُّ الدُّنيا

Any concept, 'thing' or person that provides benefit in the Hereafter is worthy of attachment in this earthly life. Indeed, love of the world is praised if it leads to spiritual elevation and healing of the heart, or if attaining wealth and position are for the benefit of the needy. Anything that is obtained from the necessities of living on earth - food, housing, shelter, and the like - is beneficial and is not considered "worldly" per se.

However, what scholars have traditionally warned against, with regard to attaining wealth, is the danger of transgression. The more wealth one acquires, the higher the probability one will become preoccupied with other than Allāh ﷻ.

'Īsā ﵇ is reported to have said "Love of this world is the root of all evil." [Al-Bayhaqī in Shu'ab Al-Īmān 9974]

It is the action of clinging to the world's 'glittering distractions', paying excessive attention to the 'things' that benefit the lower self, that ties somebody to blameworthy love of the world (ḥubb al-dunyā). The manifestation of this misdirected love includes greediness and arrogance, as well as burdening (and depending on) others with your needs. The compulsion is a desire for provision in this world only, and the salvation in the next world is dismissed in some measure. Attaining prohibited wealth and power for power's sake is normalised by the individual sufferer. Finally, it is worth remarking that 'love of wealth' (ḥubb al-māl) is undoubtedly a branch of ḥubb ad-dunyā.

Allāh ﷻ says: "Indeed, those who do not expect to meet Us, being pleased and content with this worldly life, and who are heedless of Our signs, they will have the Fire as a home because of what they have committed." [Yūnus 10: 7-8]

The Prophet ﷺ said:

- "Two hungry wolves let loose in a flock of sheep do not cause as much harm as the harm to a man's religion wrought by his desire for wealth and fame" [At-Tirmidhī 2376]
- "Whoever makes the Hereafter his goal, Allāh makes his heart rich, and organises his affairs, and the world comes to him whether it wants to or not. And whoever makes the world his goal, Allāh puts his poverty right before his eyes, and disorganises his affairs, and the world does not come to him, except what has been decreed for him" [At-Tirmidhī 2465]
- "If the son of Ādam had two valleys of money, he would wish for a third, for nothing can fill the mouth of the son of Ādam except dust" [Ṣaḥīḥ Al-Bukhārī 6436, Ṣaḥīḥ Muslim 1048:116]

Love of the world falls under 5 categories of classical legal rulings: obligatory (wājib), recommended (mandūb), permissible (mubāḥ), reprehensible (makrūh), or forbidden (ḥarām).

Love of the World

Signs & Symptoms	Qur'ānic, Prophetic & Scholarly Evidence
Forgetfulness	
Your acquisition of wealth and love of such material objects causes you to forget Allāh ﷻ	Allāh ﷻ says, "Know that this worldly life is no more than play, amusement, luxury, mutual boasting, and competition in wealth and children." [Al-Ḥadīd 57:20]
You have little or no concern for the Hereafter; you have love for ephemeral aspects of the world to the point that they suppress your spiritual yearning	
Disingenuousness	
You are disingenuous with praise, by pouring accolades upon others, worthy or not, desiring something from other than Allāh ﷻ because you want something from them	Allāh ﷻ says: o "Do not let those who rejoice in their misdeeds and love to take credit for what they have not done think they will escape torment. They will suffer a painful punishment" [Āli 'Imrān 3:188] o "Do not do a favour expecting more (in return)" [Al-Muddaththir 74:6]
You receive credit for work others have actually done, and attribute nothing to those that have actually done the work	The Prophet ﷺ said "When you see those who shower (undue) praise (upon others), throw dust upon their faces." [Ṣaḥīḥ Muslim 3002:69, Ibn Mājah 3742]
Prying & Eavesdropping	
You busy yourself with that which does not concern you	Imām Al-Ghazālī رحمه الله said, "An indication of the withdrawal of Allāh Most High from the worshipper is his busying himself with what does not concern him, and if an hour of a man's life slips by in other than that for which he was created in the way of worship, then it is proper that his affliction is protracted. Whoever passes forty without his virtue overpowering his vice, let him get ready for Hellfire!" [Letter to a Disciple/Ayyuhāl Walad p.4-5]

Love of the World

Signs & Symptoms

Vain & Sinful Pursuits (including Social Media)
You earn wealth for the purpose of vainglorious competition, competing for the things of the world and trying to gain superiority over others through them
Your vying for wealth becomes an addiction and leads to ostentation
Your love of the world results in greed and arrogance
You enjoy those things that are sinful or that lead to sinful matters, or you at least are neither bothered about righteous deeds nor abstain from evil
You spend an inordinate amount of time on social media, for instance, by browsing 'Facebook' posts, clicking suggestions on YouTube, posting updates and images about your latest experience etc.
You find that although your initial intentions may have been positive, as you move from page to page, from post to post, this results in you browsing information and images that are distasteful and may lead to sin
Your exposure to online images (such as advertisements or photographs of celebrities) displaying faces of wantonness (ecstatic postures, supreme happiness) consumes you and your time

Qur'ānic, Prophetic & Scholarly Evidence

Allāh says:

- "The life of this world is no more than the delusion of enjoyment" [Āli 'Imrān 3:185]
- When it is time for a person to die, he asks that his life be extended in order to do more good deeds: "There they will be (fervently) screaming, 'Our Lord! Take us out (and send us back). We will do good, unlike what we used to do.' (They will be told,) 'Did We not give you lives long enough so that whoever wanted to be mindful could have done so? And the warner came to you. So taste (the punishment), for the wrongdoers have no helper'" [Fāṭir 35:37]
- "Whoever desires (only) this worldly life and its luxuries, We will pay them in full for their deeds in this life - nothing will be left out. It is they who will have nothing in the Hereafter except the Fire. Their efforts in this life will be fruitless and their deeds will be useless" [Hūd 11: 15-16]

The Prophet said:

- "If the value of the world were equal to that of the wing of a mosquito, in the eyes of Allāh, He would not have allowed any unbeliever even a sip of water from it" [At-Tirmidhī 2320]
- "I fear for you the carnal desires of your bellies and private parts" [Musnad Aḥmad 19772]
- "By Allāh, it is not poverty I fear for you, but rather I fear you will be given the wealth of the world just as it was given to those before you. You will compete for it just as they competed for it and it will destroy you just as it destroyed them" [Ṣaḥīḥ Al-Bukhārī 6425, Ṣaḥīḥ Muslim 2961:6]

'Īsā is reported to have said: "Love of this world is the root of all evil." [Al-Bayhaqī in Shu'ab Al-Īmān 9974]

Love of the World

Academic Treatment	Qur'ānic, Prophetic & Scholarly Evidence
Seeking the Hereafter	
You remind yourself that this worldly life is mere play and amusement, which spawns most of the evil spiritual traits and characteristics (pride, hatred, jealousy, boasting, greed, etc.) and that your true objective of this life is to make sufficient arrangements for your travels to the Hereafter	Allāh ﷻ says, o "Do not let your eyes crave what We have allowed some of the disbelievers to enjoy; the (fleeting) splendour of this worldly life, which We test them with. But your Lord's provision (in the Hereafter) is far better and more lasting" [Ṭāhā 20:131] o "Whatever (pleasure) you have been given is (no more than a fleeting) enjoyment of this worldly life. But what is with Allāh is far better and more lasting for those who believe and put their trust in their Lord" [Ash-Shūrā 42:36] o "This worldly life is no more than play and amusement. But the Hereafter is indeed the real life, if only they knew" [Al-'Ankabūt 29:64]
You remind yourself that you will most certainly be questioned about your expenditure on the Day of Qiyāmah	
You remember death often and do not involve yourself in far-fetched hopes, avoiding making lengthly plans and preparations	
You love the things of the world that help you achieve felicity in the Hereafter, such as love of the Qur'ān, of the Ka'bah, of the Prophet ﷺ, of parents, of godly people, of books of knowledge, of children, and of brothers and sisters who help you in religious affairs, as well as love of wealth (hubb al-māl) in order to give to the needy	The Prophet ﷺ described the world in the following similitude: "What relationship with the world have I? My likeness is as a traveller on a mount, halting in the shade of a tree (for a short) while, only to leave it again and proceed along the way." [At-Tirmidhī 2377, Musnad Aḥmad 2744]

Love of the World

Academic Treatment	Qur'ānic, Prophetic & Scholarly Evidence
Using the World as a Means to Spiritual Elevation	
Your love of the world in terms of anything that is obtained from the necessities of living on Earth - food, housing, shelter, and the like - leads to your spiritual elevation and healing	Allāh ﷻ says: o "We have indeed made whatever is on earth as an adornment for it, in order to test which of them is best in deeds" [Al-Kahf 18:7] o "And as for those who were in awe of standing before their Lord and restrained themselves from (evil) desires, Paradise will certainly be (their) home" [An-Nāzi'āt 79: 40-41]
Your attainment of education, wealth and position is for the benefit of the needy, as you sow seeds, which you will reap in the Hereafter	The Prophet ﷺ said: o "The world is the prison of the believer and the paradise of the unbeliever" [Ṣaḥīḥ Muslim 2956:1] o "Be in this world as if you were a stranger or a traveller" [Ṣaḥīḥ Al-Bukhārī 6416] o "Whoever makes the Hereafter his goal, Allāh makes his heart rich, and organises his affairs, and the world comes to him whether he wants it or not. And whoever makes the world his goal, Allāh puts his poverty right before his eyes, and disorganises his affairs, and the world does not come to him, except what has been decreed for him" [At-Tirmidhī 2465] o "If the world to Allāh were equal to a mosquito's wing, then He would not allow the disbeliever to have a sip of water from it" [At-Tirmidhī 2320]
You censure or avoid loving those things that are sinful or that lead to sinful matters	
You avoid short-lived aspects of the world that suppress your spiritual yearning	Imām Al-Ghazālī said: o "The best of what one loves is what will enter one's grave and be a friend to one in it. And I found (it to be) nothing but good deeds! So I took them as the object of my love, to be a light for me in my grave, to be a friend to me in it and not to leave me alone" [Letter to a Disciple/Ayyuhāl Walad, p.28-29] o "If you read or study knowledge, your knowledge must improve your heart and purge your ego" [Letter to a Disciple/Ayyuhāl Walad, p.56-57]

Love of the World

Practical Treatment	Qur'ānic, Prophetic & Scholarly Evidence
Valuing Your Time (Social Media)	
You become more mindful of your use of time by regulating the time you spend on social networking and media by holding your own self to account at the end of each day: o What did I do that was good today? o What did I do that was blameworthy today?	**Allāh ﷻ says,** "It is Allāh Who created you in a state of weakness, then developed (your) weakness into strength, then developed (your) strength into weakness and old age. He creates whatever He wills. For He is the All-Knowing, Most Capable." [Ar-Rūm 30:54] The Prophet ﷺ said: o "There are two blessings which many people do not make the best use of: good health and free time" [Ṣaḥīḥ Al-Bukhārī 6412]
You make it your duty not to be enslaved by social media in a way that consumes your time and impacts your health and well-being	o "A person will not move on (on the Day of Judgement) until he has been asked about: his life and how he spent it, his knowledge and what he did with it, his wealth, from where he acquired it and on what he spent it, and his body and how he wore it out" [At-Tirmidhī 2417]
You make more effort to communicate in person with your spouse, with your parents, with your children, and with your relatives and friends, and even with passers-by (even just by sharing a smile)	**Abdullāh Ibn 'Umar ؓ used to say,** "When you arrive at the evening do not expect to see the morning and when you arrive at the morning do not expect to see the evening. During health, prepare for illness and while you are alive, prepare for death." [Ṣaḥīḥ Al-Bukhārī 6416]

Love of the World

Practical Treatment	Qur'ānic, Prophetic & Scholarly Evidence
Seeking Moderation	
You seek moderation by bringing your conditions of living under control so that your wealth and time (for example) may be used to reach a higher ideal (Paradise)	Allāh ﷻ says, "(They are) those who spend neither wastefully nor stingily, but moderately in between." [Al-Furqān 25:67] The Prophet ﷺ affirmed the statement of Salmān Al-Fārsi ؓ, "You have a duty to your Lord, you have a duty to your body, and you have a duty to your family, so you should give each one its rights." [Ṣaḥīḥ Al-Bukhārī 1968]
You intelligently avoid accumulating great wealth, in fear of transgressing the bounds of permissibility, since the more wealth one acquires, the higher the probability one will become preoccupied with other than Allāh ﷻ	
Expressing & Receiving Thanks	
You express gratitude to someone who has done good, and do not enjoy receiving praise yourself for something you have not done	The Prophet ﷺ also said, "Whoever is not thankful to people will not be thankful to God." [At-Tirmidhī 1955]

Love of the World

Exceptions

Physical Needs

You want things of this world for your physical necessities, and in order to be free from burdening others with your needs

Attaining the Best of the Hereafter

You desire provision from the world for the purpose of attaining the best of the Hereafter

Benefiting the Needy

Your attainment of wealth and position is for the benefit of the needy

Qur'ānic, Prophetic & Scholarly Evidence

Allāh ﷻ says, "Allāh is the One Who has subjected the sea for you so that ships may sail upon it by His command, and that you may seek His bounty, and that perhaps you will be grateful." [Al-Jāthiyah 45:12]

The Prophet Muḥammad ﷺ prohibited denunciation of the world. He said: "Lawful riches are a benefit to a pious man" [Al-Bayhaqī in Shu'ab Al-Īmān 1190]. He benefits because he spends his wealth in meritorious ways.

البُخْل

Miserliness

SIGNS & SYMPTOMS

- Withholding Charity
- Giving Shoddy & Inferior Charity
- When Fulfilling Others' Rights
- Living an Impoverished Life
- Anxiety & Fear of Poverty
- Failing to Bestow Prayers upon the Messenger of Allāh ﷺ

TREATMENTS

- Wealth & Affluence is Only Temporary
- Bad Opinion of Misers
- Bestowing Prayers Upon the Messenger of Allāh ﷺ
- Spending on Your Family
- Flexible Loans
- Giving to the Needy
- Fulfilling Rights of Others

EXCEPTIONS

- When Giving in Moderation

CHAPTER 18

Miserliness [Bukhl] البُخْل

Miserliness is when one refuses to give what is required by Sacred Law (the necessary rights due to Allāh ﷻ and to His creation) or denies the merits of giving in general. This is usually as a result of a love for the wealth of this world (hubb al-māl) for its own sake, and the dunyā, which weakens the bond of love with Allāh ﷻ.

The Messenger of Allāh ﷺ exhorted:

- "Save yourself from miserliness, for it has destroyed nations before you" [Ṣaḥīḥ Muslim 2578:56]
- "There are two habits which are never present in a believer: miserliness and bad manners" [At-Tirmidhī 1962]

Miserliness

Signs & Symptoms

Withholding Charity

You withhold or are reluctant to pay charity to the needy, deliberately paying less than is obligated (zakāh) or finding ways to avoid it, ardently clinging to and hoarding your wealth, using excuses to delay donation. All the while, you fear impoverishment

Giving Shoddy & Inferior Charity

You feel discomforted when spending on your family (this includes giving little or no child support after suffering divorce, for example). When cornered, your goodwill extends only to the minimum, even on your own spouse and children

You spend from the least of what you possess, giving away charity that is shoddy and inferior (e.g. the worst of your clothing)

When Fulfilling Others' Rights

You create difficulty over trivial matters

You hand out difficulty without reasonable cause. For instance, you become demanding and unbearable in matters of debt, especially when you are not in need and even when the debtor is facing hardship

You fulfil a trust or discharge an obligation without good cheer

Qur'ānic, Prophetic & Scholarly Evidence

Allāh ﷻ says:

- "O believers! Donate from the best of what you have earned and of what We have produced for you from the earth. Do not pick out worthless things for donation, which you yourselves would only accept with closed eyes. And know that Allāh is Self-Sufficient, Praiseworthy" [Al-Baqarah 2:267]
- "You will never achieve righteousness until you donate some of what you cherish. And whatever you give is certainly well known to Allāh" [Āli 'Imrān 3:92]
- "And do not let those who (greedily) withhold Allāh's bounties think it is good for them - in fact, it is bad for them! They will be leashed (by their necks) on the Day of Judgement with whatever (wealth) they used to withhold. And Allāh is the (sole) inheritor of the heavens and the earth. And Allāh is All-Aware of what you do" [Āli 'Imrān 3:180]
- "Surely Allāh does not like whoever is arrogant, boastful - those who are stingy, promote stinginess among people, and withhold Allāh's bounties. We have prepared for the disbelievers a humiliating punishment" [An-Nisā' 4: 36-37]

Miserliness

Signs & Symptoms	Qur'ānic, Prophetic & Scholarly Evidence
Living an Impoverished Life	
You live a grim life, though you have millions in the bank, and this choice of living is not inspired by spiritual sensibilities, rather it causes you great discomfort to spend money on yourself and your family	**Allāh ﷻ says**, "Still some of you withhold. And whoever does so, it is only to their own loss." [Muḥammad 47:38]
Anxiety & Fear of Poverty	
You hoard wealth to alleviate your fear of poverty, and you never truly feel relieved of anxiety, constantly being worried about money and devoted to servicing your worry	**Allāh ﷻ says**, "The Devil threatens you with (the prospect of) poverty and bids you to the shameful deed (of stinginess), while Allāh promises you forgiveness and (great) bounties from Him. And Allāh is All-Bountiful, All-Knowing." [Al-Baqarah 2:268] **The Messenger of Allāh ﷺ said**: "Allāh said: 'If My servant likes to meet me, then I like to meet him; and if he dislikes to meet Me, then I dislike to meet him.'" [Ṣaḥīḥ Al-Bukhārī 7504]
At the time of death, you look upon your wealth with regret and sorrow	
Your journey into the Hereafter is made with reluctance, because you have virtually no desire to meet Allāh ﷻ	
Failing to Bestow Prayers upon the Messenger of Allāh ﷺ	
You fail to recognise the immense generosity of the Messenger of Allāh ﷺ	**The Prophet ﷺ said**: "The miserly person is the one who does not bestow prayers upon me when I am mentioned in his presence." [Musnad Aḥmad 1736]
You fail to bestow prayers upon the Messenger of Allāh ﷺ when his name is mentioned in your presence	

Miserliness

Academic Treatment	Qur'ānic, Prophetic & Scholarly Evidence
Wealth & Affluence is Only Temporary You realise that those who achieve wealth do so after exhausting themselves over long periods of time, working day and night for it, whilst life passes on and time runs out You realise that just as you climb the heights of wealth and luxury, death will assail you without invitation, and that this is just the same for the poor and the wealthy, whether you are old or young, happy or sad You realise that when death takes you, your wealth stays behind for others to wrangle over and spend, so you make a personal commitment to spend your wealth purely for the pleasure of Allāh ﷻ You make a firm resolution to support the needy whilst you are in good health and possess the means to do so You constantly remind yourself of death in order to expel the love of wealth (hubb al-māl) and fear of poverty from your heart	A man came to the Prophet ﷺ and said: "O Messenger of Allāh, which charity brings a greater reward?" He said, "If you give in charity when you are healthy and miserly, fearing poverty and hoping for richness. Do not delay until you are at the point of death and you say, 'Give this to so-and-so, give this to so-and-so,' when It has already become the possession of so-and-so (the heirs)." [Ṣaḥīḥ Al-Bukhārī 1419, Ṣaḥīḥ Muslim 1032:92] The Messenger of Allāh ﷺ said, "Allāh will help a person so long as he is helping his brother." [Ṣaḥīḥ Muslim 2699:38, Sunan Abī Dawūd 4946, At-Tirmidhī 1425] Imām Al-Ghazālī said: "I saw every individual in mankind exerting himself in accumulating the ephemeral things of the world, then clutching at them, laying hold on them, and I meditated on His saying (the Exalted), 'Whatever you have will end, but whatever Allāh has is everlasting' [An-Naḥl 16:96]. So I sacrificed the gains I got from the world to Allāh the Exalted, and I distributed them among the poor so that they might become a treasure from me with Allāh the Exalted." [Letter to a Disciple/ Ayyuhāl Walad, p.30-31]
Bad Opinion of Misers You realise the level of scorn shown to misers; nobody likes a miser and misers tend to loathe other misers	The Prophet ﷺ once asked some clansmen about their leader. They mentioned his name and said, "But he is a bit of a miser." The Prophet ﷺ said, "Do you know of any disease that is worse than miserliness?" [Al-Adab Al-Mufrad 296] The Prophet ﷺ said, "A miser is far from Allāh, far from Jannah, far from the people and close to the Fire." [Al-Mu'jam Al-Awsaṭ Aṭ-Ṭabarānī 2363]

Miserliness

Practical Treatment	Qur'ānic, Prophetic & Scholarly Evidence
Bestowing Prayers Upon the Messenger of Allāh ﷺ	
You understand that a manifestation of the Prophet's ﷺ generosity is that he is the cause of everything coming into existence You recognise the immense generosity of the Messenger of Allāh ﷺ, that in his lifetime he was the most generous of people, and never said 'no' to anyone that asked him for anything You remind yourself that his generosity will be made clear in the most complete way on the Day of Judgement when even the other Prophets will be silent, that only he ﷺ will intercede on behalf of the whole of creation You bestow prayers upon the Messenger of Allāh ﷺ when his name is mentioned in your presence	Abdullāh ibn Abbās رضي الله عنهما narrates that: "The Messenger of Allāh ﷺ was the most generous of people and he was at his most generous in Ramadan when he would meet Jibrā'īl. And he would meet Jibrā'īl every night in Ramadan and review the Qur'ān with him. Truly, when Jibrā'īl would meet him, the Messenger of Allāh ﷺ was more generous than a continuously blowing wind." [Ṣaḥīḥ Al-Bukhārī 6] The Prophet ﷺ said, "If anyone invokes blessings on me once, Allāh will bless him ten times." [Sunan Abī Dawūd 1530] Abdullāh ibn Abbās رضي الله عنهما said, He ﷺ once gave a man a valley full of sheep. The man returned to his people saying, "Accept Islām, for Muḥammad gives like someone who does not fear poverty!" [Ṣaḥīḥ Muslim 2312:57]. He fulfilled people's needs whether they were material or spiritual. He fed the hungry, taught the ignorant and guided those who were astray.
Spending on Your Family	
You understand that Allāh ﷻ advises you to first be kind to the people in your home, then to your larger circle of relatives (and then to all human beings) You are pleased when spending on your family, spending generously on your wife and children, parents, and any other dependents You understand that such generous provision is classed as worshipping Allāh ﷻ because you are obeying Him by fulfilling the responsibilities He has assigned to you You understand that you gain the reward of performing good deeds, by paying for your family's food, clothes, housing, medicine, etc. At the same time, you remind yourself that Allāh ﷻ has forbidden extravagance (wasteful spending) alongside miserliness, so you spend in a balanced manner, keeping well away from these two extremes	Allāh ﷻ says about his true servants: "(They are) those who spend neither wastefully nor stingily, but moderately in between." [Al-Furqān 25:67] The Prophet ﷺ said: o "What a Muslim spends on his family, for seeking the pleasure of Allāh, is also counted as charity" [Ṣaḥīḥ Al-Bukhārī 55, Ṣaḥīḥ Muslim 1002:48] o "A dīnār which you spend in the path of Allāh, a dīnār which you spend on freeing a slave, a dīnār which you give in charity to a poor person and a dīnār which you spend on your family – the greatest of these in reward is that which you spend on your family" [Ṣaḥīḥ Muslim 995:39]

Miserliness

Practical Treatment	Qur'ānic, Prophetic & Scholarly Evidence
Flexible Loans	
You are a flexible (lenient) creditor, especially when you are not in need and when your debtor is facing hardship	The Prophet ﷺ said, "Whoever removes a worldly hardship from a believer, Allāh ﷻ will remove one of the hardships of the Day of Resurrection from him. Whoever grants respite to (a debtor) who is in difficulty, Allāh will grant him relief in this world and in the Hereafter. Whoever conceals (the fault of) a Muslim in this world, Allāh will conceal him (his faults) in this world and in the Hereafter. Allāh will help a person so long as he is helping his brother." [Ṣaḥīḥ Muslim 2699:38] A ḥadīth speaks of a wealthy man who would instruct his servants when collecting money on his behalf, "A man used to give loans to the people and used to say to his servant, 'If the debtor is poor, forgive him, so that Allāh ﷻ may forgive us.' So when he met Allāh ﷻ (after his death), Allāh ﷻ forgave him." [Ṣaḥīḥ Al-Bukhārī 3480] One of the most excellent names of Allāh ﷻ is Al-Karīm, 'The Generous'.
Giving to the Needy	Allāh ﷻ says: o "O believers! Donate from the best of what you have earned and of what We have produced for you from the earth. Do not pick out worthless things for donation, which you yourselves would only accept with closed eyes. And know that Allāh is Self-Sufficient, Praiseworthy" [Al-Baqarah 2:267] o "You will never achieve righteousness until you donate some of what you cherish. And whatever you give is certainly well known to Allāh" [Āli 'Imrān 3:92] The Prophet ﷺ said: o "Kind speech and feeding (the hungry) guarantee you Paradise" [Al-Mu'jam Al-Awsaṭ Aṭ-Ṭabarānī 5325] o "Verily there are chambers in Paradise; their insides and outsides can be seen – for he who fed (the hungry), spoke kindly, was punctual in prayer and stood (in prayer) at night whilst others were asleep" [Al-Mu'jam Al-Kabīr Aṭ-Ṭabarānī 3466] o "Who among you considers the wealth of his heirs dearer to him than his own wealth?" They replied, "O Messenger of Allāh! There is none among us but loves his own wealth more." The Prophet said, "So his wealth is whatever he sends forward (i.e. spends in Allāh's cause during his life on good deeds) while the wealth of his heirs is whatever he leaves after his death" [Ṣaḥīḥ Al-Bukhārī 6442]
You realise that by giving zakāh, you are purifying your provision from whatever unknown impurities that may have entered, and ultimately your own soul	
You repress your natural inclinations by making it a habit to spend generously, placing much emphasis on reflecting on the benefits of spending on necessary items	
You gradually expel evil thoughts and reprehensible characteristics, until you cut off miserliness at the root and you then begin spending your wealth purely for the pleasure of Allāh ﷻ	
When purchasing a burial shroud or a sacrificial animal, you do not haggle over the cost because this should be a reminder of death, and is not a worldly matter	
When purchasing anything (e.g. livestock for sacrifice, a gift or souvenir whilst on holiday), you don't haggle over the price, since your intention is to help those in need	

Miserliness

Practical Treatment	Qur'ānic, Prophetic & Scholarly Evidence
Giving to the Needy	
When paying charity, you should smile and be humble, allowing the hand of the poor and needy to be above your (the giver's) hand	Allāh ﷻ says: o "Worship Allāh (alone) and associate none with Him. And be kind to parents, relatives, orphans, the poor, near and distant neighbours, close friends, (needy) travellers, and those (bondspeople) in your possession. Surely Allāh does not like whoever is arrogant, boastful - those who are stingy, promote stinginess among people, and withhold Allāh's bounties" [An-Nisā' 4: 36-37] o "And whoever is mindful of Allāh, He will make a way out for them, and provide for them from sources they could never imagine. And whoever puts their trust in Allāh, then He (alone) is sufficient for them. Certainly Allāh achieves His Will. Allāh has already set a destiny for everything" [At-Ṭalāq 65: 2-3] o "You will never achieve righteousness until you donate some of what you cherish. And whatever you give is certainly well known to Allāh" [Āli 'Imrān 3:92]
You should think that it is a privilege to be in a position of giving charity and an honour to fulfil a divine obligation	
You are blessed enough to recognise your shortcomings, so you battle your soul by giving charity, detaching yourself from your want of wealth and its hoarding	
You give away what you love because you realise that contributions from the best of your wealth will purify your heart, especially when it is concealed (seeking thereby the pleasure of Allāh ﷻ with absolute sincerity)	
You go beyond the minimum of what Sacred Law demands when giving charity, which is an expression of gratitude to Allāh ﷻ who is the provider of all wealth and provision	The Prophet ﷺ was asked, "O Messenger of Allāh, which charity brings a greater reward?" He said, "If you give in charity when you are healthy and miserly, fearing poverty and hoping for richness. Do not delay until you are at the point of death and you say, 'Give this to so and so, give this to so and so.' When It has already become the possession of so and so (the heirs)" [Ṣaḥīḥ Al-Bukhārī 1419, Ṣaḥīḥ Muslim 1032:92]. Similarly, "The likeness of the one who frees a slave (or gives charity) at the time of his death is that of the one who gives his food away only after he has eaten his fill." [At-Tirmidhī 2123, Sunan Abī Dawūd 3968]

Miserliness

Practical Treatment	Qur'ānic, Prophetic & Scholarly Evidence
Fulfilling Rights of Others	
You make matters easier for neighbours, relatives, servants and the needy	The Prophet ﷺ said: o Jibrā'īl continued to enjoin upon me the duty of neighbours towards one another, until I thought that Allāh would make neighbours the heirs of the deceased" [Ṣaḥīḥ Al-Bukhārī 6014] o "Whoever believes in Allāh and the Last Day should treat his neighbour generously" [Ṣaḥīḥ Al-Bukhārī 6019, Ṣaḥīḥ Muslim 47:74] o "The word 'rahm' (womb) is derived from the name 'Ar-Raḥmān' (Most Gracious, one of Allāh's names), and Allāh said: I will keep good relations with the one who keeps good relations with you (the womb, meaning kith and kin) and sever relations with him who severs relations with you" [Ṣaḥīḥ Al-Bukhārī 5988]
When hosting guests, and if a guest spills something, you don't display anger or scold the guest, ensuring that your guest feels no anxiety at all	Generosity is one of the highest virtues of Islām and one of the manifest qualities of the Prophet Muḥammad ﷺ, who was known as the most generous of people.

Miserliness

Exceptions

Qur'ānic, Prophetic & Scholarly Evidence

When Giving in Moderation	
You understand that our Prophet ﷺ, in this narration and elsewhere, coupled and associated cowardice with miserliness, and that one of the manifestations of cowardice is being stingy and miserly	
However, you remind yourself that the ideal is ultimately in the middle, that generosity (sakhā) is a balance between the two extremes of miserliness on one side, and extravagance on another	Allāh ﷻ says about his true servants, "(They are) those who spend neither wastefully nor stingily, but moderately in between." [Al-Furqān 25:67] The Prophet ﷺ said, "O Allāh, I seek refuge in you from miserliness and I seek refuge in you from cowardice." [Ṣaḥīḥ Al-Bukhārī 6365]
You want to give freely, but realise that there is actually a better place for you to put your wealth, or that it is not the right time for you to give out your wealth, or (perhaps) it is not the right person or cause for you to give your wealth to	

السُخْرِيَّة

Mockery

SIGNS & SYMPTOMS

- Social Media Provocation
- Ridicule, Humiliation & Fright
- Looking Down upon Others
- Cursing Entire Races or Faiths

TREATMENTS

- Remember Your Origins & Strengthen Your Relationship With Allāh ﷻ
- Severe Warnings Regarding Mocking Others
- Loss of Self-Respect
- Social Media & Avoiding Ridicule
- Not Insulting Other Races & Faiths
- Repentance & Forgiveness

EXCEPTIONS

- Making Light of a Serious Matter
- Light-Hearted and Humble Fun

CHAPTER 19

Mockery [Sukhriyyah] السُخْرِيَّة

Mockery is when one ridicules people (making jest at their expense) with the purpose of humiliation. This is often because the one who is quick to ridicule most likely sees himself either as superior to his victim or, in fact, envious of what they possess.

The Prophet ﷺ said, "The whole of a Muslim is sanctified for another Muslim with regards to his blood, his property and his honour." [Ṣaḥīḥ Muslim 2564:32]

Humour and lightheartedness are important in human life. But humour as a way of life harms the spiritual heart. And laughter and amusement at the expense of the dignity of others is wholly inappropriate.

Mockery

Signs & Symptoms

Social Media Provocation

You share the latest news story or post a status about the latest gossip, or you like a post alleging a major incident, or you post embarrassing pictures (without consent) with the intention of mocking the said person(s)

You share devastating or upsetting news just to get a reaction out of others, and to see how many likes, views, comments, shares or hits you gather

Ridicule, Humiliation & Fright

You mock another through public criticism by way of ridicule or sarcasm

You like to make fun of others (their appearance, manner of walking or vehicle) and wink behind their backs or make indirect insulting remarks

You make another person your object of fun and the butt of your jokes

You imitate another person, exaggerating certain characteristics of theirs to create a comic effect (caricaturing)

You call another abusive or insulting names

When you see someone drunken and aggressive, vomiting in the street, you ridicule them

You take advantage of the darkness or a hiding place as a means of scaring and alarming another person

Qur'ānic, Prophetic & Scholarly Evidence

Allāh ﷻ says, "O believers! Do not let some (men) ridicule others, they may be better than them, nor let (some) women ridicule other women, they may be better than them. Do not defame one another, nor call each other by offensive nicknames. How evil it is to act rebelliously after having faith! And whoever does not repent, it is they who are the (true) wrongdoers." [Al-Hujurat 49:11]

The Prophet ﷺ said:

- "Woe to the one who talks about something to make the people laugh, in which he lies. Woe to him! Woe to him!" [Sunan Abī Dawūd 4990, At-Tirmidhī 2315]
- "A man may say something to make his companions laugh, and he will fall into Hell as far as the Pleiades (first constellation) because of it" [Musnad Aḥmad 9220]
- "Do not express malicious joy towards your brother's misfortune, for Allāh may have mercy on him and may afflict you" [At-Tirmidhī 2506]
- "(Backbiting is) your mentioning about your brother something that he dislikes" [Ṣaḥīḥ Muslim 2589:70]

Mockery

Signs & Symptoms	Qur'ānic, Prophetic & Scholarly Evidence
Looking Down upon Others	Allāh ﷻ says:
You most probably see yourself as superior to your 'victim'	o "(O believers!) Do not insult what they invoke besides Allāh or they will insult Allāh spitefully out of ignorance. This is how We have made each people's deeds appealing to them. Then to their Lord is their return, and He will inform them of what they used to do" [Al An'ām 6:108] o "As for those who abuse believing men and women unjustifiably, they will definitely bear the guilt of slander and blatant sin" [Al-Aḥzāb 33:58]
In the context of triumph, you are joyful and boastful, resulting in degrading others	The Prophet ﷺ said, "Whoever taunts a brother with a sin (which the brother has committed), will not die until he (the taunter) commits the same sin." [At-Tirmidhī 2505]
Cursing Entire Races or Faiths	
You create enmity, cursing another race or faith outright and calling them names because of the actions of a few	The Companions of Muḥammad ﷺ said that they were travelling with the Prophet ﷺ and a man among them fell asleep. Some of them got a rope and tied him up, and he got scared. The Messenger of Allāh ﷺ said' "It is not permissible for a Muslim to frighten another Muslim." [Sunan Abī Dawūd 5004]

Mockery

Academic Treatment

Qur'ānic, Prophetic & Scholarly Evidence

Remember Your Origins & Strengthen Your Relationship With Allāh ﷻ

You treat your mockery in the same way you would treat arrogance, by remembering:

- o Your humble origins
- o The source of your health and wealth
- o The importance of strengthening your relationship with Allāh ﷻ, and
- o The consequences of arrogance

Allāh ﷻ says, "O believers! Do not let some (men) ridicule others, they may be better than them, nor let (some) women ridicule other women, they may be better than them. Do not defame one another, nor call each other by offensive nicknames. How evil it is to act rebelliously after having faith! And whoever does not repent, it is they who are the (true) wrongdoers." [Al-Hujurāt 49:11]

Severe Warnings Regarding Mocking Others

You understand that there is a severe warning about looking down on any Muslim, belittling them or making fun of them

You remind yourself that those who mock people (causing ridicule and enmity) in this life shall be mocked in the Hereafter, for it is a divine law that Allāh ﷻ recompenses people with the like of what they have done

The Prophet ﷺ said:

- o "A person may say a word that is pleasing to Allāh ﷻ, not paying it any heed, for which Allāh will raise him in status, and a person may say a word that is displeasing to Allāh ﷻ, not paying it any heed, for which he will fall into Hell" [Ṣaḥīḥ Al-Bukhārī 6478]
- o "A person may say a word, not realising its repercussions, for which he will be thrown down into Hell further than the distance between the East and the West" [Ṣaḥīḥ Al-Bukhārī 6477, Ṣaḥīḥ Muslim 2988:49]
- o "It is not permissible for a Muslim to frighten another Muslim" [Sunan Abī Dawūd 5004]

Loss of Self-Respect

You remind yourself that overly jesting and making excessive jokes kills the heart, and a 'blind spot' or darkness is created in the heart's ability to obey and recognise Allāh ﷻ

You realise that such behaviour causes harm to your dignity and self-respect, resulting in your honour falling in the sight of others, to such an extent that other people end up developing a hatred and dislike towards you

Mockery

Practical Treatment	Qur'ānic, Prophetic & Scholarly Evidence
Social Media & Avoiding Ridicule	
You refrain from mocking people and hurting their feelings, because you realise that is the path that leads to hatred and grudges	**Allāh ﷻ says,** "The hypocrites fear that a sūrah should be revealed about them, exposing what is in their hearts. Say (O Prophet), 'Keep mocking! Allāh will bring to light what you fear.' If you question them, they will certainly say, 'We were only talking idly and joking around.' Say, 'Was it Allāh, His revelations, and His Messenger that you ridiculed?'" [At-Tawbah 9: 64-65]
Before you share the latest news story or post a status about the latest gossip, or 'like' a post alleging a major incident, or post embarrassing pictures without consent, you check your intention, ensuring you avoid anything that involves mockery or ridicule	**The Prophet ﷺ said:** o "Do not express malicious joy towards your brother's misfortune, for Allāh may have mercy on him and may afflict you" [At-Tirmidhī 2506] o "A man may say something to make his companions laugh, and he will fall into Hell as far as the Pleiades (first constellation) because of it" [Musnad Aḥmad 9220] o "Actions are judged by their intentions, so each man will have what he intended. Therefore, he whose migration was for Allāh and His Messenger, his migration is for Allāh and His Messenger. But he whose migration was for some worldly benefit, or for a wife he might marry, his migration is to that for which he migrated" [Ṣaḥīḥ Al-Bukhārī 1]
You remind yourself not to judge others, and instead to focus on yourself and your own ills (self-reflection), many of which Allāh ﷻ has concealed	

Mockery

Practical Treatment	Qur'ānic, Prophetic & Scholarly Evidence
Not Insulting Other Races & Faiths	
You understand that only Allāh ﷻ knows the seal of people and their destinies When you see someone drunken and out of control, vomiting in the street, you do not ridicule them, for now you understand that you do not know what their future holds	Allāh ﷻ commanded: o "(O believers!) Do not insult what they invoke besides Allāh or they will insult Allāh spitefully out of ignorance. This is how We have made each people's deeds appealing to them. Then to their Lord is their return, and He will inform them of what they used to do" [Al An'ām 6:108] o "O believers! Do not let some (men) ridicule others, they may be better than them, nor let (some) women ridicule other women, they may be better than them. Do not defame one another, nor call each other by offensive nicknames. How evil it is to act rebelliously after having faith! And whoever does not repent, it is they who are the (true) wrongdoers" [Al-Hujurāt 49:11]
You guard yourself against insulting others (other people, races, religions), for if people start to curse Allāh ﷻ , this may invite the worse kind of harm	The Prophet ﷺ, in his victories, was never boastful. He was completely magnanimous and grateful to Allāh ﷻ. When he entered Makkah in the final conquest of his beloved city, whose people tortured, mocked, and reviled him, he entered with his head bowed and granted clemency to its inhabitants. He was entirely beautiful in character and compassion.
Repentance & Forgiveness	
You repent (thinking back to when you scoffed at others), reflecting on the Qur'ānic ethic that there is strength in dealing nobly with people (that it is simply a better way to live)	The Prophet ﷺ said:, "Among my people, the one who is bankrupt is the one who – after praying, fasting, and paying charity – arrives on the Day of Judgement having cursed one person and slandered another, assaulted another, and misappropriated the wealth of someone else. Then those people will be given of his good deeds, and if his good deeds run out before redress is made, then some of their sins will be taken from them and put upon him. Then he will be cast into Hell." [Ṣaḥīḥ Muslim 2581:59]

Mockery

Exceptions	Qur'ānic, Prophetic & Scholarly Evidence
Making Light of a Serious Matter You make humour and light of a serious matter when this will benefit the affected, but only on occasions (and when applied with wisdom), because your commentary may be taken as mockery, which is sinful	The Prophet ﷺ once told an old lady, "There will be no old ladies in Jannah" [Shamāil Al-Muḥammadiyyah by At-Tirmidhī 240]. He ﷺ implied that everyone who enters Jannah will do so as young people and not old, so he eventually clarified to the lady that she will enter Jannah as a young woman!
Light-Hearted and Humble Fun You make a little light-hearted joke, especially if the intention is to keep the spouse and children happy, however, such joking must be something which is truthful, and not based on fiction or lies	Once a man came to the Prophet ﷺ and asked for a mount. The Prophet replied, "I will give you a baby camel as a mount." The man then wondered: "O Messenger of Allāh, what will I do with a baby camel?" The Prophet replied, "Are not all camels the babies of a mother camel?" [At-Tirmidhī 1991]

الأَفْكَارُ السَّلْبِيَّة

Negative Feelings

SIGNS & SYMPTOMS

- Bad Opinion of Others & Being Judgemental
- Backbiting of the Limbs, Tongue, Mind & Heart (Ghībah)
- Social Media Gossip

TREATMENTS

- Understanding Backbiting & the Consequences of Negative Feelings or Suspicion (Social Media)
- Avoiding Potential Harm on Social Media
- Keeping Good Company
- You Seek Forgiveness from Others
- Protecting the Honour of a Muslim
- Busy Yourself With Your Own Faults & Forgive Others

EXCEPTIONS

- Alleviating Oppression, Highlighting Evil-Doing or Seeking Help
- Being Conscious of Deceit & Corruption, and Therefore Asking for Proof
- Supporting Important Decisions

CHAPTER 20

Negative Feelings

[Al-Afkār as-Salbiyyah] الأفْكارُ السَّلْبِيَّة

For the purposes of this book, 'negative feelings' are those that a person harbours towards someone behaving in a righteous way. One has become bothered by the positive words or deeds of another, and has judged that person based on the heart's suspicions (ẓann) without proof. By far the most likely root cause of these negative feelings is jealousy, fed by pride of course, but there are a variety of accessories to this disease: weakness of faith and a lack of consciousness of Allāh ﷻ; the frustrated venting of anger; unfounded dislike and unjustified animosity towards the other person; and the desire to elevate oneself by declaring the faults of others.

Allāh ﷻ says, "O believers! Avoid many suspicions, (for) indeed, some suspicions are sinful." [Al-Hujurāt 49:12]

The Messenger of Allāh ﷺ said, "Allāh says, 'I am as My servant thinks of Me. If he thinks good of Me then so it shall be, and if he thinks ill of Me then so it shall be.'" [Musnad Aḥmad 9076]

Imām As-Shafi'ī رحمه الله said in one of his poems: "Let not your tongue mention the shame of another, for you yourself are covered in shame and all men have tongues. If your eye falls upon the sins of your brother, shield them and say: 'O my eye! All men have eyes!'" [Dīwān As-Shafi'ī, p.144]

We need to distinguish between these negative feelings that stem from a certain inadequacy of character, and the socially constructive mechanism which allows for relevant evidence to be shown against someone for their negative actions, in order that further damage can be prevented.

Negative Feelings

Signs & Symptoms

Qur'ānic, Prophetic & Scholarly Evidence

Bad Opinion of Others & Being Judgemental

Based upon your own assumptions (i.e. without sound reasoning or evidence), you hold a bad opinion about someone who actually demonstrates righteous behaviour

You form your own conclusions based on a perceived 'bad' appearance of someone (it could be that Allāh ﷻ is veiling their goodness from you)

Your suspicion is judgemental, often superficially plausible and almost always incorrect

You divulge the flaws and complain about an oppressor to such people who have no control over the oppressor and are unable to alleviate the suffering of the complainant

Backbiting of the Limbs, Tongue, Mind & Heart (Ghībah)

You communicate about another by means of backbiting (ghībah), often finding yourself saying:

- 'Brother, but it's the truth'
- 'I would say it to his face, it doesn't matter'
- 'I'm not backbiting but...' and then you mention a weakness of that someone else
- 'Sister, what do you think about so and so?'
- 'This is what he is like...'
- 'Did you hear about this person, he's involved in such and such an action'

You harbour suspicion in your heart that affects your thoughts and opinion of another person (ghībah tul-qalb or 'backbiting of the heart')

Allāh ﷻ **said**, "O believers! Avoid many suspicions, (for) indeed, some suspicions are sinful. And do not spy, nor backbite one another. Would any of you like to eat the flesh of their dead brother? You would despise that! And fear Allāh. Surely Allāh is (the) Accepter of Repentance, Most Merciful." [Al-Hujurāt 49:12]

The Prophet ﷺ **said**:

- "Among my people, the one who is bankrupt is the one who – after praying, fasting, and paying charity – arrives on the Day of Judgement having cursed one person and slandered another, assaulted another, and misappropriated the wealth of someone else. Then those people will be given of his good deeds, and if his good deeds run out before redress is made, then some of their sins will be taken from them and put upon him. Then he will be cast into Hell" [Ṣaḥīḥ Muslim 2581:59]
- "Do you know what 'ghībah' (backbiting) is?" **The listeners said**, "Allāh and His Messenger know best." **He** ﷺ **said**, "Saying something about your brother that he dislikes." **It was said**, "What if what I say about my brother is true?" **He** ﷺ **said**, "If what you say is true then you have backbitten about him, and if it is not true, then you have slandered him" [Ṣaḥīḥ Muslim 2589:70]
- "The person who spreads calumnies will never enter Paradise" [Ṣaḥīḥ Al-Bukhārī 6056, Ṣaḥīḥ Muslim 105:168]
- "Beware of sitting in the roads." **The listeners said**, "O Messenger of Allāh, we have nowhere else to sit and talk." **The Prophet** ﷺ **said**, "If you insist, then give the road its right." **They said**, "What is its right, O Messenger of Allāh?" **The Prophet** ﷺ **said**, "Lower the gaze, refrain from harming others, return greetings of peace, enjoin good and forbid evil" [Ṣaḥīḥ Al-Bukhārī 2565, Ṣaḥīḥ Muslim 2121:114]
- "When I was taken up to Heaven I passed by people who had nails of copper and were scratching their faces and their breasts. I said, 'Who are these people, Jibrāīl?' He replied, 'They are those who were given to backbiting and who aspersed people's honour" [Sunan Abī Dawūd 4878]
- "The faith of a servant is not upright until his heart is upright, and his heart is not upright until his tongue is upright. A man will not enter Paradise if his neighbour is not secure from his evil" [Musnad Aḥmad 13048]
- "Whoever taunts a brother with a sin (which the brother has committed), will not die until he (the taunter) commits the same sin" [At-Tirmidhī 2505]
- "When the son of Ādam wakes up in the morning, all the limbs humble themselves before the tongue and say, 'Fear Allāh for our sake, (for) we are with you; if you are upright, we will be upright; and if you are crooked, we will become crooked" [At-Tirmidhī 2407]

Negative Feelings

Signs & Symptoms	Qur'ānic, Prophetic & Scholarly Evidence
Social Media Gossip	
You speak ill of another person over social media, or spread the latest gossip (namīmah), or even enjoy reading others' comments, with no constructive purpose but to malign their reputation because you (or someone else) hold some issue against that other person	Allāh ﷻ said, "Indeed, those who love to see indecency spread among the believers will suffer a painful punishment in this life and the Hereafter. Allāh knows and you do not know." [An-Nūr 24:19] The Prophet ﷺ said: o "Do you know what calumny is?" They said, "No, Allāh and His Messenger know best." He said, "Telling people what other people have said in order to create dissension between them" [Al-Adab Al-Mufrad 425] o "It is enough lying for a man to speak of everything that he hears" [Ṣaḥīḥ Muslim 5:5]
You harbour negative thoughts about someone who has posted something you do not like, which results in you not talking to them and/or holding a grudge against them, and this impacts your relationship	The Prophet ﷺ asked his Companions, "Do you know what 'ghībah' (backbiting) is?" They said, "Allāh and His Messenger know best." He said, "Saying something about your brother that he dislikes." It was said, "What if what I say about my brother is true?" He said, "If what you say is true then you have backbitten about him, and if it is not true, then you have slandered him." [Ṣaḥīḥ Muslim 2589:70] Two Companions once criticised a man who had been punished for committing adultery. The Prophet ﷺ was travelling and he passed by the carcass of a donkey. He said, "Where are those two people? Get down and eat from the flesh of this donkey!" They said, "O Prophet of Allāh! Who would eat this?" He said, "What the two of you have recently done by defaming the honour of your brother is far worse than eating from this." [Sunan Abī Dawūd 4428] Imām Al-Ghazālī رحمه الله said: "Know that the unrestrained tongue, and the heart that is rusted over and full of negligence and greed, are a sign of misfortune, and if you do not kill the ego with sincere exertion your heart will not be animated by the light of gnosis." [Letter to a Disciple/Ayyuhāl Walad, p.24-25]

Negative Feelings

Academic Treatment	Qur'ānic, Prophetic & Scholarly Evidence
Understanding Backbiting & the Consequences of Negative Feelings or Suspicion (Social Media)	
You remind yourself of all that backbiting involves, when it is permissible to speak about an absent person, and what to do after you backbite	Allāh ﷻ said, "Exalted is Allāh, the True King! Do not rush to recite (a revelation of) the Qur'ān (O Prophet) before it is (properly) conveyed to you, and pray, 'My Lord! Increase me in knowledge.'" [Ṭāhā 20:114]
You restrain yourself from negative thoughts (e.g. a feeling of anger) and backbiting, by reflecting on the punishments and harms of it	
You realise that it is easy to jump to false conclusions or assume the worst about others on social media, and that it is also easy to get offended, upset, or even angry based on what you perceive someone else is saying	The Prophet ﷺ said, "Beware of suspicion, for suspicion is the most false of speech." [Ṣaḥīḥ Al-Bukhārī 5143, At-Tirmidhī 1988]
You learn to give people the benefit of the doubt, whilst also avoiding posting passive-aggressive updates that others may misinterpret	The Prophet ﷺ said (while circumambulating the Ka'bah), "(O Ka'bah!) You are beautiful and your scent is beautiful. I admire your majesty and sacredness. I swear by Allāh, in whose hand is Muḥammad's life, that the honour of the believer is superior to your honour in the eye of Allāh. A believer's wealth, blood and sacredness of having positive thoughts about him is superior to yours." [Ibn Mājah 3932]
You understand that harbouring negative feelings has a devastating effect on your own virtuous deeds	
You remind yourself that you will only experience regret and remorse on the Day of Judgement when you find your account has been diminished and your good deeds have been transferred to that person for whom you harboured a bad opinion	
You understand the importance of having positive thoughts about others	

Negative Feelings

Practical Treatment

Avoiding Potential Harm on Social Media

You refrain from online 'commentary' because you realise that 'just a few words' can have a devastating impact on a long-standing relationship

You instead adopt patience and take up your issue in person, ensuring you have a good opinion (expectations, thoughts) of others

You realise that though negative thoughts are very easy to have, they are harmful to brotherhood and injurious to your own spiritual growth, so you take steps to:

- Ensure you never help further any type of split between two people
- Try to develop an ability to see in people signs of goodness
- Never despise anyone no matter how bad their actions may seem, as you never know who is more beloved than you in the eyes of Allāh ﷻ
- Avoid people who talk about others, including places of gossip where spreading negativity is the norm, such as internet chat rooms, blogs, lunchroom settings and other notorious places for spreading rumours
- Mind your own business when things look interesting but do not concern you, which may require that you cut down on your overall consumption of information (e.g. reducing your membership of WhatsApp groups)
- Avoid seemingly 'innocent' questions that can lead to backbiting, such as: "I haven't seen so-and-so for a while. How is she doing?" because you realise that instead of getting a simple reply, the response might be: "Did you hear that she ..."
- Avoid talking about people who are not present in your conversation because you realise that this drastically limits the risk of backbiting
- Stop backbiting the first time it happens
- Let others know immediately that you cannot be involved in such conversations, without seeming self-righteous or hostile
- Change the topic or at least despise 'in your heart' what is being discussed
- Remind yourself of the brevity of your life and the consequences in the Hereafter by seeking refuge in Allāh ﷻ from punishment in the grave

Qur'ānic, Prophetic & Scholarly Evidence

Allāh ﷻ says:

- "O believers! Be mindful of Allāh and be with the truthful" [At-Tawbah 9:119]
- "O believers! Avoid many suspicions, (for) indeed, some suspicions are sinful. And do not spy, nor backbite one another" [Al-Hujurāt 49: 12]
- "Not a word does a person utter without having a (vigilant) observer ready (to write it down)" [Qāf 50:18]

The Prophet ﷺ said:

- "A strong man is not one who defeats (another) in physical combat. Verily, a strong man is he who controls his self at the time of anger" [Ṣaḥīḥ Al-Bukhārī 6114, Ṣaḥīḥ Muslim 2609:107]
- "Whoever believes in Allāh and the Last Day should speak good or remain silent" [Ṣaḥīḥ Al-Bukhārī 6018, Ṣaḥīḥ Muslim 47:74]
- "Keep to gentleness, for gentleness is not found in anything without adorning it, and is not withdrawn from anything without shaming it" [Ṣaḥīḥ Muslim 2594:79]
- "He who keeps silent will be safe" [At-Tirmidhī 2501]
- "From the excellence of a person's Islām is that he leaves what does not concern him" [At-Tirmidhī 2317]
- "Whosoever of you sees an evil, let him change it with his hand; and if he is not able to do so, then (let him change it) with his tongue; and if he is not able to do so, then with his heart, and that is the weakest of faith" [Ṣaḥīḥ Muslim 49:78]

Once a person grew very angry before the Prophet ﷺ, who then noticed how when the face shows extreme anger it resembles Satan; the Prophet ﷺ then said, "I have a word, if spoken, will remove it from him. It is, 'I seek refuge in Allāh from Satan the accursed.'" [Ṣaḥīḥ Al-Bukhārī 3282, Ṣaḥīḥ Muslim 2610:109]

Some scholars advise not to ask about an absent person for fear of backbiting; some scholars reportedly dug graves in their homes and lay in them to remind themselves that one day they would be in the grave and no longer able to repent for their sins.

Negative Feelings

Practical Treatment	Qur'ānic, Prophetic & Scholarly Evidence
Keeping Good Company	
You understand that you will be influenced by your friends and acquaintances, so you look carefully for those who maintain positivity and encourage you towards what is good and help you avoid what is harmful	Allāh ﷻ said: o "O believers! Be mindful of Allāh and be with the truthful" [At-Tawbah 9:119] o "And (beware of) the Day the wrongdoer will bite his nails (in regret) and say, 'Oh! I wish I had followed the Way along with the Messenger!' Woe to me! I wish I had never taken so-and-so as a close friend" [Al-Furqān 25: 27-28] The Prophet ﷺ said: o "A person is upon the religion of his close friend, so beware whom you befriend" [Sunan Abī Dawūd 4833, At-Tirmidhī 2378] o "A good friend and a bad friend are like a perfume-seller and a blacksmith: The perfume-seller might give you some perfume as a gift, or you might buy some from him, or at least you might smell its fragrance. As for the blacksmith, he might singe your clothes, and at the very least you will breathe in the fumes of the furnace" [Ṣaḥīḥ Al-Bukhārī 2101]
You Seek Forgiveness from Others	
You make tawbah, and you praise this individual and/or mention his virtues in the gathering (if the other person does not know of your negative feelings)	The Prophet ﷺ said, "Whoever has oppressed another person concerning his reputation or anything else, he should beg him to forgive him today (before the Day of Resurrection) when there will be no dīnār or dirham (to compensate for wrong deeds), but if he has good deeds, those good deeds will be taken from him according to his oppression which he has done, and if he has no good deeds, the sins of the oppressed person will be loaded on him." [Ṣaḥīḥ Al-Bukhārī 2449]
You seek his forgiveness and express regret at having voiced negative feelings (where your news has reached the other person)	

Negative Feelings

Practical Treatment	Qur'ānic, Prophetic & Scholarly Evidence
Protecting the Honour of a Muslim	
You work hard to cover the faults of others and to defend their honour as you would defend your own (i.e. not spending time seeking them out and exposing them)	The Prophet ﷺ said: o "Whoever defends his brother's honour, Allāh will protect his face from the fire of Hell on the Day of Resurrection" [At-Tirmidhī 1931] o "The servant who conceals the faults of others in this world, Allāh will conceal his faults on the Day of Resurrection" [Ṣaḥīḥ Al-Bukhārī 2442, Ṣaḥīḥ Muslim 2580:58] o "A person may say a word that is pleasing to Allāh, not paying it any heed, for which Allāh will raise him in status, and a person may say a word that is displeasing to Allāh, not paying it any heed, for which he will fall into Hell" [Ṣaḥīḥ Al-Bukhārī 6478]
You do not resign and stay quiet leaving others to backbite, where you have the ability to change the course of action	
You censure the backbiters and prevent them from persisting as it relates to the honour of your Muslim brother or sister	

Negative Feelings

Practical Treatment	Qur'ānic, Prophetic & Scholarly Evidence
Busy Yourself With Your Own Faults & Forgive Others	
You remind yourself that you also make mistakes, that you have your own shortcomings in your duties towards Allāh ﷻ, that you would like Allāh ﷻ to pardon you and conceal your faults	Allāh ﷻ says: o "Do not let the people of virtue and affluence among you swear to suspend donations to their relatives, the needy, and the emigrants in the cause of Allāh. Let them pardon and forgive. Do you not love to be forgiven by Allāh? And Allāh is All-Forgiving, Most Merciful" [An-Nūr 24:22] o "Be gracious, enjoin what is right, and turn away from those who act ignorantly" [Al-'A'rāf 7:199]
You therefore ask Allāh ﷻ, the Most Forgiving, the Most Merciful, for His forgiveness	o "We have not created the heavens and the earth and everything in between except for a purpose. And the Hour is certain to come, so forgive graciously" [Al-Ḥijr 15:85] o "The reward of an evil deed is its equivalent. But whoever pardons and seeks reconciliation, then their reward is with Allāh. He certainly does not like the wrongdoers" [Ash-Shūrā 42:40]
You also forgive others as mentioned in the Qur'ān, reminding yourself that perhaps you will be treated in the same fashion	The Prophet ﷺ said: o "Charity does not decrease wealth, no one forgives except that Allāh increases his honour, and no one humbles himself for the sake of Allāh except that Allāh raises his status" [Ṣaḥīḥ Muslim 2588:69] o "Be merciful to others and you will receive mercy. Forgive others and Allāh will forgive you" [Musnad Aḥmad 6541, 7041]

Negative Feelings

Exceptions

Alleviating Oppression, Highlighting Evil-Doing or Seeking Help

- You have doubts or a bad opinion about someone based on sound reasoning and observable evidence
- You wish to complain about an oppressor to his senior, a judge or the authorities (i.e. someone who has control over the oppressor) and make him aware of the oppression thereby alleviating yourself or someone else of the suffering
- You wish to warn someone about a person, i.e. 'do you know such and such, he is spreading lies', or 'he is a thief so guard your property'
- You describe how you have been wronged because you seek help to remove an evil, or to right a wrong

Qur'ānic, Prophetic & Scholarly Evidence

Allāh ﷻ says, "You are the best community ever raised for humanity - you encourage good, forbid evil, and believe in Allāh. Had the People of the Book believed, it would have been better for them. Some of them are faithful, but most are rebellious." [Āli 'Imrān 3:110]

The Prophet ﷺ said, "Whosoever of you sees an evil, let him change it with his hand; and if he is not able to do so, then (let him change it) with his tongue; and if he is not able to do so, then with his heart – and that is the weakest of faith" [Ṣaḥīḥ Muslim 49:78]

Being Conscious of Deceit & Corruption, and Therefore Asking for Proof

- You remind yourself that there are many people who have no qualms in deceiving and cheating people, adorning their faces with smiles and communicating that they are wonderful people, but that they will cheat a person whenever the opportunity arises
- Because corruption and fraud are prevalent, you are rigorous in your investigation because some people often present themselves as mired in poverty, though they are well-off
- You ensure you ask for proof if someone says to you that a given person is bad because you know that without proof, what has been said is almost a lie
- You do not accept the news, without circumspection, from someone known to openly indulge in major sins
- You always test someone's sincerity and trustworthiness before entrusting him with anything significant (until their goodness becomes manifest), especially where there is much corruption in a given generation
- You are circumspect with your dispensation of charity (zakāh) because charity is considered a trust from Allāh ﷻ, and its dispensation must be performed with care

Qur'ānic, Prophetic & Scholarly Evidence

Allāh ﷻ says, "O believers, if an evildoer brings you any news, verify (it) so you do not harm people unknowingly, becoming regretful for what you have done." [Al-Hujurāt 49:6]

The Prophet ﷺ said, "It is enough lying for a man to speak of everything that he hears" [Ṣaḥīḥ Muslim 5]

Supporting Important Decisions

- You make someone aware of important facts so that an informed decision can be made (otherwise he may be disadvantaged, e.g. related to marriage, a business deal, in court)
- You only divulge what is necessary and pertaining to the issue and nothing further

كُفْرَانُ النِّعَم

Obliviousness to Blessings or Ingratitude

SIGNS & SYMPTOMS

- Forgetful of Seen & Unseen Blessings
- Misinterpretation of Blessings
- Short-Term Relief
- Hopelessness at Loss

TREATMENTS

- Showing Gratitude for Allāh's ﷻ Innumerable Blessings
- Wealth & Restriction are Both Tests
- Demonstrating Gratefulness
- Being Patient & Pursuing Long-Term Benefits
- Compare with Those Worse than You

NO EXCEPTIONS

- Any Obliviousness to Blessings is Blameworthy

CHAPTER 21

Obliviousness to Blessings or Ingratitude

[Kufrān an-Ni'am] كُفْرَانُ النِّعَم

Allāh ﷻ states in the Qur'ān: "Whatever blessings you have are from Allāh." [An-Naḥl 16:53]

To be bitterly hostile in disregarding this blessing can be an active and obvious personal choice, a kind of barefaced 'thumbing of the nose' at Allāh's ﷻ grace. In a more passive manner, ignorance of His blessings can originate from a person's lack of understanding and realisation. Either way, this lack of acknowledgement constitutes ingratitude.

Allāh ﷻ also says:

- "And (remember) when your Lord proclaimed, 'If you are grateful, I will certainly give you more. But if you are ungrateful, surely My punishment is severe'" [Ibrāhīm 14:7]
- "Remember Me; I will remember you. And thank Me, and never be ungrateful" [Al-Baqarah 2:152]

The Prophet ﷺ said, "If happiness reaches him (the believer), he is grateful (to Allāh)." [Ṣaḥīḥ Muslim 2999:64]

Obliviousness to Blessings or Ingratitude

Signs & Symptoms

Forgetful of Seen & Unseen Blessings

You find yourself forgetting blessings that come in all forms, both what you can see and what you cannot: food, clothing, shelter, wealth, safety, friendship, love, family, health, and protection from harm and calamity

Misinterpretation of Blessings

You are oblivious of the concept of istidrāj, in which Allāh ﷻ allows you to flaunt your blessings, while He does not diminish your blessings in the least, and in fact, He may increase them. Indeed, you begin to think that Allāh ﷻ really loves and favours you, when in actuality, Allāh ﷻ may be giving you a lot of fortune in order to destroy you

Short-Term Relief

You see only short-term relief as a blessing and ignore the benefits of patience and temporary discomfort

Hopelessness at Loss

You fall apart and plunge into dejection when losing something valuable

Qur'ānic, Prophetic & Scholarly Evidence

Allāh ﷻ says:

- "Now, whenever a human being is tested by their Lord through (His) generosity and blessings, they boast, 'My Lord has (deservedly) honoured me!' But when He tests them by limiting their provision, they protest, 'My Lord has (undeservedly) humiliated me!'" [Al-Fajr 89: 15-16]
- "We already showed them the Way, whether they (choose to) be grateful or ungrateful" [Al-Insān 76:3]
- "Have you (O Prophet) not seen those who fled their homes in the thousands for fear of death? Allāh said to them, 'Die!' then He gave them life. Surely Allāh is ever Bountiful to humanity, but most people are ungrateful" [Al-Baqarah 2:243]
- Iblīs said, "I will approach them from their front, their back, their right, their left, and then You will find most of them ungrateful" [Al-'A'rāf 7:17]

The Prophet ﷺ said:

- "When you see Allāh ﷻ giving good fortune to his slaves who are always committing sins (being disobedient), know that the person is being given istidrāj by Allāh ﷻ" [Al-Mu'jam Al-Kabīr Aṭ-Ṭabarānī 913, Musnad Aḥmad 17311, Al-Bayhaqī in Shu'ab Al-Īmān 4220]
- "I saw Hellfire and I never saw a scene like today, and I saw that most of its people are women." They (the Companions) asked, "O Messenger of Allāh, why?" He said, "Because of their ungratefulness." They asked, "Do they disbelieve in (are they ungrateful to) Allāh ﷻ?" He replied, "They are ungrateful to their companions (husbands) and are ungrateful for the favours done to them; Even if you do good to one of them all your life, when she sees some mistake from you, she will say, 'I have never seen any good from you'" [Ṣaḥīḥ Al-Bukhārī 5197]

Obliviousness to Blessings or Ingratitude

Academic Treatment	Qur'ānic, Prophetic & Scholarly Evidence
Showing Gratitude for Allāh's ﷻ Innumerable Blessings	
You remind yourself that the best of blessings are those connected with entering Paradise, i.e. faith, patience, good character, swiftness in doing good, and promptness in worship (because these are everlasting) You understand that whatever blessings come to you (night and day), are from Allāh ﷻ, and are beyond numeration You understand that blessings come in all forms - what we can see and touch (by way of material goods: food, clothing, shelter, wealth, and the like), as well as what we cannot see (like safety, friendship, love, health, and protection from harm and calamity) You remind yourself of just a few of the countless blessings: o You blink, for example, thousands of times a day without thought, however there are people who require artificial lubrication because their tear glands do not function; and that there are countless other blessings related to the eye o Your ability to walk in balance even the slightest distance without needing to consciously stimulate dozens of muscles o Your thumbs permit you to do with your hands what most creatures cannot attempt o Your food has been made delicious instead of bland o You have been given dignity in your partaking of nutrition, compared to the inelegant fashion in which carnivores ravage and devour their prey	Allāh ﷻ says: o "Whatever blessings you have are from Allāh. Then whenever hardship touches you, to Him (alone) you cry (for help)" [An-Naḥl 16:53] o "Let people then consider their food: how We pour down rain in abundance and meticulously split the earth open (for sprouts), causing grain to grow in it, as well as grapes and greens, and olives and palm trees, and dense orchards, all as (a means of) sustenance for you and your animals" ['Abasa 80: 24-32] o "Remember Me; I will remember you. And thank Me, and never be ungrateful" [Al-Baqarah 2:152] o "And proclaim the blessings of your Lord" [Ad-Duḥā 93:11] o "And He has granted you all that you asked Him for. If you tried to count Allāh's blessings, you would never be able to number them. Indeed humankind is truly unfair, (totally) ungrateful" [Ibrāhīm 14:34] o "Say (O Prophet), 'He is the One Who brought you into being and gave you hearing, sight, and intellect. (Yet) you hardly give any thanks'" [Al-Mulk 67:23] The Prophet ﷺ said: o "If happiness reaches him (the believer), he is grateful" [Ṣaḥīḥ Muslim 2999:64] o "By Allāh, I love you, Mu'ādh. I advise you to never abandon this supplication after every (prescribed) prayer, say: "O Allāh, help me in remembering You, in giving You thanks, and worshipping You well'" [Sunan Abī Dawūd 1522] o "Allāh is pleased with a person who eats some food and then praises Him for it, or who drinks some drink and then praises Him for it" [Ṣaḥīḥ Muslim 2734:88] 'Āishah ؓ reports that the Prophet ﷺ used to offer prayer at night (for such a long time) that his ankles used to swell. She said, "O Rasūlullah! Why do you do it since Allāh has forgiven you your faults of the past and those to follow?" He said, "Should I not be a grateful slave?" [Ṣaḥīḥ Al-Bukhārī 4837]

Obliviousness to Blessings or Ingratitude

Academic Treatment

Qur'ānic, Prophetic & Scholarly Evidence

Wealth & Restriction are Both Tests	
You remind yourself that the enemy of Allāh ﷻ, Iblīs, applies all his efforts in making you negligent and unwary of the lofty rank of shukr (thankfulness)	Allāh ﷻ says: o "And (remember) when your Lord proclaimed, 'If you are grateful, I will certainly give you more. But if you are ungrateful, surely My punishment is severe'" [Ibrāhīm 14:7] o "In this way We have tested some by means of others, so those (disbelievers) may say, 'Has Allāh favoured these (poor believers) out of all of us?' Does Allāh not best recognise the grateful?" [Al An'ām 6:53]
You understand that engaging in thankfulness towards Allāh ﷻ will protect you from the retraction of His blessings	
You remember that wealth is a test for you, and that the more you have of the 'ornaments of this world', the more you will be accountable for them	
You use His bounties and favours to obtain His good pleasure	

Practical Treatment

Qur'ānic, Prophetic & Scholarly Evidence

Demonstrating Gratefulness	
You employ the use of your eyes, your ears, your tongue and your limbs correctly, to obtain His good pleasure	Allāh ﷻ says, "And (remember) when your Lord proclaimed, 'If you are grateful, I will certainly give you more. But if you are ungrateful, surely My punishment is severe.'" [Ibrāhīm 14:7] The Prophet ﷺ said, "Allāh is pleased with a person who eats some food and then praises Him for it, or who drinks some drink and then praises Him for it." [Ṣaḥīḥ Muslim 2734:88]
You adopt a self-discipline of the heart, in which you are indifferent (i.e. not attached) to the material world, such that your character and level of faith do not change if and when you lose your blessings	
When your wealth is restricted, this is also a test, so you adopt patience and contentment (rather than hopelessness and bitterness)	

Obliviousness to Blessings or Ingratitude

Practical Treatment	Qur'ānic, Prophetic & Scholarly Evidence
Being Patient & Pursuing Long-Term Benefits	Allāh ﷻ says:
You understand that things may be somewhat uncomfortable in the short term, yet beneficial in the long term	o "Surely Allāh is with those who persevere" [Al-'Anfāl 8:46] o "If you retaliate, then let it be equivalent to what you have suffered. But if you patiently endure, it is certainly best for those who are patient" [An-Naḥl 16:126]
You control your lustful desires (shahawāt) because you understand that sexual intimacy and being patient until marriage is far greater than any temporary pleasure and the dishonour of descent into sin. This self control can become difficult: uncomfortable and even frustrating	o "They replied (in shock), 'Are you really Joseph?' He said, 'I am Joseph, and here is my brother (Benjamin)! Allāh has truly been gracious to us. Surely whoever is mindful (of Allāh) and patient, then certainly Allāh never discounts the reward of the good-doers'" [Yūsuf 12:90]
You avoid overeating because you realise that it invites health problems in the longer term (though you may enjoy some gratification in the short term)	o "These (believers) will be given a double reward for their perseverance, responding to evil with good, and for donating from what We have provided for them" [Al-Qaṣaṣ 28:54]
Compare with Those Worse than You	The Prophet ﷺ said:
Even when you encounter problems or inconveniences, you think about those who are in a worse condition	o "Look at those who are inferior to you and do not look at the ones above you: this is worthier, so you do not despise Allāh's blessings" [Ṣaḥīḥ Muslim 2963:8] o "How wonderful is the case of a believer! There is good for him in whatever happens to him, and none, apart from him, enjoys this blessing. If he receives some bounty, he is grateful to Allāh and this bounty brings good to him. And if some adversity befalls him, he is patient, and this affliction, too, brings good to him" [Ṣaḥīḥ Muslim 2999:64]

Obliviousness to Blessings or Ingratitude

NO Exceptions	Qur'ānic, Prophetic & Scholarly Evidence
Any Obliviousness to Blessings is Blameworthy	
You remind yourself that Allāh ﷻ is most deserving of your thanks and praise because of the great favours and blessings that He has bestowed upon you in both spiritual and worldly terms	Allāh ﷻ says, "Remember Me; I will remember you. And thank Me, and never be ungrateful." [Al-Baqarah 2:152]
You remind yourself that Allāh ﷻ has commanded you to give thanks to Him for those blessings, and not to deny them	

OBLIVIOUSNESS TO BLESSINGS

الرِيَاء

Ostentation or Showing Off

TREATMENTS

SIGNS & SYMPTOMS

- Virtuous Deeds for Personal Gain
- Lazy & Lethargic When Alone
- Preparing to Engage in Blameworthy Showing Off
- Heedless of the Evil of Envy
- Using Complex Language
- Seeking the Pleasure of Others & Social Media
- A Slave to Fashion

- Struggling Within Yourself to Correct Your Intention
- Righteousness, Not Wealth
- Only Allāh ﷻ can Benefit or Harm You
- Remembering the Life Hereafter
- Reflecting on those Less Fortunate & the Harms of Showing Off
- Reflecting on the Temporary & Transitory
- Seek Allāh's ﷻ Help in Overcoming Ostentation
- Performing Deeds in Private & in Abundance
- Avoid Boasting on Social Media
- Reflect Upon One's Own Shortcomings
- Managing Evil Whisperings
- Regular Qur'ānic Recital, Forgiveness & Remembrance in Private

EXCEPTIONS

- Cause of Inspiration
- Beautification Only for the Sake of Allāh ﷻ

CHAPTER 22

Ostentation or Showing Off [Riyā'a] الرِيَاء

Ostentation is when you perform an act of devotion for other than the Creator's sake, for the purpose of seeking some worldly benefit, praise or admiration from His creation. Ostentation is a branch of ḥubb al-jāh, love of fame and glory.

When you split the purpose of worship by endeavouring to attain both public acclaim as well as the pleasure of Allāh ﷻ (i.e. partnering with Allāh ﷻ), therein lies a hint of polytheism (lesser shirk).

The Messenger of Allāh ﷺ said:

- "If anyone wants to have his deeds widely publicised, Allāh will publicise (his humiliation). And if anyone makes a hypocritical display of his deeds, Allāh will make a display of him" [Ṣaḥīḥ Muslim 2986:47]
- "Verily, even a little ostentation is shirk" [Ibn Mājah 3989]
- "Shall I not tell you about what I fear for you more than the presence of the False Messiah?" We said, "Of course!" He said, "Hidden polytheism; that a man stands for prayer and beautifies his prayer because he sees another man looking at him" [Ibn Mājah 4204]

People are known to commit riyā'a due to:

- Craving praise and acclaim (the admiration of people) over the pleasure of Allāh ﷻ because their faith in Him has become weak
- Fear of criticism or humiliation, by making a display of good deeds (for example, praying in the mosque out of fear of being criticised by people for not doing so)
- An envious greed for worldly wealth: seeing the possessions of others, they hanker after them, largely in the hope that one day they will be able to parade similar trophies and trinkets

Ostentation or Showing Off

Signs & Symptoms	Qur'ānic, Prophetic & Scholarly Evidence
Virtuous Deeds for Personal Gain	
You pretentiously display virtue so that you can be entrusted with the wealth of another (e.g. an orphan, funds raised for religious purposes), and then misuse it for personal need	Allāh ﷻ says: o "Surely the hypocrites seek to deceive Allāh, but He outwits them. When they stand up for prayer, they do it half-heartedly only to be seen by people: hardly remembering Allāh at all" [An-Nisā' 4:142] o "O believers! Do not waste your charity with reminders (of your generosity) or hurtful words, like those who donate their wealth just to show off and do not believe in Allāh or the Last Day. Their example is that of a hard barren rock covered with a thin layer of soil hit by a strong rain – leaving it just a bare stone. Such people are unable to preserve the reward of their charity. Allāh does not guide (such) disbelieving people" [Al-Baqarah 2:264]
Lazy & Lethargic When Alone	
You become lazy and lack action for Allāh's ﷻ sake when you are alone and out of view of others	
When alone, you become lethargic, unable (or unwilling) to perform acts of devotion. However in public places of worship, you somehow find the drive to recite the Qur'ān or meditate	

Ostentation or Showing Off

Signs & Symptoms

Qur'ānic, Prophetic & Scholarly Evidence

Preparing to Engage in Blameworthy Showing Off

You come across a matter that is difficult to understand, and thinking that it would be good to mention in public, write it down or memorise it, preparing for the grand moment when you will unveil this newfound knowledge before people

The Prophet said, "If anyone wants to have his deeds widely publicised, Allāh will publicise (his humiliation). And if anyone makes a hypocritical display of his deeds, Allāh will make a display of him." [Ṣaḥīḥ Muslim 2986:47]

Heedless of the Evil of Envy

You forget to realise that it takes just one envious eye for your blessing to be destroyed, i.e. that you (who have means) will have someone who envies you for what you possess

The Prophet said, "Resort to secrecy for the fulfilment and success of your needs for, verily, everyone who has a blessing is envied." [Al-Mu'jam Al-Kabīr Aṭ-Ṭabarānī 183, Al-Bayhaqī in Shu'ab Al-Īmān 6228]

Using Complex Language

You use complex language when a simple explanation will suffice

Imām Al-Ghazālī said, "Be careful of... pretentiousness in talking, by way of idioms, allusions, outbursts, verses and poems, for God the Exalted detests the pretentious." [Letter to a Disciple/Ayyuhāl Walad, p.48-49]

Ostentation or Showing Off

Signs & Symptoms	Qur'ānic, Prophetic & Scholarly Evidence
Seeking the Pleasure of Others & Social Media	
You increase your actions when praised and decrease them in the absence of such praise	The Prophet ﷺ said: o "They (the believers) will not worship the sun, the moon, a rock or an idol, but they will be ostentatious in their deeds" [Musnad Aḥmad 17120] o "What I fear for you the most is the minor shirk, that is riyā'a. Allāh will say on the Day of Judgement when He is rewarding the people for their actions: Go to those for whom you did riyā'a in the world: then see if you find the reward with them" [Musnad Aḥmad 23630] o "All of my followers will have their sins pardoned except those who publicise them. An example of this is that of a man who commits a sin at night, and even though Allāh screens it from the public, he comes in the morning and says, 'I committed such-and-such sin last night.' He spent the night screened by his Lord (none knowing about his sin), and in the morning he removed Allāh's screen from himself" [Ṣaḥīḥ Al-Bukhārī 6069] o "There are three (types of) people to whom Allāh will neither speak on the Day of Resurrection nor look at them nor purify them, and they will have a painful chastisement." The Messenger of Allāh ﷺ repeated it three times. Abū Dharr (may Allah be pleased with him) remarked: "They are ruined. Who are they, O Messenger of Allāh?" Upon this, the Messenger of Allāh ﷺ said, "One who lets down his lower garments below his ankles (out of arrogance), one who boasts of his favours done to another; and he who sells his goods by taking a false oath" [Ṣaḥīḥ Muslim 106:171] o "A man will be brought forward (on the Day of Judgement) whom Allāh had made abundantly rich and had granted every kind of wealth. He will be brought and Allāh will make him recount His blessings and he will recount them and (admit having enjoyed them in his lifetime). Allāh will (then) ask: 'What have you done (with these blessings)?' He will say: 'I spent money in every cause in which You wished that it should be spent.' Allāh will say: 'You are lying. You did (so) that it might be said about (you): 'He is a generous person' and so it was said.' Then Allāh will pass the orders and he will be dragged with his face downward and thrown into Hell" [Ṣaḥīḥ Muslim 1905:152] Imām Al-Ghazālī (may Allah have mercy on him) said, "Know that insincerity is produced by overestimating mankind." [Letter to a Disciple/ Ayyuhāl Walad, p.40-41]
You expend much energy seeking the pleasure of others, trying to seek prestige, recognition or promotion by pleasing someone in authority	
You use social media (e.g. Snapchat) to 'post and boast' your latest achievement or experience, forwarding updates, media clips, etc. desperate to establish and maintain your presence	
You announce your engagement before the event is certain, your best wedding photos, your new job or car, holiday pictures, latest baby scans, and your cute-looking children on Instagram, WhatsApp and Facebook	

Ostentation or Showing Off

Signs & Symptoms	Qur'ānic, Prophetic & Scholarly Evidence
A Slave to Fashion	Allāh ﷻ says:
You keep yourself updated on the trends, styles and designs at the expense of common sense, to the extent that you are consumed by the glitter of fashion, resulting in lavishness that exceeds the limits of sharī'ah and ignores the plight of the needy	o "Surely those (pagans) love this fleeting world, (totally) neglecting a weighty Day ahead of them" [Al-Insān 76:27] o "O humanity! Your transgression is only against your own souls. (There is only) brief enjoyment in this worldly life, then to Us is your return, and then We will inform you of what you used to do" [Yūnus 10:23]
You are obsessed with luxury consumption or the 'ostentatious use of goods or services' so that you can demonstrate your status to family, friends and other members of society	o "Whatever (pleasure) you have been given is no more than (a fleeting) enjoyment and adornment of this worldly life. But what is with Allāh is far better and more lasting. Will you not then understand?" [Al-Qaṣaṣ 28:60] o "O humanity! Indeed, Allāh's promise is true. So do not let the life of this world deceive you, nor let the Chief Deceiver deceive you about Allāh" [Fāṭir 35:5]
You dress extravagantly, keeping in mind that 'no one has the clothes I have', or 'no one looks or should look like me', or 'my clothes show that I am better than everyone else'	o "Know that this worldly life is no more than play, amusement, luxury, mutual boasting, and competition in wealth and children. This is like rain that causes plants to grow, to the delight of the planters. But later the plants dry up and you see them wither, then they are reduced to chaff. And in the Hereafter there will be either severe punishment or forgiveness and pleasure of Allāh, whereas the life of this world is no more than the delusion of enjoyment" [Al-Ḥadīd 57:20]
You reflect little on the less fortunate who are unemployed or simply less fortunate and may not have the basic means to survive	o "Whoever desires (only) this worldly life and its luxuries, We will pay them in full for their deeds in this life – nothing will be left out. It is they who will have nothing in the Hereafter except the Fire. Their efforts in this life will be fruitless and their deeds will be useless" [Hūd 11: 15-16]
You forget the inescapable reality of death	o "Say (O Prophet), 'Shall we inform you of who will lose the most deeds? (They are) those whose efforts are in vain in this worldly life, while they think they are doing good!'" [Al-Kahf 18: 103-104]
You rarely stop to think that one day, very soon, you will leave this world wrapped in a simple kafan (shroud), the pattern and style of which has no designer names or brands, and which has remained and will always remain the same	The Prophet ﷺ said: o "Allāh does not look at your outward appearance and your wealth, rather He looks at your hearts and deeds" [Ṣaḥīḥ Muslim 2564:33] o "When lewdness is a part of anything, it becomes defective; and when ḥayā (modesty) is a part of anything it becomes beautiful" [At-Tirmidhī 1974]

Ostentation or Showing Off

Academic Treatment

Struggling Within Yourself to Correct Your Intention

You understand that when your basic motive is to be seen by others (from the start), this invalidates your act of worship, and you are liable for punishment

You develop riyā'a during an act of worship (the intention for which was originally sincere) where your showing off develops and you begin to, for instance, lengthen your prayer, so you fight this thought and restore your niyyah only for Allāh's sake. You are fully aware of the punishment for riyā'a

You struggle within yourself, fearing that your entire action will become null and void if you do not correct your intention

You know that Satan discourages you from doing good deeds, but you do not abandon the deed out of fear of riyā'a: you instead take a moment, re-align your intention, and then proceed

You develop a sense of pride after a good action, as people begin to praise you, however you understand that this is simply a sign of a believer, and whether you are praised by others or not becomes irrelevant

Qur'ānic, Prophetic & Scholarly Evidence

Allāh says, "Say, (O Prophet) 'I am only a man like you, (but) it has been revealed to me that your God is only One God. So whoever hopes for the meeting with their Lord, let them do good deeds and associate none in the worship of their Lord.'" [Al-Kahf 18:110]

The Prophet said, "Actions are according to intentions, and everyone will get what was intended." [Ṣaḥīḥ Al-Bukhārī 1]

Imām Al-Ghazālī said, "You questioned me about sincerity. It is that all your deeds be for God the Exalted, and that your heart be not gladdened by men's praises nor that you care about their censure." [Letter to a Disciple/Ayyuhāl Walad, p.40-41]

Ostentation or Showing Off

Academic Treatment	Qur'ānic, Prophetic & Scholarly Evidence
Righteousness, Not Wealth	
You become conscious of Allāh ﷻ, that He is watching you, and this arouses in you respect and fear of Him; what others think then becomes insignificant	Allāh ﷻ says: o "O humanity! Indeed, We created you from a male and a female, and made you into peoples and tribes so that you may (get to) know one another. Surely the most noble of you in the sight of Allāh is the most righteous among you. Allāh is truly All-Knowing, All-Aware" [Al-Hujurāt 49:13] o "It is not your wealth or children that bring you closer to Us. But those who believe and do good – it is they who will have a multiplied reward for what they did, and they will be secure in (elevated) mansions" [Sabā' 34:37] o "Even though they were only commanded to worship Allāh (alone) with sincere devotion to Him in all uprightness, establish prayer, and pay alms-tax. That is the upright Way" [Al-Bayyinah 98:5]
You remind yourself that the more importance you give to this world, the more it entangles you in a web of never-ending desires and ever-expanding ambitions that trap you in its fleeting pleasures	
You remind yourself that Islām prohibits you to adopt an extravagant display of wealth and superiority, and lays emphasis on modesty	
Your heart is therefore inclined towards preparation for the eternal life, and you therefore seek the pleasure of Allāh ﷻ before leaving the world and entering your grave, by striving to abide by the teachings of Islām in your daily life	Abu Hurairah ؓ reported that in answer to Jibreel's ؑ question about 'Iḥsān' the Prophet ﷺ explained, "Iḥsān is to worship Allāh as if you see Him, and if you do not achieve this state of devotion, then (take it for granted that) Allāh sees you." [Ṣaḥīḥ Al-Bukhārī 4777, Ṣaḥīḥ Muslim 8:1]
Only Allāh ﷻ can Benefit or Harm You	The Prophet ﷺ said, "Be mindful of Allāh, and Allāh will protect you. Be mindful of Allāh, and you will find Him in front of you. If you ask, ask Allāh; if you seek help, seek help from Allāh. Know that if the nation were to gather to benefit you with anything, it would only benefit you with something that Allāh has already prescribed for you, and that if they gather to harm you with anything, they would only harm you with something Allāh has already prescribed for you. The pen has been lifted and the pages have dried." [At-Tirmidhī 2516]
You actively and sincerely seek out purification of your heart by nurturing the certainty that only Allāh ﷻ can benefit or harm you	
You attempt to remove the following things: love of praise, and the desire for worldly benefit from people	
You realise that He alone possesses rewards for your actions in both abodes, that He is All-Powerful	Imām Al-Ghazālī ؒ said, "The cure for it (insincerity) is for you to see them (mankind) as subject to omnipotence, and for you to reckon them as though inanimate objects, powerless to bestow ease or hardship, so you become free of insincerity towards them. As long as you reckon them as having control and free-will, insincerity will not keep away from you." [Letter to a Disciple/ Ayyuhāl Walad, p.40-41]
You realise that if all of creation were to join forces to oppose you or support you, they would not be able to do so except by His permission	

Ostentation or Showing Off

Academic Treatment	Qur'ānic, Prophetic & Scholarly Evidence
Remembering the Life Hereafter You remind yourself of the Hereafter and the difficulties that may lie ahead for you	Imām Al-Ghazālī said, "The idea for admonition is for the worshipper to recollect the fire of the Hereafter...to consider his own past life which he has spent in what did not concern him, and consider what difficulties lie before him such as the absence of firmness of faith in his life's final moments, the nature of his state in the clasps of the Angel of Death, and whether he will be capable of answering Munkar and Nakīr, and that he worry about his state during the Resurrection and its episodes, and whether he will cross the Bridge safely or tumble into the abyss." [Letter to a Disciple/Ayyuhāl Walad, p.48-49]
Reflecting on those Less Fortunate & the Harms of Showing Off You reflect on the situation of the less fortunate, those who may have less than you, those who are unemployed, and those who do not have the basic means to survive You remind yourself that these bounties you are about to flaunt may lead to the jealousy and envy of others so you preserve and protect them You become conscious of the vanity and harm of ostentation, resulting in your detesting it and thus warding it off You are conscious of the fact that if Allāh so wishes, He can make people displeased with you, which will lead to them rebuking and criticising you rather than praising you	Allāh says, "Do not be like those (pagans) who left their homes arrogantly, only to be seen by people and to hinder others from Allāh's Path. And Allāh is Fully Aware of what they do." [Al-'Anfāl 8:47] The Prophet said, "A deed contaminated by even an atom of ostentation is unacceptable to Allāh." [At-Targhīb wa At-Tarhīb by Al-Mundhirī 54] Consider that Prophet Ya'qūb didn't want his son, Sayyidunā Yūsuf to tell his brothers about a dream he had because he worried that it would trigger ill feelings in their hearts. He rightly suspected that the brothers would then try to harm Yūsuf. Then what should be our case when we display all the gifts Allāh has given us? Recent poverty statistics: o 'In 2015, 10 percent of the world's population lived on less than US$1.90 a day' [The World Bank, 2018] o 'There were 4.1 million children living in poverty in the UK in 2016-17. That's 30 per cent of children, or 9 in a classroom of 30. Families experience poverty for many reasons, but its fundamental cause is not having enough money to cope with the circumstances in which they are living' [Department for Work and Pensions, 2018]

Ostentation or Showing Off

Academic Treatment	Qur'ānic, Prophetic & Scholarly Evidence
Reflecting on the Temporary & Transitory	
You reflect on the temporary and fleeting nature of fame, that it is merely a superficial thing which is not worthy of consideration	
You remind yourself how foolish it would be to exchange the praises and plaudits of this temporary world for the anger and displeasure of Allāh	The Prophet said, "What I fear for you the most is the minor shirk, that is riyā'a. Allāh will say on the Day of Judgement when He is rewarding the people for their actions: Go to those for whom you did riyā'a in the world: then see if you find the reward with them." [Musnad Aḥmad 23630]
You also consider that when you die, all your praises and commendations will be left behind, to no benefit, that all your efforts will have been in vain and the difficulty which you experienced in executing these acts will be confiscated and lost	
You remind yourself that your ostentation will be a cause for disgrace tomorrow on the plains of Qiyamah, where you will be humiliated in front of the entire creation	
Seek Allāh's Help in Overcoming Ostentation	
Your recitation of this ayah from Surah Fatihah strengthens your faith; when you say that you worship Allāh alone, you follow up this assertion with your actions	Allāh, the Most Merciful, knows every human's weakness and has given us the cure as well. The best means is supplication to Him. Allāh says that we should say: "You (alone) we worship and You (alone) we ask for help." [Al-Fatihah 1:5]
Your worship signifies your obedience and trust, followed by deeds that have Allāh's acceptance as their only goal	
You disregard your desire for worldly praise	

Ostentation or Showing Off

Practical Treatment	Qur'ānic, Prophetic & Scholarly Evidence
Performing Deeds in Private & in Abundance	Allāh says:
You understand that Satan is always on the lookout for when you show any inclination and weakness towards impressing others, and he therefore arouses in you the desire for showing off	o "Say (O Prophet), 'I am only a man like you, (but) it has been revealed to me that your God is only One God. So whoever hopes for the meeting with their Lord, let them do good deeds and associate none in the worship of their Lord'" [Al-Kahf 18:110]
You therefore perform your act of worship in private in order to train your soul and purify your intention, and guard it from ostentation (however regarding congregational prayer, the removal of love of fame is enough)	o "To give charity publicly is good, but to give to the poor privately is better for you, and will absolve you of your sins. And Allāh is All-Aware of what you do" [Al-Baqarah 2:271] The Prophet said, "Actions are according to intentions, and everyone will get what was intended." [Ṣaḥīḥ Al-Bukhārī 1]
Avoid Boasting on Social Media	The Prophet said:
You remind yourself that not everyone who has befriended you on social media is actually your friend or necessarily wishes good for you, so you utilise social networks with caution	o "Shall I not tell you who among you is most beloved to me and will be closest to me on the Day of Resurrection?" He repeated it two or three times, and they said, "Yes, O Messenger of Allāh." He said, "Those of you who are the best in manners and character" [Musnad Aḥmad 7035]
Before sharing your latest post, you first assess: o Why are you sharing something or posting a particular status update? o What is the underlying message you're trying to convey? o Who are you really writing it for?	o "When lewdness is a part of anything, it becomes defective; and when ḥayā (modesty) is a part of anything it becomes beautiful" [At-Tirmidhī 1974]
Where others unexpectedly become aware of your good deed (without you doing it for their attention or pleasure), you make 'shukr' to Allāh who has publicised your acts and concealed your sins and evils from the eyes of the people, ensuring your deed remains praiseworthy	o "Actions are judged by their intentions, so each man will have what he intended. Therefore, he whose migration was for Allāh and His Messenger, his migration is for Allāh and His Messenger. But he whose migration was for some worldly benefit, or for a wife he might marry, his migration is for that for which he migrated" [Ṣaḥīḥ Al-Bukhārī 1]
You are not proud about how many followers (on social media) you have because in reality, you begin to appreciate that this holds little or no value or substance	
You avoid posting images of yourself, your experiences, your achievements, your family, etc. because wealth, health, status, beauty, etc. are all unstable, and therefore can be removed with one fell swoop (that these bounties are only from Allāh and He can select any which way He chooses to restrict and diminish them)	

Ostentation or Showing Off

Practical Treatment	Qur'ānic, Prophetic & Scholarly Evidence
Reflect Upon One's Own Shortcomings	
You are aware of your own weaknesses and therefore keep a constant check on your own shortcomings, not allowing yourself to get carried away by any praise that comes your way You become conscious that it is Allāh alone who makes you capable of all that you might achieve, so you thank Him for your achievements, and this effectively restricts your desire to take credit for your good deeds	Allāh says: o "(This is) a blessed Book which We have revealed to you (O Prophet) so that they may contemplate its verses, and people of reason may be mindful" [Ṣād 38:29] o "O believers! Be mindful of Allāh and let every soul look to what (deeds) it has sent forth for tomorrow. And fear Allāh, (for) certainly Allāh is All-Aware of what you do" [Al-Ḥashr 59:18] o "Remember Me; I will remember you. And thank Me, and never be ungrateful" [Al-Baqarah 2:152]
Managing Evil Whisperings	
You do not abandon a good act out of fear of ostentation, as you realise that this is simply an irrational fear that is perhaps inspired by evil whisperings engineered to side-track you	Allāh says, "If you are tempted by Satan, then seek refuge with Allāh. Surely He is All-Hearing, All-Knowing." [Al-A'rāf 7:200]
Just as Satan arouses in you vanity and the yearning for self-glorification, you realise that he also uses his devious strategies to make you avoid doing good out of fear of showing off When you realise your intention is contaminated, you purify your intention and firmly resolve to perform the deed for the pleasure of Allāh You remind yourself that if your heart is fortified with strong faith and sincerity of intention, it will not be troubled by Satan's whispers when practising virtues secretly or openly	Jibreel asked, "O Allāh's Apostle, what is iḥsān?" The Prophet said, "Iḥsān is to worship Allāh as if you see Him, and if you do not achieve this state of devotion, then (take it for granted that) Allāh sees you." [Ṣaḥīḥ Al-Bukhārī 4777, Ṣaḥīḥ Muslim 8:1] It is recommended to recite Surah Al-Ikhlāṣ often, a surah which affirms the oneness of Allāh and negates the possibility of there being anything comparable to Him.

Ostentation or Showing Off

Practical Treatment	Qur'ānic, Prophetic & Scholarly Evidence
Regular Qur'ānic Recital, Forgiveness & Remembrance in Private	
You regularly recite Surat Al-Ikhlāṣ (112) and Sayyid al-Istighfār (the master supplication of forgiveness)	Allāh ﷻ says, "Say (O Prophet), 'I am only a man like you, (but) it has been revealed to me that your God is only One God. So whoever hopes for the meeting with their Lord, let them do good deeds and associate none in the worship of their Lord.'" [Al-Kahf 18:110] **The Prophet ﷺ said about the beautiful supplication known as Sayyid al-Istighfar (the master supplication for forgiveness) that,** "If somebody recites it during the day with firm faith in it, and dies on the same day before the evening, he will be from the people of Paradise; and if somebody recites it at night with firm faith in it, and dies before the morning, he will be from the people of Paradise." [Ṣaḥīḥ Al-Bukhārī 6306] **The Prophet ﷺ said,** "O people, beware of this shirk (form of polytheism), for it is more subtle than the footsteps of an ant" **When a person asked,** "How can we beware of it when it is more subtle than the footsteps of an ant, O Messenger of Allāh?" **He said,** "Say: O Allāh, we seek refuge with You from knowingly associating anything with You, and we seek Your forgiveness for that which we do unknowingly." [Musnad Aḥmad 19606]
You pray the night prayer vigil (tahajjud), engage in dhikr litanies (remembrance of Allāh ﷻ), recite Qur'ān, and the like, all in privacy	
You memorise a supplication to help you stay away from associating partners with Allāh ﷻ	

Ostentation or Showing Off

Exceptions

Cause of Inspiration
You do good deeds openly because you are inspired in the company of people who are also doing good deeds
You learn or do something in public so that others may also benefit

Beautification Only for the Sake of Allāh ﷻ
When you dress and adorn yourself, you make the following intentions: o To acquire the pleasure of Allāh ﷻ only o To follow the sunnah of Rasūlullāh ﷺ o To please your near and dear ones, e.g. your spouse, your parents, your children, thus pleasing Allāh ﷻ in turn

Qur'ānic, Prophetic & Scholarly Evidence

Allāh ﷻ says:

- o "Those who spend their wealth in charity day and night, secretly and openly - their reward is with their Lord, and there will be no fear for them, nor will they grieve" [Al-Baqarah 2:274]
- o "And those who do whatever (good) they do with their hearts fearful, (knowing) that they will return to their Lord - it is they who race to do good deeds, always taking the lead" [Al-Mu'minūn 23: 60-61]

The Messenger of Allāh ﷺ said:

- o "Whoever directs someone to do good will be rewarded equivalent to him who practises that good action" [Ṣaḥīḥ Muslim 1893:133]
- o "Whoever sets a good precedent in Islām will have the reward for that and the reward of those who do it after him, without that detracting from their reward in the slightest. And whoever sets a bad precedent in Islām will bear the burden of sin for that, and the burden of those who do it after him, without that detracting from their burden in the slightest" [Ṣaḥīḥ Muslim 1017:15]
- o "Indeed, Allāh is beautiful and loves beauty" [Ṣaḥīḥ Muslim 91:147]

التَوَكُّلُ علي غَيْرِ الله

Relying on Other than Allāh ﷻ

SIGNS & SYMPTOMS

- Lacking Certainty in Allāh ﷻ
- Neglecting Obligations
- Delusion of Self-Sufficiency

TREATMENTS

- Only Allāh ﷻ can Benefit or Harm You
- Allāh ﷻ Tests & also Provides Relief
- Producing an Inner Strength of Patience, Contentment & Obedience
- Keeping the Right Company
- Turning Away from Wrong Company
- Confidence and Success

EXCEPTIONS

- Striving for Provision & Relying on Allāh ﷻ Alone

CHAPTER 23

Relying on Other than Allāh ﷻ

[At-Tawakkul 'ala Ghayrillāh]

التَّوَكُّلُ علي غَيْرِ الله

Allāh ﷻ is the possessor of unlimited power and grace. Knowing this, the ideal for the believer is to have full 'tawakkul' (trust and reliance) that Allāh ﷻ is in control of mankind's affairs. When a lack of certainty is allowed to develop within the inner heart, the believer's weakened sense of faith is transformed into a reliance on created beings and the material realm.

Allāh ﷻ says, "Say, 'He is the Most Compassionate – in Him (alone) we believe, and in Him (alone) we trust. You will soon know who is clearly astray.'" [Al-Mulk 67:29]

The Prophet ﷺ said, "When you ask something then (only) ask of Allāh, and when you seek aid, then (only) seek assistance from Allāh." [At-Tirmidhī 2516]

Relying on Other than Allāh ﷻ

Signs & Symptoms	Qur'ānic, Prophetic & Scholarly Evidence
Lacking Certainty in Allāh ﷻ	Allāh ﷻ says: o "And who could be more astray than those who call upon others besides Allāh – (others) that cannot respond to them until the Day of Judgement, and are (even) unaware of their calls? And when (such) people will be gathered together, those (gods) will be their enemies and will disown their worship" [Al-Aḥqāf 46: 5-6] o "Whoever invokes, besides Allāh, another god - for which they can have no proof – they will surely find their penalty with their Lord. Indeed, the disbelievers will never succeed" [Al-Mu'minūn 23:117]
Your sense of faith and trust in Allāh ﷻ has diminished, and you seek benefit from people, rather than the Almighty	
Your obsession with other mortals and created things such as money, wealth, property and business has compromised your certainty (yaqīn) in Allāh ﷻ	
Neglecting Obligations	
Your desire to place your trust in other than Allāh ﷻ results in you falling into the trap of neglecting simple obligations, as well as those praiseworthy acts that invite untold blessings	
Delusion of Self-Sufficiency	
You believe yourself to be self-sufficient, evaluating yourself only by worldly standards, and craving approval	
Your heart's striving to connect with Allāh ﷻ is weakened as a result	

Relying on Other than Allāh ﷻ

Academic Treatment

Only Allāh ﷻ can Benefit or Harm You

You remind yourself of the certainty that only Allāh ﷻ can benefit or harm you

You realise that if all of creation were to join forces to oppose you or support you, they would not be able to do so except by His permission

Qur'ānic, Prophetic & Scholarly Evidence

Allāh ﷻ says:

- "Say, 'Nothing will ever befall us except what Allāh has destined for us. He is our Protector.' So in Allāh let the believers put their trust" [At-Tawbah 9:51]
- "And whoever puts their trust in Allāh, then He (alone) is sufficient for them. Certainly Allāh achieves His Will. Allāh has already set a destiny for everything" [At-Ṭalāq 65:3]
- "Once you make a decision, put your trust in Allāh. Surely Allāh loves those who trust in Him" [Āli 'Imrān 3:159]

The Prophet ﷺ said:

- "Be mindful of Allāh, and Allāh will protect you. Be mindful of Allāh, and you will find Him in front of you. If you ask, ask Allāh; if you seek help, seek help from Allāh. Know that if the nation were to gather to benefit you with anything, it would only benefit you with something that Allāh has already prescribed for you, and that if they gather to harm you with anything, they would only harm you with something Allāh has already prescribed for you. The pen has been lifted and the pages have dried" [At-Tirmidhī 2516]
- "If you were to rely upon Allāh with the required reliance, then He would provide for you just as a bird is provided for, it goes out in the morning empty, and returns full" [At-Tirmidhī 2344]
- "Seventy thousand people of my followers will enter Jannah without reckoning; and they are those who do not use charms, do not see an evil omen in things, they do not get themselves cauterized (branded) and they put their trust in their Lord" [Ṣaḥīḥ Al-Bukhārī 5752]

Relying on Other than Allāh ﷻ

Academic Treatment

Allāh ﷻ Tests & also Provides Relief

You reflect on the attributes and names of Allāh ﷻ, especially His Oneness and that He is Al-Wakeel, the Disposer of Affairs, the One entrusted, relied upon, depended upon and sufficient to take care of all your matters

You understand that 'At-Tawakkul 'alā Allāh' is the Islāmic concept of complete reliance on Allāh ﷻ or 'trusting in Allāh's ﷻ plan'

You always keep in mind that Allāh ﷻ tests people and provides relief and provision

You reflect on Allāh's ﷻ favours and promises in guiding you in past successes, in strengthening you in the face of challenges

Producing an Inner Strength of Patience, Contentment & Obedience

You remind yourself that you are totally dependent upon Allāh ﷻ at every moment, and you cannot achieve anything by your own efforts and abilities unless He wills it

You understand that one of the foremost attributes of a believer is his inner and outward peace and tranquillity, all of which stems from his reliance on the Beneficent and Merciful Allāh ﷻ

You understand that practising reliance on only Allāh ﷻ fortifies you with inner strength, patience, tolerance, determination, contentment, happiness and an acceptance of His will and decree

You are given a renewed energy to take account of yourself and lead a life of obedience, to exert effort, to repent from sins and to contemplate the power and majesty of the Lord you worship

You keep any level of worry, distress, disappointment and depression at a minimum

Qur'ānic, Prophetic & Scholarly Evidence

Allāh ﷻ says:

- "And whoever is mindful of Allāh, He will make a way out for them, and provide for them from sources they could never imagine. And whoever puts their trust in Allāh, then He (alone) is sufficient for them" [At-Ṭalāq 65: 2-3]
- "(He is the) Lord of the east and the west. There is no god (worthy of worship) except Him, so take Him (alone) as a Trustee of Affairs" [Al-Muzzammil 73:9]
- "Say, 'Nothing will ever befall us except what Allāh has destined for us. He is our Protector.' So in Allāh let the believers put their trust'" [At-Tawbah 9:51]
- "There will certainly be no fear for the close servants of Allāh, nor will they grieve" [Yūnus 10:62]
- "Those who were warned, 'Your enemies have mobilised their forces against you, so fear them,' the warning only made them grow stronger in faith and they replied, 'Allāh (alone) is sufficient (as an aid) for us and (He) is the best Protector'" [Āli 'Imrān 3:173]
- In the most distressful situations, the words of the Prophet Muḥammad ﷺ, the greatest example of complete reliance on Allāh, were "Do not worry, for Allāh is certainly with us" [At-Tawbah 9:40]

The Prophet ﷺ said, "If you were to rely upon Allāh with the required reliance, then He would provide for you just as a bird is provided for: it goes out in the morning empty, and returns full." [At-Tirmidhī 2344, Ibn Mājah 4164]

The Messenger of Allāh ﷺ was ordered to tell the believers that no calamity or difficulty will befall them unless Allāh ﷻ wills it.

Relying on Other than Allāh ﷻ

Practical Treatment	Qur'ānic, Prophetic & Scholarly Evidence
Keeping the Right Company	
You socialise with people who possess attributes of tawakkul (trust and reliance in Allāh ﷻ)	
You associate with those who have created a calm and peaceful life for themselves, and who can help you develop and enhance this characteristic	Allāh ﷻ says: o "When you recite the Qur'ān, seek refuge with Allāh from Satan, the accursed. He certainly has no authority over those who believe and put their trust in their Lord. His authority is only over those who take him as a patron and who – under his influence – associate (others) with Allāh (in worship)" [An-Naḥl 16: 98-100] o "So turn away from them, and put your trust in Allāh. And Allāh is sufficient as a Trustee of Affairs" [An-Nisā' 4:81] o "But if they turn away, then say, (O Prophet) 'Allāh is sufficient for me. There is no god (worthy of worship) except Him. In Him I put my trust. And He is the Lord of the Mighty Throne'" [At-Tawbah 9:129]
Turning Away from Wrong Company	
You are able to free yourself from the control and dominance of Satan: an awareness that is informed by your faith and trust in Allāh ﷻ	
You turn away from the path that Satan keeps placing in front of you, and you are not intimidated by the doubts that the Devil whispers into your heart because you trust in Allāh ﷻ	
You persevere in this path with reliance on Allāh ﷻ and you do not fear any obstacles or problems you encounter	

Relying on Other than Allāh ﷻ

Practical Treatment	Qur'ānic, Prophetic & Scholarly Evidence
Confidence and Success You understand that the key to reliance on Allāh ﷻ alone is to strive without any fears or worries, to fulfil your needs within the sharī'ah framework that Allāh ﷻ has placed in this world, while asking for His assistance As you rely on Allāh ﷻ and His unlimited power, you feel a great amount of confidence within yourself when encountering difficulties and hardships	Allāh ﷻ says: o "And whoever puts their trust in Allāh, then He (alone) is sufficient for them" [At-Ṭalāq 65:3] o "If Allāh helps you, none can defeat you. But if He denies you help, then who else can help you? So in Allāh let the believers put their trust" [Āli 'Imrān 3:160] o "(Remember) when the hypocrites and those with sickness in their hearts said, 'These (believers) are deluded by their faith.' But whoever puts their trust in Allāh, surely Allāh is Almighty, All-Wise" [Al-'Anfāl 8:49] o "Consult with them in (conducting) matters. Once you make a decision, put your trust in Allāh. Surely Allāh loves those who trust in Him" [Āli 'Imrān 3:159] o "What is with Allāh is far better and more lasting for those... Who respond to their Lord, establish prayer, conduct their affairs by mutual consultation, and donate from what We have provided for them" [Ash-Shūrā 42: 36&38]
While relying on your God-given talents and the facilities that have been granted to you, you make certain decisions and then ask Allāh ﷻ for His assistance in reaching your goal	The Prophet ﷺ said, "A strong believer is better and is more lovable to Allāh ﷻ than a weak believer, and there is good in everyone, (but) cherish that which gives you benefit (in the Hereafter) and seek help from Allāh ﷻ and do not lose heart, and if anything (in the form of trouble) comes to you, don't say, 'If I had not done that, such-and-such would not have happened', but say, 'Allāh ﷻ did that what He had ordained to do, and know that your "if" opens the (gate) for Satan.'" [Ṣaḥīḥ Muslim 2664:34]

Relying on Other than Allāh ﷻ

Exceptions

Striving for Provision & Relying on Allāh ﷻ Alone

You understand clearly that Allāh ﷻ has ordered you to both depend upon Him and to work, to take the necessary steps needed to achieve your goals

You remind yourself that the act of striving for your sustenance is an act of physical worship while trusting and depending upon Allāh ﷻ is faith in Him

Qur'ānic, Prophetic & Scholarly Evidence

Allāh ﷻ says, "So seek provision from Allāh (alone), worship Him, and be grateful to Him. To Him you will (all) be returned." [Al-'Ankabūt 29:17]

السُمْعَة

Seeking Reputation

SIGNS & SYMPTOMS

- Displaying Insincerity
- Unnecessary Competitive Drive
- Ostentation in Good Deeds & Receiving Praise
- Heedlessness of Allāh's ﷻ Power
- Occupied with Worldly Pursuits
- Desperate for Social Media Presence

TREATMENTS

- No Good or Harm Except by Allāh's ﷻ Permission
- Secrecy & Repentance
- Seeking Reputation with Allāh ﷻ
- Futility of Fame & Certainty of Death
- Humiliation & Deprivation
- Reflect on Your True State
- Avoiding Pursuit of Fame (Social Media)
- Protecting Your Morality
- Seeking Guidance from & Refuge in Allāh ﷻ

EXCEPTIONS

- Encouraging Good
- Enabling Safety, Justice & Ultimately Worship
- Allāh ﷻ Exposes your Goodness

CHAPTER 24

Seeking Reputation

[Sum'a] السُّمْعَة

Islām is a 'transactional' way of life. The mature believer accepts that ultimate success is dependant on Allāh's ﷻ favour: the Almighty looks at all words, deeds, sacrifices and relationships, and rewards or penalises them accordingly, with His perfect justice. An individual who outwardly professes that they wish to seek Allāh's ﷻ pleasure, yet inwardly they crave admiration, respect and honour from others in humanity, is walking a dangerous high-wire of hypocrisy. They long to be in a permanent state of 'high profile', tiptoeing across the peaks of spiritual or material endeavour, their hearts cheered by the feeling that others are marvelling at their progress.

While walking this tightrope, they communicate their achievements 'back to ground level' by all manner of modes of communication, whether obvious or underhand. People come to know about them, and the hunger for 'sum'a' is fulfilled when tongues start chattering, and compliments come cascading. Because of the 'show' of it all, the seeking of reputation is the close cousin of 'riyā'a', or ostentation. The person who suffers from the affliction of 'sum'a' is often sadly unaware or even dismissive of the fact that their position on the high-wire is not secure, and that they can take a tumble at any time.

The Prophet ﷺ however said:

- "Know that if the nation were to gather to benefit you with anything, it would only benefit you with something that Allāh has already prescribed for you, and that if they gather to harm you with anything, they would only harm you with something Allāh has already prescribed for you. The pen has been lifted and the pages have dried" [At-Tirmidhī 2516]
- "If the son of Ādam had two valleys of money, he would wish for a third, for nothing can fill the mouth of the son of Ādam except dust" [Ṣaḥīḥ Al-Bukhārī 6436]
- "Two hungry wolves let loose in a flock of sheep do not cause as much harm as the harm to a man's religion wrought by his desire for wealth and fame" [At-Tirmidhī 2376]

Seeking Reputation

Signs & Symptoms	Qur'ānic, Prophetic & Scholarly Evidence
Displaying Insincerity	
You are involved with backbiting, lying, or you habitually invoke insincere praise of others (particularly people of position and authority), all because you are seeking to enhance your reputation. The fundamental driving factor is your greedy excess of desire	**Whomever Allāh ﷻ debases, none can elevate:** "Say (O Prophet), 'O Allāh! Lord over all authorities! You give authority to whoever You please and remove it from who You please.'" [Āli 'Imrān 3:26] **The Prophet ﷺ also said,** "If anyone wants to have his deeds widely publicised, Allāh will publicise (his humiliation). And if anyone makes a hypocritical display of his deeds, Allāh will make a display of him." [Ṣaḥīḥ Al-Bukhārī 6499, Ṣaḥīḥ Muslim 2986:47] **Imām Al-Ghazālī** رحمه الله **said,** "The spectacle of them (princes and rulers), gatherings with them and socialising with them are a serious danger." [Letter to a Disciple/Ayyuhāl Walad, p.52-53]
Unnecessary Competitive Drive	**The Prophet ﷺ said:** o "By Allāh, it is not poverty I fear for you, but rather I fear you will be given the wealth of the world just as it was given to those before you. You will compete for it just as they competed for it and it will destroy you just as it destroyed them" [Ṣaḥīḥ Al-Bukhārī 4015] o "My nation will be afflicted by the diseases of the former nations." **They said,** "O Messenger of Allāh, what are the diseases of the former nations?" **The Prophet ﷺ said,** "Insolence, hubris, turning their backs on one another, competing for worldly possessions, hating each other, and miserliness, until there comes oppression and then bloodshed" [Al-Mu'jam Al-Awsaṭ Aṭ-Ṭabarānī 9016]
You say just about anything to, for instance, sell your product or service (by way of lies, flattery, embellishing the truth)	
You support cut-throat strategies (labelled as 'smart business'), whereby destroying the competition is encouraged and celebrated	
Your drive for (unnecessary) competition grows into animosity, leaving you with an insatiable desire to be at odds with real and imagined competitors	

Seeking Reputation

Signs & Symptoms

Ostentation in Good Deeds & Receiving Praise

- Your heart is preoccupied with seeking the attention of others during prayers
- You want others to hear about how much money you gave in charity
- When expected honour does not come to you, it is clear that you love fame and hanker after reputation
- When others praise you, you are overtaken by pride and vanity

Qur'ānic, Prophetic & Scholarly Evidence

Allāh ﷻ says, "Do not let those who rejoice in their misdeeds and love to take credit for what they have not done think they will escape torment. They will suffer a painful punishment." [Āli 'Imrān 3:188]

The Prophet ﷺ said:

- "If anyone wants to have his deeds widely publicised, Allāh will publicise (his humiliation). And if anyone makes a hypocritical display of his deeds, Allāh will make a display of him" [Ṣaḥīḥ Muslim 2986:47]
- "When you see those who shower undue praises upon others, throw dust upon their faces" [Ṣaḥīḥ Muslim 3002:69]

Once, the Prophet ﷺ heard a man praising another, and he ﷺ responded to him, "May Allāh's mercy be upon you! You have cut the neck of your friend." [Ṣaḥīḥ Al-Bukhārī 6061]

Signs & Symptoms

Heedlessness of Allāh's ﷻ Power

- You have become so terribly preoccupied with seeking things from other people that you have become heedless of Allāh's ﷻ power and ownership, and you permit yourself to forget that blessings are from Allāh ﷻ alone
- You have become sceptical of the wisdom behind the distribution of material provisions among different people
- You start to believe that your wealth is in the hands of others, which leads to you craving what others have, doing whatever it takes to get it, and becoming angry or frustrated when you do not receive what you expect

Qur'ānic, Prophetic & Scholarly Evidence

Allāh ﷻ says, "If Allāh touches you with harm, none can undo it except Him. And if He touches you with a blessing, He is Most Capable of everything." [Al An'ām 6:17]

The Prophet ﷺ said, "Know that if the nation were to gather to benefit you with anything, it would only benefit you with something that Allāh has already prescribed for you, and that if they gather to harm you with anything, they would only harm you with something Allāh has already prescribed for you. The pen has been lifted and the pages have dried." [At-Tirmidhī 2516]

Seeking Reputation

Signs & Symptoms

Occupied with Worldly Pursuits

You seek knowledge, however you are distracted or occupied with simply gratifying your ego, believing that knowledge alone will suffice, and that you can do without good deeds

Desperate for Social Media Presence

It has become more important for you to post and comment about your latest achievement or experience, forwarding updates and media clips, than to enjoy the company of others

You are desperate to establish and maintain your presence and increase the number of 'followers' you have, supplementing human interaction (family and friends) with 'likes' to gain popularity or other vested interests, trying to create a footprint in the virtual world hoping for its reflection in reality

You are constantly seeking the approval of others, by carefully monitoring your status updates to see the number of likes, retweets, and comments you get

Your phone is set to alert you for every status update, and you know off the top of your head how many friends and followers you have

Qur'ānic, Prophetic & Scholarly Evidence

The Prophet ﷺ said:

- "The man most severely punished on the Day of Resurrection is a scholar whose knowledge did not benefit himself" [Al-Mu'jam Aṣ-Ṣaghīr Aṭ-Ṭabarānī 507]
- "What I fear for you the most is the minor shirk, that is riyā'a (showing off). Allāh will say on the Day of Judgement when He is rewarding the people for their actions: 'Go to those for whom you did riyā'a in the world: then see if you find the reward with them'" [Musnad Aḥmad 23630]

Imām Al-Ghazālī (raḥimahullāh) said, "O disciple, advice is easy – what is difficult is accepting it, for it is bitter to those who pursue vain pleasures, since forbidden things are dear to their hearts. (This is) particularly so for whoever is the student of conventional knowledge, who is occupied with gratifying his ego and with worldly exploits, for he supposes that his knowledge alone will be his salvation and that his deliverance is in it, and that he can do without deeds – and this is the conviction of the philosophers. Glory be to God Almighty! This conceited fool does not know that when he acquires knowledge, if he does not act on the strength of it, the evidence against him will become decisive." [Letter to a Disciple/Ayyuhāl Walad, p.6-7]

Seeking Reputation

Academic Treatment	Qur'ānic, Prophetic & Scholarly Evidence
No Good or Harm Except by Allāh's ﷻ Permission	
You do not allow yourself to forget that blessings are from Allāh ﷻ alone, and that no good or harm can come to one except by Allāh's ﷻ leave	Allāh ﷻ says: o "There is no moving creature on earth whose provision is not guaranteed by Allāh. And He knows where it lives and where it is laid to rest. All is (written) in a perfect Record" [Hūd 11:6] o "Say (O Prophet), 'O Allāh! Lord over all authorities! You give authority to whoever You please and remove it from who You please; You honour whoever You please and disgrace who You please – all good is in Your Hands. Surely You (alone) are Most Capable of everything'" [Āli 'Imrān 3:26] o "If Allāh touches you with harm, none can undo it except Him. And if He touches you with a blessing, He is Most Capable of everything" [Al An'ām 6:17]
You remind yourself that you must trust in Allāh ﷻ and seek refuge in Him from resorting to unlawful livelihood out of fear of not having enough wealth	The Prophet ﷺ said: o "Do good deeds properly, sincerely and moderately, and give good news because one's good deeds will not make him enter Paradise." **They asked,** "Even you, O Allāh's Messenger?" **He said,** "Even I, unless and until Allāh protects or covers me with His pardon and His mercy" [Ṣaḥīḥ Al-Bukhārī 6467] o "Know that if the nation were to gather to benefit you with anything, it would only benefit you with something that Allāh has already prescribed for you, and that if they gather to harm you with anything, they would only harm you with something Allāh has already prescribed for you. The pen has been lifted and the pages have dried" [At-Tirmidhī 2516] o "No soul will die until it completes the provision that was allotted to it" [Ibn Mājah 2144]
You realise that Allāh ﷻ will bestow upon you reputation and fame without you requesting it	

Seeking Reputation

Academic Treatment	Qur'ānic, Prophetic & Scholarly Evidence
Secrecy & Repentance	
You realise that your good deeds become corrupted when telling others about them, however when this does occur, you repent sincerely (that the deed's goodness might be restored)	**Allāh ﷻ says**, "That (eternal) Home in the Hereafter We reserve (only) for those who seek neither tyranny nor corruption on the earth. The ultimate outcome belongs (only) to the righteous." [Al-Qaṣaṣ 28:83]
As a true servant of Allāh ﷻ you love obscurity and concealment (you prefer to remain anonymous), because the safest is that person who remains the most reclusive and concealed	**Whomever Allāh ﷻ exalts, none can debase**: "Say (O Prophet), 'O Allāh! Lord over all authorities! You give authority to whoever You please and remove it from who You please; You honour whoever You please and disgrace who You please - all good is in Your Hands. Surely You (alone) are Most Capable of everything.'" [Āli 'Imrān 3:26]
Seeking Reputation with Allāh ﷻ	
You abide by the hope that, if you can be straight with Allāh ﷻ, then none of the spiteful prayers or animosity held towards you in the heart of others will result in anything harmful	**Sahl ibn Sa'd رضي الله عنه said**, "A man came to the Prophet ﷺ and said, 'O Messenger of Allāh, direct me to an act, which if I do it, Allāh will love me and people will love me.' The Prophet ﷺ said, 'Detach yourself from the world, and Allāh will love you. Detach yourself from what is with the people, and the people will love you.'" [Ibn Mājah 4102]
You are observant of His commands, avoiding what He has prohibited, and go beyond what is merely obligated and remember Him often through routine prayers, voluntary acts of worship, and generosity in charity	

Seeking Reputation

Practical Treatment	Qur'ānic, Prophetic & Scholarly Evidence
Futility of Fame & Certainty of Death	
You meditate upon the transitory nature of fame, from the basis that neither the one who honours nor the one who is honoured will remain; all will perish	Allāh says, "That (eternal) Home in the Hereafter We reserve (only) for those who seek neither tyranny nor corruption on the earth. The ultimate outcome belongs (only) to the righteous." [Al-Qaṣaṣ 28:83] The Prophets, Rightly Guided Khulafā', and the pious friends of Allāh found perfection in that thing which is not adversely affected at all by death, and that is recognition of Allāh. Though they also passed away, their lofty ranks and stages of recognition do not terminate or come to naught.
Humiliation & Deprivation	
You realise that seeking reputation from others eventually leads to humiliation and in the end will deprive you of the very thing you long for	Whomever Allāh exalts, none can debase: "Say (O Prophet), "O Allāh! Lord over all authorities! You give authority to whoever You please and remove it from who You please; You honour whoever You please and disgrace who You please – all good is in Your Hands. Surely You (alone) are Most Capable of everything.'" [Āli 'Imrān 3:26]
You avoid praising and complimenting wrongdoers, or people who are cruel or oppressive	Imām Al-Ghazālī said, "If you are put to the test by this (meeting people of leadership and importance), avoid praising them and complimenting them, for God the Exalted is angered if a wrongdoer or tyrant is praised, and whoever prays for their long life wants God to be disobeyed on His Earth." [Letter to a Disciple/Ayyuhāl Walad, p52-53]
Reflect on Your True State	
When you are praised, you reflect on your true deeds, and the fact that only Allāh knows the state in which you will die	
You reflect on your spiritual flaws and illnesses and think to yourself that if the one praising knew all this, he would never praise you again	

Seeking Reputation

Practical Treatment	Qur'ānic, Prophetic & Scholarly Evidence
Avoiding Pursuit of Fame (Social Media)	
You realise that reputation or fame can lead to many envious enemies who engage in conspiracies to harm you	The Prophet ﷺ said: o "Resort to secrecy for the fulfilment and success of your needs for, verily, everyone who has a blessing is envied" [Al-Mu'jam Al-Awsaṭ Aṭ-Ṭabarānī 2455] o "Shall I not tell you who among you is most beloved to me and will be closest to me on the Day of Resurrection?" He repeated it two or three times, and they said, "Yes, O Messenger of Allāh." He said, "Those of you who are the best in manners and character" [Musnad Aḥmad 6735]
You remind yourself that your virtual 'followers' and 'likes' will never replace genuine human interaction with family and friends, and that indeed the true source and cause of reputation and fame is Allāh ﷻ	
You decide against posting and commenting about your latest achievement or experience, and instead enjoy and respect the company of those with whom you have agreed to spend your valuable time	
Protecting Your Morality	
As a businessman or woman, or the like, you do not sacrifice your morality or ethics for reputation or profit, and you acknowledge that any success is from Allāh ﷻ alone	The Prophet ﷺ says, "The trustworthy, honest merchant will be with the Prophets, the honest, and martyrs on the Day of Resurrection." [At-Tirmidhī 1209]
You take steps to purify yourself of covetousness (greed), and no longer support strategies that encourage unnecessary competition	
Seeking Guidance from & Refuge in Allāh ﷻ	
You seek help and guidance from Allāh ﷻ alone, and seek refuge with Him from even minor shirk, knowingly and unknowingly	Allāh ﷻ says, "You (alone) we worship and You (alone) we ask for help." [Al-Fatihah 1:5] The Prophet ﷺ said, "O Allāh, we seek refuge with You from knowingly associating anything with You, and we seek Your forgiveness for that which we do unknowingly." [Musnad Aḥmad 19606]

Seeking Reputation

Exceptions

Encouraging Good

There is no harm when you inform others of your works for the purpose of encouraging them to do good, but even in this case you must tread very carefully

Enabling Safety, Justice & Ultimately Worship

As you need wealth to a certain degree, so do you stand in need of reputation or fame to a certain degree, enabling you to remain in safety and be protected against injustice and oppression, which in itself enables you to engage in worship of Allāh ﷻ without fear and in peace

Allāh ﷻ Exposes your Goodness

If without any desire of your own, Allāh ﷻ reveals you to the people then it would be inappropriate to remain anonymous

Qur'ānic, Prophetic & Scholarly Evidence

Allāh ﷻ says, "They believe in Allāh and the Last Day, encourage good and forbid evil, and race with one another in doing good. They are (truly) among the righteous." [Āli 'Imrān: 3:114]

"It was said to **the Prophet** ﷺ, "What is your opinion about the person who has done good deeds and the people praise him?" He said, "It is glad tidings for a believer (which he has received in this mortal world)." [Ṣaḥīḥ Muslim 2642:166]

The Prophets, Rightly Guided Khulafā', and most of the pious friends of Allāh ﷻ never desired or hoped for fame and yet they gained unparalleled popularity and fame.

العُجْب

Vanity

SIGNS & SYMPTOMS

- Forgetting the Source & Purpose of Blessings
- Impressed with Yourself
- Vanity on Social Media

TREATMENTS

- Inner Character, Not Outward Appearance
- Considering Your Own Faults
- Temporary Nature of Accomplishments & Bounties
- Showing Gratitude for Allāh's ﷻ Voluntary & Involuntary Bounties
- Avoiding Glorification & Haughtiness (including Social Media)

EXCEPTIONS

- Conscious of the Source of Bounty & Favour

CHAPTER 25

Vanity [Ujub] العُجْب

Vanity is to attribute one's excellence to oneself while forgetting that it came from Allāh ﷻ and being oblivious of the possibility of such excellence being snatched away by Allāh ﷻ. The vain person labours under the notion that these bounties they have accrued are everlasting and noteworthy. The word 'vanity' comes from the Latin word 'vanus', which means 'empty', implying that the source of our vanity is devoid of substance, and will vanish.

The Prophet ﷺ said, "On the Day of Resurrection, the man of vanity, strutting about in overconfidence, will meet Allāh, and He (Allāh) will be irate." [Al-Adab Al-Mufrad 549]

Vanity is related to arrogance, which - it is said - requires two people for its outward manifestation: the arrogant one and the one to whom the arrogance is shown. Contrastingly, the vain person is always preoccupied with the agony of wondering what other people think of him, yet this worry continues regardless of whether there are any other people passing judgement on him. In other words, vanity does not need a second person. In a very similar vein, in the case of the close cousin, pride (takabbur), the proud person must be noticeably superior to the other(s). With vanity, this does not apply: there can be a fluctuating sense of inferiority with the insecure and vain individual.

Vanity

Signs & Symptoms	Qur'ānic, Prophetic & Scholarly Evidence
Forgetting the Source & Purpose of Blessings	
You think of only years of tireless preparation, perseverance, long training and repetition to master your trade, deceiving yourself into thinking, "I worked so hard, and I did this all by myself, so therefore I deserve this"	Allāh ﷻ says: o "Now, whenever a human being is tested by their Lord through (His) generosity and blessings, they boast, 'My Lord has (deservedly) honoured me!' But when He tests them by limiting their provision, they protest, 'My Lord has (undeservedly) humiliated me!'" [Al-Fajr 89: 15-16] o "Surely Allāh is ever Bountiful to humanity, but most people are ungrateful" [Al-Baqarah 2:243]
As a businessperson, you are truly talented and bold, admiring yourself and praising your financial prowess, but you forget the source of your blessings	
You are oblivious to the possibility that such excellence might be snatched away by Allāh ﷻ	
You become neglectful and fail to see that the bounty in your possession is in fact a gift from Allāh ﷻ, and that you think yourself entitled to these bounties	
You have become complacent and content with yourself, to the extent that you are deprived of striving for the Hereafter	
Impressed with Yourself	Allāh ﷻ says: o "So do not (falsely) elevate yourselves. He knows best who is (truly) righteous" [An-Najm 53:32] o "And do not turn your nose up to people, nor walk pridefully upon the earth. Surely Allāh does not like whoever is arrogant, boastful" [Luqmān 31:18] The Prophet ﷺ says, "When you see Allāh giving good fortune to his slaves who are always committing sins (being disobedient), know that the person is being given istidrāj by Allāh." [Al-Mu'jam Al-Kabīr Aṭ-Ṭabarānī 913, Musnad Aḥmad 17311, Al-Bayhaqī in Shu'ab Al-Īmān 4220]
You are impressed with yourself, considering yourself to be of lofty rank, and so you admire your own talents, possessions, looks, and status, considering yourself better than others	
You show delight, for example, when looking at yourself in the mirror or gazing upon your accomplishments or property, but you forget the source of your blessings	
You are oblivious of the concept of istidrāj, in which Allāh ﷻ allows you to flaunt your blessings, while He does not diminish your blessings in the least, and in fact, He may increase them for a short time; indeed you begin to think that Allāh ﷻ really loves and favours you	

Vanity

Signs & Symptoms

Vanity on Social Media

You spend an inordinate amount of time on social media because you feel a need to project a positive image at all times, using social media to promote the highlights of your life, focusing on parties, holidays, times with family and friends etc.

You hope that if you post something revealing about yourself, or something provocative, then you get more comments, likes, etc. For example:

- You travel across the globe for vacations, and announce your arrival in airport X or resort Y, with little or no consideration for your friends' feelings and circumstances
- You've just visited the world's fanciest hotel or exclusive restaurant, and feel the urge to share your current location or endless images of the latest fashionable foods on Facebook or Instagram
- You extend your expression of love for your spouse to social media on a daily / frequent basis
- You host dinner parties for relatives and friends, with the intention of keeping family ties, yet you cannot resist flaunting your culinary skills: the inevitable uploading of photos or video clips follows
- You extend advice to other scholars, whilst also sharing a scholar's mistake, believing that you are doing a service to Islām
- You help the poor and needy on a daily basis, but you document your every act of charity with endless images
- You showcase your latest wardrobe labels, which saddens your friends as they find themselves being forced to make label and style comparisons of a personal nature
- The normally intimate act of sharing personal gifts between husband and wife becomes a public social media event
- You make more du'ā' on social media than you ordinarily make in your private worship, failing to invoke Allāh ﷻ in secret during your prostrations
- You spend an inordinate amount of time getting your profile picture on social media 'just right'

You sometimes spend hours thinking about what to post next to get a reaction, thinking about what your followers want, and also what you want them to think about you, with no incentive except excessive vanity

Qur'ānic, Prophetic & Scholarly Evidence

The Prophet ﷺ said:

- "Might is His (Allāh) garment and pride is His cloak; (Allāh says) whoever seeks to compete with Me concerning them, I will punish him" [Ṣaḥīḥ Muslim 2620:136]
- "Whoever wears a garment of pride and vanity in this world, Allāh will clothe him in a garment of humiliation on the Day of Resurrection, then set it ablaze" [Ibn Mājah 3607]
- "The effect of the evil eye is a fact" [Ṣaḥīḥ Muslim 2188:42]

'More than 80 million photographs are uploaded to Instagram every day, more than 3.5bn 'likes' every day, and some 1.4bn people - 20% of the world's population - publish details of their lives on Facebook.' [The Guardian, 2016]

Vanity

Academic Treatment	Qur'ānic, Prophetic & Scholarly Evidence
Inner Character, Not Outward Appearance	Allāh ﷻ says: o "O humanity! Indeed, We created you from a male and a female, and made you into peoples and tribes so that you may (get to) know one another. Surely the most noble of you in the sight of Allāh is the most righteous among you. Allāh is truly All-Knowing, All-Aware" [Al-Hujurāt 49:13] o "That (eternal) Home in the Hereafter We reserve (only) for those who seek neither tyranny nor corruption on the earth. The ultimate outcome belongs (only) to the righteous" [Al-Qaṣaṣ 28:83] The Prophet ﷺ said: o "Allāh does not look at your outward appearance and your wealth, rather He looks at your hearts and deeds" [Ṣaḥīḥ Muslim 2564:33] o "Shall I not tell you who among you is most beloved to me and will be closest to me on the Day of Resurrection?" **He repeated it two or three times, and they said,** "Yes, O Messenger of Allāh." **He said,** "Those of you who are the best in manners and character" [Musnad Aḥmad 6735]
You understand that it is the garment of taqwā that will help you adorn your inner self with the faḍā'il (i.e. the praiseworthy traits of the heart), such as humility and generosity, which will ultimately beautify your character	
You understand that it is the garment of taqwā that will provide you with protection from all the trials of this world and the Hereafter	
You learn that taqwā or God-consciousness (piety, fear of Allāh ﷻ) is the true criterion of superiority, not your outward appearance	
Considering Your Own Faults	Allāh ﷻ says, "Successful indeed is the one who purifies their soul." [As-Shams 91:9] The Prophet ﷺ said, "The servant who conceals the faults of others in this world, Allāh would conceal his faults on the Day of Resurrection." [Ṣaḥīḥ Muslim 2580:58]
You remember that you possess faults, both internal and external, so that any ideas you have of perfection and self-righteousness are abolished	
Temporary Nature of Accomplishments & Bounties	Allāh ﷻ says, "Whatever (pleasure) you have been given is (no more than a fleeting) enjoyment of this worldly life. But what is with Allāh is far better and more lasting for those who believe and put their trust in their Lord." [Ash-Shūrā 42:36] The Prophet ﷺ described the world with the following similitude: "What relationship with the world have I? My likeness is as a traveller on a mount, halting in the shade of a tree (for a short) while, only to leave it again and proceed along the way." [At-Tirmidhī 2377, Ibn Mājah 4109, Musnad Aḥmad 2744] The Prophet ﷺ said, "The value of the world in comparison with the Hereafter is as if one of you dips a finger in the ocean and observes how much moisture sticks to it when he pulls it back." [Ṣaḥīḥ Muslim 2858:55]
You also consider that when you die, all your self-praising and self-aggrandisement will be of no benefit, that all your worldly efforts have been in vain and the difficulty which you experienced in executing these acts will be confiscated and lost	

Vanity

Academic Treatment	Qur'ānic, Prophetic & Scholarly Evidence
Showing Gratitude for Allāh's ﷻ Voluntary & Involuntary Bounties	
You realise that Allāh ﷻ the Exalted is the Fashioner and the Bestower of blessings, and that your talent to achieve remarkable things is a gift and great mercy from Allāh ﷻ	Allāh ﷻ says: o "Whatever blessings you have are from Allāh. Then whenever hardship touches you, to Him (alone) you cry (for help)" [An-Naḥl 16:53] o "Remember Me; I will remember you. And thank Me, and never be ungrateful" [Al-Baqarah 2:152] o "And proclaim the blessings of your Lord" [Ad-Duhā 93:11] o "And He has granted you all that you asked Him for. If you tried to count Allāh's blessings, you would never be able to number them. Indeed humankind is truly unfair, (totally) ungrateful" [Ibrāhīm 14:34] The Prophet ﷺ said, "If happiness reaches him (the believer), he is grateful." [Ṣaḥīḥ Muslim 2999:64] 'Āishah ؓ reports that the Prophet ﷺ used to offer prayer at night (for such a long time) that his ankles used to swell. She said, "O Rasūlullah! Why do you do it since Allāh has forgiven you your faults of the past and those to follow?" He said, "Should I not be a grateful slave?" [Ṣaḥīḥ Al-Bukhārī 4837]
You realise that when men and women are blessed with exceptional outward beauty, they introduce ugliness when they have vanity for it	
You reflect long and hard on the fact that all blessings are entirely from Allāh ﷻ and that you cannot produce any benefit or harm without His permission in an attempt to rid yourself of vanity, or even prevent it from entering your heart	
When you are granted bounties like strength, talent, beauty, etc. then you reflect on the fact that you actually had absolutely nothing to do with acquiring such qualities	
You remind yourself that it is totally through the mercy of Allāh ﷻ that He has blessed you with these traits, and it has nothing to do with you earning or deserving them	
When you feel a growing sense of vanity because of the benefit of knowledge, qualifications gained, or your occupation, etc. then you reflect on how you were blessed with these qualities	
You remind yourself that had Allāh ﷻ not blessed you with intelligence, strength, enthusiasm, brain, limbs, etc. you would not have been able to achieve any of these outcomes	
You realise that your thankfulness to Allāh ﷻ and acknowledgement and praise of Him means that your accomplishment outlasts your earthly life and the memory of people	
You realise that you have been blessed with the ability to express shukr and make His 'ibādat, whereas many others have been deprived of this	

Vanity

Practical Treatment	Qur'ānic, Prophetic & Scholarly Evidence
Avoiding Glorification & Haughtiness (including Social Media)	
You are conscious of the fact that Allāh detests anyone who considers himself distinguished, praiseworthy, and a purveyor of excellence	Allāh says: o "And do not walk on the earth arrogantly. Surely you can neither crack the earth nor stretch to the height of the mountains" [Al-'Isrā' 17:37] o "Be moderate in your pace. And lower your voice, for the ugliest of all voices is certainly the braying of donkeys" [Luqmān 31:19]
You avoid posting images of yourself, your experiences, your achievements, etc. because you have come to realise that wealth, health, status, beauty, etc. can be removed at one fell swoop	The Prophet would make the following supplication: "O Allāh, as You have made my countenance most excellent, make my character most excellent." [Musnad Aḥmad 3823]
You remember that these bounties are only from Allāh and He can, by innumerable means, restrict and diminish them to the point of obsolescence	Mūsa was once asked if he was the most knowledgeable of people, and he answered "Yes." Mūsa was then told that there was a man who had knowledge that he did not have. This man was Khidr, and despite his not being a Prophet, Mūsa shunned vanity and became his student. [The story is told in Surah Al-Kahf (18) of the Qur'ān]
You avoid sharing intimate details (e.g. via 'selfies', Instagram) with strangers or with those whom you would never ordinarily share personal details, even though you may be modestly dressed	"It's not our outward behaviour that we need to concentrate on, we need to look inward" says McMahon, "People are using external validation on social media for a reason. We need to examine what is missing at the heart of people." Psychologist Ciarán McMahon, Director at the Institute of Cyber Security. [The Guardian, 2016]
You protect yourself and your personal space because you know that you might very easily become a victim of 'naẓr' (the evil eye) and this may lead to physical and spiritual harm	
You are wary of over-glorifying your own feats and the accomplishment of those close to you, as this may lead to harm (e.g. envy, hatred)	
You adopt humility and avoid haughtiness by remembering Allāh and being grateful: you realise that if you do not humble yourself, Allāh will humble you	

Vanity

Exceptions

Conscious of the Source of Bounty & Favour

When you are pleased and appreciative of any bounty or favour that is afforded you by Allāh ﷻ, and you also have the fear that it can be snatched away at any time, then you are not a victim of vanity

Your appreciation, whether inward or displayed, does not amount to pride or your looking down on others

Qur'ānic, Prophetic & Scholarly Evidence

Allāh ﷻ says, "Whatever blessings you have are from Allāh." [An-Naḥl 16:53]

The Prophet ﷺ said:

- "No one will enter Paradise who has an atom's weight of pride in his heart." A man said, "What if a man likes his clothes to look good and his shoes to look good?" He ﷺ said, "Allāh is Beautiful and loves beauty. Pride means denying the truth and looking down on people" [Ṣaḥīḥ Muslim 91:147]
- "Eat what you wish and wear what you wish, as long as you avoid two things: extravagance and arrogance" [Ibn Mājah 3605]

البَطَر/ الحِرْص

Wantonness or Greed

SIGNS & SYMPTOMS

- Extravagance
- Bribery
- Taking Debt
- Constant Exposure to Desired Items & Affairs (on Social Media)
- Ungratefulness
- Bad Companionship
- Distraction from Obedience

TREATMENTS

- Remembrance of Death & the Hereafter
- Being Grateful
- Correcting Your Intention & Adopting the Dress of Taqwā
- Seeking Good Company
- Fasting as a Protective Shield
- Reduced Exposure to Images of Wantonness (including Social Media)

EXCEPTIONS

- Physical Needs
- Attaining the Best of the Hereafter
- Benefiting the Needy

CHAPTER 26

Wantonness [Baṭar] البَطَر or Greed [Ḥirṣ] الحِرْص

WANTONNESS OR GREED

Wantonness or baṭar, is when one demonstrates reckless extravagance; there exists an excessive desire to need and want more, usually because one places significant value on what the fleeting things of this world have to offer, whether it is wealth, prestige, fame, or the like. Wantonness is also defined as exuberance or excessive amusement.

Something similar to wantonness is greed (ḥirṣ), stemming from the heart's obsession with wealth, which leads to people-plundering and usurping the rights of others. Something similar is covetousness (ṭama'), which is when one prefers things that conflict with the sharī'ah.

Allāh ﷻ says:

- "(Imagine) how many societies We have destroyed that had been spoiled by their (comfortable) living! Those are their residences, never inhabited after them except passingly. And We (alone) were the Successor" [Al-Qaṣaṣ 28:58]
- "(Some of) his people advised him, 'Do not be prideful! Surely Allāh does not like the prideful'" [Al-Qaṣaṣ 28:76] (relating to wealth, status etc.)
- "And whoever is saved from the selfishness of their own souls, it is they who are (truly) successful" [Al-Ḥashr 59:9]

The Prophet ﷺ said, "The son of Adām grows old and so also two (desires) grow old with him, love for wealth and (a wish for) a long life." [Ṣaḥīḥ Al-Bukhārī 6421]

Wantonness or Greed

Signs & Symptoms	Qur'ānic, Prophetic & Scholarly Evidence
Extravagance	
You are extremely pleased with your standard of living, being oblivious to your extravagance and self-importance	Allāh ﷻ says: o "Or should every person (simply) have whatever (intercessors) they desire?" [An-Najm 53:24] By means of a rhetorical question, Allāh ﷻ is reminding mankind that it is not possible for all desires to be fulfilled o "And do not follow (your) desires or they will lead you astray from Allāh's Way. Surely those who go astray from Allāh's Way will suffer a severe punishment for neglecting the Day of Reckoning" [Ṣād 38:26] o "And do not spend wastefully. Surely the wasteful are (like) brothers to the devils. And the Devil is ever ungrateful to his Lord" [Al-Isra 17: 26-27]
Before such a time as one of your desires is fulfilled, another develops, and where this wish is not fulfilled, the result is frustration and worry	

Wantonness or Greed

Signs & Symptoms

Bribery

You are greedy for income that is dishonestly acquired, and involve yourself in doubtful practices centred on money. You will even stoop low enough to become involved in bribery, persuading another to act in your favour via a gift or monetary incentive

Taking Debt

You enter debt (and indeed you may pay interest on this debt) and live quite contentedly with it, living beyond your means in order to maintain the appearance of wealth, and in order to achieve a certain material standard of living

Constant Exposure to Desired Items & Affairs (on Social Media)

Your exposure to social media and what others have in terms of their wealth, health, status, beauty, etc. encourages an excessive desire and inclination towards similar

You are constantly exposed to (advertisements that show) faces of wantonness (e.g. Facebook images), people in ecstatic postures, exaggerated smiles and gaping mouths, calling towards a supremely constructed happiness and improbable standard of living, which inclines you towards that product or service and increases your desire for that lifestyle

Ungratefulness

You find yourself forgetting your innumerable seen and unseen blessings: food, clothing, shelter, wealth, safety, friendship, love, health, and protection from harm and calamity

Bad Companionship

You seek and enjoy the constant company of companions who are only occupied with the ephemeral 'stuff' of this life and make it the substance of conversation

Distraction from Obedience

You are distracted from obedience, straying away from the Straight Path (ultimately leading to disbelief and associating others with Allāh ﷻ)

Qur'ānic, Prophetic & Scholarly Evidence

Allāh ﷻ says:

- "And leave those who take this faith (of Islām) as mere play and amusement and are deluded by (their) worldly life. Yet remind them by this (Qur'ān), so no one should be ruined for their misdeeds. They will have no protector or intercessor other than Allāh. Even if they were to offer every (possible) ransom, none will be accepted from them. Those are the ones who will be ruined for their misdeeds. They will have a boiling drink and painful punishment for their disbelief" [Al An'ām 6:70]
- "Surely Allāh is ever Bountiful to humanity, but most people are ungrateful" [Al-Baqarah 2:243]

The Prophet ﷺ said:

- "By Allāh, it is not poverty I fear for you, but rather I fear you will be given the wealth of the world just as it was given to those before you. You will compete for it just as they competed for it and it will destroy you just as it destroyed them" [Ṣaḥīḥ Al-Bukhārī 6425, Ṣaḥīḥ Muslim 2961:6]
- "The fool is the one who pursues vain pleasures and counts on Allāh the Exalted to realise his wishes" [At-Tirmidhī 2459]
- "Beware of greed for it destroyed those that came before you: it commanded them to be miserly and they were, it commanded them to be oppressive and they were and it commanded them to break the ties of kinship and they did" [Ṣaḥīḥ Muslim 2578:56]

Wantonness or Greed

Academic Treatment	Qur'ānic, Prophetic & Scholarly Evidence
Remembrance of Death & the Hereafter	
You reflect seriously (with exertion) on death and the Hereafter, and its various states and chaotic scenes You reflect on the state of the grave, which will be either a parcel of Paradise or a pit of Hell You learn more about the various stations and passages of the Hereafter, including the 'traverse' (Sirāt), over which people must cross and below which lies the awesome inferno of Hellfire Your consistent reflection lessens the lure of extravagance and, in general, all the fleeting things of this world, whether it is wealth, prestige, fame, or the like You remind yourself of the ruins of the past and make note of the utter silence of these towns, that each soul that lived there is now in another state, awaiting Allāh's ﷻ final judgement	Allāh ﷻ says: o "(Imagine) how many societies We have destroyed that had been spoiled by their (comfortable) living! Those are their residences, never inhabited after them except passingly. And We (alone) were the Successor" [Al-Qaṣaṣ 28:58] o "And when their time arrives, they cannot delay it for a moment, nor could they advance it" [An-Naḥl 16:61] The Prophet ﷺ said, o "Race to do good deeds before seven things. Are you waiting but for overwhelming poverty, or distracting richness, or debilitating illness, or babbling senility, or sudden death, or the Dajjal, the worst hidden thing that is being awaited, or the Hour? The Hour is more calamitous and more bitter" [At-Tirmidhī 2306] o "Remember often the destroyer of pleasures (death)" [At-Tirmidhī 2307]
Being Grateful	
When you are exposed to images displaying forced happiness and a higher standard of living, you remind yourself of the innumerable blessings that you have (food, clothing, shelter, wealth, safety, friendship, love, health, and protection from harm and calamity), and also those who are in a worse condition than yourself You remind yourself that Allāh ﷻ will not take away a blessing unless you show ingratitude; gratitude to Allāh ﷻ protects one from having blessings removed	Allāh ﷻ says, "Remember Me; I will remember you. And thank Me, and never be ungrateful." [Al Baqarah 2:152] The Prophet ﷺ said: o "If happiness reaches him (the believer), he is grateful" [Ṣaḥīḥ Muslim 2999:64] o "Look at those who are inferior to you and do not look at the ones above you: this is worthier of you so you do not despise Allāh's blessings" [Ṣaḥīḥ Muslim 2963:9]

Wantonness or Greed

Practical Treatment	Qur'ānic, Prophetic & Scholarly Evidence
Correcting Your Intention & Adopting the Dress of Taqwā	Allāh ﷻ says: o "O children of Ādam! We have provided for you clothing to cover your nakedness and as an adornment. However, the best clothing is righteousness. This is one of Allāh's bounties, so perhaps you will be mindful" [Al-'A'rāf 7:26] o About his true servants "(They are) those who spend neither wastefully nor stingily, but moderately in between" [Al-Furqān 25:67] The Prophet ﷺ said, "Actions are judged by their intentions, so each man will have what he intended. Therefore, he whose migration was for Allāh and His Messenger, his migration is for Allāh and His Messenger. But he whose migration was for some worldly benefit, or for a wife he might marry, his migration is for that for which he migrated." [Ṣaḥīḥ Al-Bukharī 1] Imām Al-Ghazālī said, "I saw mankind being guided by their pleasures and hurrying to what their egos desired, so I meditated on His saying (the Exalted), "whereas for the one who feared to stand before his Lord, and restrained his self from the (evil) desire, the Paradise will be his abode." [An-Nāzi'āt 79: 40-41]. I was certain that the Qur'ān is genuine truth, so I hurried to what my ego was opposed to, and I set to work combating it and restraining it from its pleasures, until it was satisfied with obedience to Allāh the Glorified and Exalted, and gave it up." [Letter to a Disciple/ Ayyuhāl Walad, p.28-31]
You understand that extravagance is usually the consequence of your misplaced and fruitless intention to show off, to feel better than others and to display your greatness; there is a fine line between beautification and extravagance, so you check your intention (i.e. 'what is driving me to do this?')	
You reverse your incorrect intention, shunning the idea of spending to satisfy your inner pride, 'status' or 'exclusivity' (which has led to your extravagance in spending), so you are able to remain within your 'true' limits (whilst not rejecting adornment and beautification completely)	
You reduce your expenditure, which lessens your concern with and desire for more earnings, also bearing in mind that the greedy are ever-loathsome	
You understand that it is the garment of taqwā that will help you adorn your inner self with the faḍā'il (i.e. the praiseworthy traits of the heart), such as humility and generosity, which will ultimately beautify your character	
You understand that it is the garment of taqwā that will provide you with protection from all the trials of this world and the Hereafter	

Wantonness or Greed

Practical Treatment	Qur'ānic, Prophetic & Scholarly Evidence
Seeking Good Company	
You surround yourself with people who are sincere and trustworthy, and who are not driven by an excessive desire to need and want more	Allāh ﷻ says: o "And (beware of) the Day the wrongdoer will bite his nails (in regret) and say, 'Oh! I wish I had followed the Way along with the Messenger!'" [Al-Furqān 25:27] o "And do not obey those whose hearts We have made heedless of Our remembrance, who follow (only) their desires and whose state is (total) loss" [Al-Kahf 18:28]
You avoid the company of wealthy people because you realise that this opens you up to craving what they have	The Prophet ﷺ said, "A good friend and a bad friend are like a perfume-seller and a blacksmith: The perfume-seller might give you some perfume as a gift, or you might buy some from him, or at least you might smell its fragrance. As for the blacksmith, he might singe your clothes, and at the very least you will breathe in the fumes of the furnace." [Ṣaḥīḥ Al-Bukhārī 2101]
When it comes to the Hereafter, you associate with people who are superior to you in their desire for and understanding of it	The Prophet ﷺ was reportedly asked, "Which of our companions is the best?" He replied, "One whose appearance reminds you of Allāh, and whose speech increases you in knowledge, and whose actions remind you of the Hereafter." [Al-Bayhaqī in Shu'ab Al-Īmān 9000]
You seek out the company of those who help you achieve contentment with Allāh ﷻ, because when you are content, modest material means will suffice	
Fasting as a Protective Shield	Allāh ﷻ says, "O believers! Fasting is prescribed for you – as it was for those before you – so perhaps you will become mindful (of Allāh)." [Al-Baqarah 2:183]
You understand that fasting weakens your excessive desire for wanting more, which makes you more able to resist any temptation to commit acts of wantonness	The Prophet ﷺ said: o "Fasting is a shield" [Ṣaḥīḥ Al-Bukhārī 7492] o "It is sufficient for you to fast three days every month, because for every good deed you will have (the reward of) ten like it, so that will be like fasting for a lifetime" [Ṣaḥīḥ Al-Bukhārī 1976]
You wilfully experience hunger through voluntary fasting (ṣawm) because it is a protective shield against wantonness	

Wantonness or Greed

Practical Treatment	Qur'ānic, Prophetic & Scholarly Evidence
Reduced Exposure to Images of Wantonness **(including Social Media)**	Allāh ﷻ says: o "(O Prophet!) Tell the believing men to lower their gaze and guard their chastity. That is purer for them. Surely Allāh is All-Aware of what they do" [An-Nūr 24:30] o "And tell the believing women to lower their gaze and guard their chastity" [An-Nūr 24:31] o "And as for those who were in awe of standing before their Lord and restrained themselves from (evil) desires, Paradise will certainly be (their) home" [An-Nāzi'āt 79: 40-41] The Prophet ﷺ said: o "Beware of sitting in the roads." They said, "O Messenger of Allāh, we have nowhere else to sit and talk." The Prophet ﷺ said, "If you insist, then give the road its right." They said, "What is its right, O Messenger of Allāh?" The Prophet ﷺ said, "Lower the gaze, refrain from harming others, return greetings of peace, enjoin good and forbid evil" [Ṣaḥīḥ Al-Bukhārī 2465, Ṣaḥīḥ Muslim 2121:114]
You reduce your exposure to images (such as advertisements or pictures on social media) displaying faces of wantonness (ecstatic postures, supreme joy)	
You reduce your inclinations towards such material products and lifestyles (including the company of such people), giving you more opportunity to reflect on the meaning of your life and your ultimate destiny	
You reject the lifestyle and culture associated with advertisements, that glorifies wantonness and subtly discourages reflection	
You keep in mind that a greedy person is always sliding down the scale of Allāh's ﷻ favour	

Wantonness or Greed

Exceptions

Physical Needs

You want things of this world for your physical necessities, and in order to be free from burdening others with your needs

Attaining the Best of the Hereafter

You desire provision from the world for the purpose of attaining the best of the Hereafter

Benefitting the Needy

Your attainment of wealth and position is for the benefit of the needy

Qur'ānic, Prophetic & Scholarly Evidence

Allāh ﷻ says, "He (also) subjected for you whatever is in the heavens and whatever is on the earth – all by His grace. Surely in this are signs for people who reflect." [Al-Jāthiyah 45:13]

The Prophet Muḥammad ﷺ prohibited vilification of the world. He said: "Lawful riches are a benefit to a pious man" [Al-Bayhaqī in Shu'ab Al-Īmān 1190]. He benefits because he spends his wealth in virtuous ways.

Index SIGNS & SYMPTOMS

Disease	SIGNS & SYMPTOMS	Page No
Anger	Rising Tempers & Evils of the Tongue	32
Anger	Rage & Hatred	32
Anger	Cutting off Family (& Friendly) Ties	32
Anger	Creating an Oppressive Environment	32
Anger	Displeasure with the Divine Decree	32
Anger	Angry Comments on Social Media	32
Antipathy Towards Death	Strong Aversion to Death	46
Antipathy Towards Death	Clutching and Grasping at Past Times	46
Antipathy Towards Death	Death & the Hereafter Hold Little Importance	46
Blameworthy Modesty	Failure through Shyness	52
Blameworthy Modesty	Supporting the Oppressor	52
Boasting, Arrogance & Pride	Self-Righteousness	58
Boasting, Arrogance & Pride	Bragging About Lineage	58
Boasting, Arrogance & Pride	Generally Boastful & Arrogant	59
Boasting, Arrogance & Pride	Boasting on Social Media	59
Boasting, Arrogance & Pride	Bragging About Knowledge	59
Boasting, Arrogance & Pride	Arrogance Because of Beauty	60
Boasting, Arrogance & Pride	Arrogance due to Wealth, Status & Position	60
Boasting, Arrogance & Pride	Arrogance due to Strength	60
Boasting, Arrogance & Pride	Arrogance due to Possessing a Lot of Something	60
Boasting, Arrogance & Pride	Arrogance due to a Dislike of Submitting to Allāh ﷻ	60
Displeasure with Blame or Disapproval	Not Encouraging Right & Forbidding Wrong	72
Displeasure with Blame or Disapproval	Social Media & Spoiling Your Intention	72
Displeasure with Blame or Disapproval	Engaging in Forbidden Matters & Neglecting Obligations	72
Displeasure with the Divine Decree	Perceived Injustices	78
Displeasure with the Divine Decree	Abuse of Blessings	78

INDEX

Index SIGNS & SYMPTOMS

Disease	SIGNS & SYMPTOMS	Page No
Displeasure with the Divine Decree	Regret & Frustration	78
Displeasure with the Divine Decree	Showing Contempt Towards Others	78
Envy	Casting Criticism Towards Other Nations	86
Envy	Envious of Others' Possessions	86
Envy	Competing on Social Media	86
Envy	Intention & Actions to Remove Blessings	87
Extravagance	Over-Eating: Going Beyond Moderation	94
Extravagance	Wasting Water & Food	94
Extravagance	Extravagant Purchases & Brand Flaunting	95
Extravagance	Hoarding Unused Items	96
Extravagance	Falling Short in Your Responsibilities	96
Extravagance	Excessive Love & Attention	96
False Hope	Indifference, Laziness & Neglecting Obligatory Duties	102
False Hope	Superstitions	103
Fantasizing	Reflecting on What is Prohibited	110
Fear of Poverty	Preoccupied with Loss of Wealth	118
Fear of Poverty	Constant Worry	118
Fear of Poverty	Keeping Bad Company	119
Fraud	Rumouring & Social Media	128
Fraud	Fake Persona on Social Media	128
Fraud	Concealing the Truth (e.g. Product or Service Defects)	129
Fraud	Breaking Promises	130
Fraud	Excessive use of Ambiguity or Indirectness in Speech	130
Hard-Heartedness	No Care for Your Relationship with Allāh	142
Hard-Heartedness	Unaffected by the Words of the Qur'ān	142

Index SIGNS & SYMPTOMS

Disease	SIGNS & SYMPTOMS	Page No
Hard-Heartedness	Indifferent to what is Permissible or Impermissible	142
Hard-Heartedness	Indifferent to Actions of Worship	142
Hard-Heartedness	Avoid Religious Gatherings & Advice	142
Hard-Heartedness	Indifferent to the Difficulties of the Ummah	143
Hard-Heartedness	Stubbornness in Times of Hardship	143
Hard-Heartedness	Consumed by the Life of this World & Material Desires	144
Hard-Heartedness	Unmoved by Funerals	144
Hard-Heartedness	Persistent Harshness with Children	145
Hatred	Illegitimate Hate	154
Hatred	Preventing you from Allāh's ﷻ Remembrance & Prayer	154
Hatred	Desiring Harm	154
Heedlessness	Heedless of Accountability	162
Heedlessness	Keeping Bad Company & Not Defending the Truth	163
Heedlessness	Enslaved by Technology & Social Media	164
Iniquity	Oppressing Others for Authority or Position	174
Iniquity	Committing Injustices (including Social Media)	174
Iniquity	Turning Away from Allāh ﷻ Towards Others	175
Love of the World	Forgetfulness	183
Love of the World	Disingenuousness	183
Love of the World	Prying & Eavesdropping	183
Love of the World	Vain & Sinful Pursuits (including Social Media)	184
Miserliness	Withholding Charity	192
Miserliness	Giving Shoddy & Inferior Charity	192
Miserliness	When Fulfilling Others' Rights	192
Miserliness	Living an Impoverished Life	193

Index SIGNS & SYMPTOMS

Disease	SIGNS & SYMPTOMS	Page No
Miserliness	Anxiety & Fear of Poverty	193
Miserliness	Failing to Bestow Prayers upon the Messenger of Allāh ﷺ	193
Mockery	Social Media Provocation	202
Mockery	Ridicule, Humiliation & Fright	202
Mockery	Looking Down upon Others	203
Mockery	Cursing Entire Races or Faiths	203
Negative Feelings	Bad Opinion of Others & Being Judgemental	210
Negative Feelings	Backbiting of the Limbs, Tongue, Mind & Heart (Ghībah)	210
Negative Feelings	Social Media Gossip	211
Obliviousness to Blessings or Ingratitude	Forgetful of Seen & Unseen Blessings	220
Obliviousness to Blessings or Ingratitude	Misinterpretation of Blessings	220
Obliviousness to Blessings or Ingratitude	Short-Term Relief	220
Obliviousness to Blessings or Ingratitude	Hopelessness at Loss	220
Ostentation or Showing Off	Virtuous Deeds for Personal Gain	228
Ostentation or Showing Off	Lazy & Lethargic When Alone	228
Ostentation or Showing Off	Preparing to Engage in Blameworthy Showing Off	229
Ostentation or Showing Off	Heedless of the Evil of Envy	229
Ostentation or Showing Off	Using Complex Language	229
Ostentation or Showing Off	Seeking the Pleasure of Others & Social Media	230
Ostentation or Showing Off	A Slave to Fashion	231
Relying on Other than Allāh	Lacking Certainty in Allāh ﷻ	242
Relying on Other than Allāh	Neglecting Obligations	242
Relying on Other than Allāh	Delusion of Self-Sufficiency	242
Seeking Reputation	Displaying Insincerity	250
Seeking Reputation	Unnecessary Competitive Drive	250

Index SIGNS & SYMPTOMS

Disease	SIGNS & SYMPTOMS	Page No
Seeking Reputation	Ostentation in Good Deeds & Receiving Praise	251
Seeking Reputation	Heedlessness of Allāh's ﷻ Power	251
Seeking Reputation	Occupied with Worldly Pursuits	252
Seeking Reputation	Desperate for Social Media Presence	252
Vanity	Forgetting the Source & Purpose of Blessings	260
Vanity	Impressed with Yourself	260
Vanity	Vanity on Social Media	261
Wantonness or Greed	Extravagance	268
Wantonness or Greed	Bribery	269
Wantonness or Greed	Taking Debt	269
Wantonness or Greed	Constant Exposure to Desired Items & Affairs (on Social Media)	269
Wantonness or Greed	Ungratefulness	269
Wantonness or Greed	Bad Companionship	269
Wantonness or Greed	Distraction from Obedience	269

Index TREATMENTS

Disease	TREATMENTS	Page No
Anger	Recognise Allāh's ﷻ Power & Rights	33
Anger	Recognising Your Own Shortcomings	33
Anger	Recognise Others' Rights (including Social Media)	33
Anger	Follow the Prophetic Example	34
Anger	Counsel Children at a Young Age	34
Anger	Maintain Balance between Anger & Mercy	35
Anger	Understand Pitfalls of Anger	35
Anger	Silence, Sitting, Reclining & Ablution	36
Anger	Diversion & Withdrawal	36
Anger	Seek Refuge in Allāh ﷻ & Repentance	36
Anger	Exercise Your Willpower & Take Control (including Social Media)	37
Anger	Seeking Forgiveness & Pardon	38
Anger	Controlled Decision-Making	38
Anger	Forbearance & Humility	39
Anger	Greater Wisdom in Forgiving	40
Antipathy Towards Death	**Reality of Death**	**47**
Antipathy Towards Death	**Remembrance of Death, Pursuit of Good Deeds & Taking Oneself to Account**	**48**
Blameworthy Modesty	Forthright & Courageous in Condemning Evil & Seeking Knowledge	53
Boasting, Arrogance & Pride	Remember Your Humble Origins	61
Boasting, Arrogance & Pride	Remember the Source of Your Blessings	61
Boasting, Arrogance & Pride	Follow the Prophetic Example & Approach to Social Media	62
Boasting, Arrogance & Pride	Follow the Honourable Actions of Our Pious Predecessors	62
Boasting, Arrogance & Pride	God-Consciousness is the True Criterion	63
Boasting, Arrogance & Pride	Reality of Your Lineage	63
Boasting, Arrogance & Pride	Avoid Your Own Vanity & Condescending or Belittling Others	64

Index TREATMENTS

Disease	TREATMENTS	Page No
Boasting, Arrogance & Pride	Humble Yourself & Strengthen Your Relationship with Allāh	65
Boasting, Arrogance & Pride	Recognise that Beauty is Deceptive & Temporary	65
Boasting, Arrogance & Pride	Recognise the Consequences of Arrogance	66
Boasting, Arrogance & Pride	Silence on Social Media	67
Boasting, Arrogance & Pride	Avoiding People of Arrogance	67
Boasting, Arrogance & Pride	Showing Humility Towards Others	67
Displeasure with Blame or Disapproval	Only Allāh Benefits & Harms	73
Displeasure with Blame or Disapproval	Self-Reflection	73
Displeasure with Blame or Disapproval	Defend the Truth for the Sake of Allāh	74
Displeasure with Blame or Disapproval	Use Wisdom to Inform the Truth	74
Displeasure with the Divine Decree	Love for Allāh	79
Displeasure with the Divine Decree	Acknowledging the Prophet's Tribulations	79
Displeasure with the Divine Decree	Response to Afflictions & Trials	80
Displeasure with the Divine Decree	Repentance to Allāh for Disobedience	80
Displeasure with the Divine Decree	Showing Gratitude	81
Displeasure with the Divine Decree	Being Thankful by Fulfilling Obligatory Actions	81
Envy	Content that Allāh is All-Wise	88
Envy	Shunning Envy & Avoiding Depression	88
Envy	Knowing that Envy Consumes Good Deeds	88
Envy	Acting Contrary to Caprice (Hawā)	89
Envy	Supplicate for the One You Envy	89
Envy	You Seek Your Own Provision	90
Envy	Protecting Your Blessings (Social Media)	90

Index TREATMENTS

Disease	TREATMENTS	Page No
Extravagance	Identify Your Extravagance	97
Extravagance	Remove Unnecessary Purchases	97
Extravagance	Control Your Food Purchases	97
Extravagance	Control Your Eating Habits	97
Extravagance	Managing Leftover Food	97
Extravagance	Avoid Becoming a Shopaholic	98
Extravagance	Control Your Brand Purchases	98
False Hope	Good Opinion of Allāh ﷻ	104
False Hope	Establishing a Balance Between Hope & Fear	105
False Hope	Contemplating the Hereafter	105
False Hope	Avoiding Superstitions	106
False Hope	Prioritising the Hereafter by Focusing on Action in Accordance with the Pillars	106
Fantasizing	Repenting to Allāh ﷻ & Doing Good Deeds	111
Fantasizing	Being Conscious of Allāh ﷻ	111
Fantasizing	Better Use of Time & Moderation in Friendship (Social Media)	112
Fantasizing	Cutting off Thoughts & Lowering Your Gaze (Social Media)	113
Fear of Poverty	Good Opinion of Allāh ﷻ	120
Fear of Poverty	Trusting in Allāh ﷻ & Severing Hope in Others	120
Fear of Poverty	Contentment	120
Fear of Poverty	Recognising & Deflecting Whisperings	121
Fear of Poverty	Spending on the Poor & Needy	122
Fear of Poverty	Seeking Forgiveness Abundantly	123
Fear of Poverty	Keeping Transactions Free from Sin	124
Fear of Poverty	Constantly Worshipping & Making Du'ā (Supplicating) to Allāh ﷻ	124
Fear of Poverty	Establishing Ties of Kinship	124
Fraud	Being Conscious of Deceit & Corruption	131

Index TREATMENTS

Disease	TREATMENTS	Page No
Fraud	Honesty & Trustworthiness in Social Life & in Business	132
Fraud	Avoiding Deceit	133
Fraud	Acknowledging Wrongful Doing & Rectifying Your Affairs	133
Fraud	Keeping Good Company	134
Fraud	Consistency in Honesty & Forgiveness	134
Fraud	Honesty in Speech	135
Fraud	Intention & Verification (Social Media)	135
Fraud	Asking for Proof	136
Hard-Heartedness	Importance of the Condition of Your Heart & its Spiritual Health	146
Hard-Heartedness	Re-Connecting with Allāh ﷻ	146
Hard-Heartedness	Reflect on the Qur'ān & Remembrance of Allāh ﷻ	147
Hard-Heartedness	Remembrance of Death	148
Hard-Heartedness	Righteous Deeds	148
Hard-Heartedness	Keeping Righteous Company	149
Hard-Heartedness	Showing Compassion	149
Hard-Heartedness	Forgiveness	150
Hatred	Accepting Allāh's ﷻ Decree	155
Hatred	Adopting Universal Brotherhood	155
Hatred	Understanding the Deceptions of Satan	156
Hatred	Adopt Moderation (Social Media)	157
Hatred	Suppressing the Ego & Reconciliation with Others	157
Heedlessness	Fulfilling Allāh's ﷻ Rights	165
Heedlessness	Reflecting on the Value of Time	165
Heedlessness	The Value of Keeping Good Company	166
Heedlessness	Reality of Death	167
Heedlessness	Counsel Children at a Young Age (Social Media)	167
Heedlessness	Valuing Time & Your Environment (Social Media)	168

Index TREATMENTS

Disease	TREATMENTS	Page No
Heedlessness	Seeking Good Company & Using Social Media to Encourage Good	168
Heedlessness	Limiting Your Laughter	169
Heedlessness	Accounting for One's Deeds & Seeking Allāh's ﷻ Forgiveness	169
Heedlessness	Honouring Righteous People	169
Heedlessness	Invoking Salutations on the Prophet ﷺ	170
Heedlessness	Recitation & Contemplation of the Qur'ān	170
Iniquity	Certainty of Death	175
Iniquity	Treating Others Fairly (& Yourself)	176
Iniquity	Satan Creates Dissension in the Hearts of People	177
Iniquity	Being Patient & Remaking Bonds, Seeking the Pleasure of Allāh ﷻ Only	177
Love of the World	Seeking the Hereafter	185
Love of the World	Using the World as a Means to Spiritual Elevation	186
Love of the World	Valuing Your Time (Social Media)	187
Love of the World	Seeking Moderation	188
Love of the World	Expressing & Receiving Thanks	188
Miserliness	Wealth & Affluence is Only Temporary	194
Miserliness	Bad Opinion of Misers	194
Miserliness	Bestowing Prayers Upon the Messenger of Allāh ﷺ	195
Miserliness	Spending on Your Family	195
Miserliness	Flexible Loans	196
Miserliness	Giving to the Needy	196-197
Miserliness	Fulfilling Rights of Others	198
Mockery	Remember Your Origins & Strengthen Your Relationship With Allāh ﷻ	204
Mockery	Severe Warnings Regarding Mocking Others	204
Mockery	Loss of Self-Respect	204
Mockery	Social Media & Avoiding Ridicule	205
Mockery	Not Insulting Other Races & Faiths	206

Index TREATMENTS

Disease	TREATMENTS	Page No
Mockery	Repentance & Forgiveness	206
Negative Feelings	Understanding Backbiting & the Consequences of Negative Feelings or Suspicion (Social Media)	212
Negative Feelings	Avoiding Potential Harm on Social Media	213
Negative Feelings	Keeping Good Company	214
Negative Feelings	You Seek Forgiveness from Others	214
Negative Feelings	Protecting the Honour of a Muslim	215
Negative Feelings	Busy Yourself With Your Own Faults & Forgive Others	216
Obliviousness to Blessings or Ingratitude	Showing Gratitude for Allāh's ﷻ Innumerable Blessings	221
Obliviousness to Blessings or Ingratitude	Wealth & Restriction are Both Tests	222
Obliviousness to Blessings or Ingratitude	Demonstrating Gratefulness	222
Obliviousness to Blessings or Ingratitude	Being Patient & Pursuing Long-Term Benefits	223
Obliviousness to Blessings or Ingratitude	Compare with Those Worse than You	223
Ostentation or Showing Off	Struggling Within Yourself to Correct Your Intention	232
Ostentation or Showing Off	Righteousness, Not Wealth	233
Ostentation or Showing Off	Only Allāh ﷻ can Benefit or Harm You	233
Ostentation or Showing Off	Remembering the Life Hereafter	234
Ostentation or Showing Off	Reflecting on those Less Fortunate & the Harms of Showing Off	234
Ostentation or Showing Off	Reflecting on the Temporary & Transitory	235
Ostentation or Showing Off	Seek Allāh's ﷻ Help in Overcoming Ostentation	235
Ostentation or Showing Off	Performing Deeds in Private & in Abundance	236
Ostentation or Showing Off	Avoid Boasting on Social Media	236
Ostentation or Showing Off	Reflect Upon One's Own Shortcomings	237
Ostentation or Showing Off	Managing Evil Whisperings	237

Index TREATMENTS

Disease	TREATMENTS	Page No
Ostentation or Showing Off	Regular Qur'ānic Recital, Forgiveness & Remembrance in Private	238
Relying on Other than Allāh	Only Allāh can Benefit or Harm You	243
Relying on Other than Allāh	Allāh Tests & also Provides Relief	244
Relying on Other than Allāh	Producing an Inner Strength of Patience, Contentment & Obedience	244
Relying on Other than Allāh	Keeping the Right Company	245
Relying on Other than Allāh	Turning Away from Wrong Company	245
Relying on Other than Allāh	Confidence & Success	246
Seeking Reputation	No Good or Harm Except by Allāh's Permission	253
Seeking Reputation	Secrecy & Repentance	254
Seeking Reputation	Seeking Reputation with Allāh	254
Seeking Reputation	Futility of Fame & Certainty of Death	255
Seeking Reputation	Humiliation & Deprivation	255
Seeking Reputation	Reflect on Your True State	255
Seeking Reputation	Avoiding Pursuit of Fame (Social Media)	256
Seeking Reputation	Protecting Your Morality	256
Seeking Reputation	Seeking Guidance from & Refuge in Allāh	256
Vanity	Inner Character, Not Outward Appearance	262
Vanity	Considering Your Own Faults	262
Vanity	Temporary Nature of Accomplishments & Bounties	262
Vanity	Showing Gratitude for Allāh's Voluntary & Involuntary Bounties	263
Vanity	Avoiding Glorification & Haughtiness (including Social Media)	264
Wantonness or Greed	Remembrance of Death & the Hereafter	270
Wantonness or Greed	Being Grateful	270
Wantonness or Greed	Correcting Your Intention & Adopting the Dress of Taqwā	271
Wantonness or Greed	Seeking Good Company	272
Wantonness or Greed	Fasting as a Protective Shield	272
Wantonness or Greed	Reduced Exposure to Images of Wantonness (including Social Media)	272

Index EXCEPTIONS

Disease	EXCEPTIONS	Page No
Anger	Addressing Injustices	41
Anger	Witness to Impermissible Acts	41
Anger	Lacking Basic Needs	41
Anger	Belittlement	42
Anger	Protective Jealousy	42
Antipathy Towards Death	Fear of Not Being Prepared for the Day of Judgement	49
Blameworthy Modesty	Ill-Timed or Ill-Conceived Modesty is always Blameworthy	54
Boasting, Arrogance & Pride	When Not Belittling Others & Showing Gratefulness	68
Displeasure with Blame or Disapproval	When Allāh ﷻ or Someone Rightly Guided Disapproves	75
Displeasure with the Divine Decree	Displeased with Immorality	82
Envy	Your Fear of Allāh ﷻ Prevents Harm	91
Envy	Wealth for Righteous Deeds	91
Envy	Righteous Wisdom	91
Envy	Focused on the Hereafter	91
Extravagance	Allāh ﷻ Loves Beauty	99
Extravagance	Moderation, without Extravagance or Arrogance	99
False Hope	Extended Hope is a Human Condition	107
False Hope	Preparing for the Hereafter	107
False Hope	Absolute Hope in Allāh ﷻ	107
Fantasizing	Not Dwelling on What Crosses One's Mind	114
Fear of Poverty	Inability to Support the Needy	125
Fraud	In Reconciliation	137
Fraud	Concealing Sins for Fear of Admonishment	137
Fraud	Ambiguity or Indirectness in Speech	138
Hard-Heartedness	Any Level of Hard-Heartedness is Blameworthy	151

Index EXCEPTIONS

Disease	EXCEPTIONS	Page No
Hatred	Hating Corruption	158
Hatred	Mere Dislike, with No Intent or Desire to Harm	158
Heedlessness	Humankind is Forgetful	171
Iniquity	All Iniquity is Blameworthy	178
Love of the World	Physical Needs	189
Love of the World	Attaining the Best of the Hereafter	189
Love of the World	Benefiting the Needy	189
Miserliness	When Giving in Moderation	199
Mockery	Making Light of a Serious Matter	207
Mockery	Light-Hearted and Humble Fun	207
Negative Feelings	Alleviating Oppression, Highlighting Evil-Doing or Seeking Help	217
Negative Feelings	Being Conscious of Deceit & Corruption, and Therefore Asking for Proof	217
Negative Feelings	Supporting Important Decisions	217
Obliviousness to Blessings or Ingratitude	Any Obliviousness to Blessings is Blameworthy	224
Ostentation or Showing Off	Cause of Inspiration	239
Ostentation or Showing Off	Beautification Only for the Sake of Allāh	239
Relying on Other than Allāh	Striving for Provision & Relying on Allāh ﷻ Alone	247
Seeking Reputation	Encouraging Good	257
Seeking Reputation	Enabling Safety, Justice & Ultimately Worship	257
Seeking Reputation	Allāh ﷻ Exposes your Goodness	257
Vanity	Conscious of the Source of Bounty & Favour	265
Wantonness or Greed	Physical Needs	274
Wantonness or Greed	Attaining the Best of the Hereafter	274
Wantonness or Greed	Benefiting the Needy	274

BIBLIOGRAPHY

Qur'ān source:

- Dr. Mustafa Khattab, The Clear Qur'ān: A Thematic English Translation of the Message of the Final Revelation, Book of Signs Foundation, 2016

Aḥādīth sources (sayings of the Prophet ﷺ):

- Imām Al-Bukhārī رحمه الله, Ṣaḥīḥ Al-Bukhārī using the numbering of Muhammad Fuad Abdul Baqi
- Imām Muslim رحمه الله, Ṣaḥīḥ Muslim using the numbering of Muhammad Fuad Abdul Baqi
- Imām Nasai رحمه الله, Sunan Nasai using the numbering of Muhammad Fuad Abdul Baqi
- Imām Abū Dāwūd رحمه الله, Sunan Abī Dāwūd using the numbering of Muhammad Fuad Abdul Baqi
- Imām At-Tirmidhī رحمه الله, Sunan At-Tirmidhī, using the numbering of Muhammad Fuad Abdul Baqi
- Imām Ibn Majah رحمه الله, Sunan Ibn Majah using the numbering of Muhammad Fuad Abdul Baqi
- Imām Aḥmad ibn Ḥanbal رحمه الله, Musnad Aḥmad, 'Ālam Al-Kutub Beirut, 1998, First Edition, verified by Sayyid Abu Al-Ma'āṭī An-Nūrī
- Imām Mālik رحمه الله, Al-Muwaṭṭa, Zayed Foundation for Charity and Humanitarian Works Abu Dhabi, 2004, First Edition, verified by Dr. Muhammad Mustafa Azmi

- Imām Al-Bayhaqī, Shu'ab Al-Īmān, Al-Rushd Publishers Riyadh in collaboration with Ad-Dar As-Salafiyya Mumbai, 2003, First Edition, verified by Dr. Abdul 'Ālī Abdul Ḥamīd Ḥāmid
- Imām Al-Ḥākim, Al-Mustadrak, Dar Al-Kotob Al-ilmiyah Beirut, 1990, First Edition, verified by Mustafā Abdul Qādir 'Aṭā
- Imām Aṭ-Ṭabarānī, Al-Mu'jam Aṣ-Ṣaghir, Dar Ammar Publishing & Distribution Amman, 1985, First Edition, verified by Muḥammad Shakūr Maḥmūd Al-Hajj Amrīr
- Imām Aṭ-Ṭabarānī, Al-Mu'jam Al-Awsaṭ, Dar Elharamen Cairo, 1995, First Edition, verified by Abdul Muḥsin ibn Ibrahim Al-Ḥusaini and Ṭāriq ibn 'Awaḍullāh ibn Muḥammad
- Imām Aṭ-Ṭabarānī, Al-Mu'jam Al-Kabīr, Maktaba Ibn Taymiyyah Cairo, Second Edition, verified by Ḥamdī ibn 'Abdul Majīd As-Salafī
- Imām Abū Bakr ibn Abī Shaybah, Muṣannaf Ibn Abī Shaybah, Dar Al-Qiblah Jeddah, 2006, First Edition, verified by Muḥammad 'Awwamah
- Ibn Ḥibbān, Ṣaḥīḥ Ibn Ḥibbān, Muassasah Ar-Risālah Beirut, 1993, Second Edition, verified by Shuaib Al Arna'ut
- Imām Al-Bukhārī, Al-Adab Al-Mufrad, Dar Al-Bashāir Al-Islāmiyyah Beirut, 1989, Third Edition, verified by Muhammad Fuad Abdul Baqi
- Imām Abū Dawūd, Marāsīl of Abū Dawūd, Muassasah Ar-Risālah Beirut, 1988, First Edition, verified by Shuaib Al Arna'ut
- Imām Ibn Abī Dunyā, Al-Jū'u, Dar Ibn Ḥazm Beirut, 1997 First Edition, verified by Muḥammad Khayr Ramaḍān Yūsuf
- Imām As-Suyuṭī, Fayḍ Al-Qadīr fi Sharh Al-Jām'i Aṣ-Ṣaghīr, Dar Al-Kotob Al-ilmiyah Beirut, 1994

BIBLIOGRAPHY

- Imām At-Tirmidhī ﵀, Shamāil Al-Muḥammadiyyah, Muassasah Al-Kutub At-Thaqafiyya (Cultural Books Publishing) Beirut, 1992, First Edition, verified by Sayyid Abbās Al-Jalīmī
- Imām Zakī Ad-Dīn Al-Mundhirī ﵀, At-Targhīb wa At-Tarhīb, Dar Al-Kotob Al-ilmiyah Beirut, 1996, First Edition, verified by Ibrāhīm Shams Ad-Dīn
- Imām Abū Al-Qasim Al-Aṣbahanī ﵀, At-Targhīb wa At-Tarhīb, Dar Al-Hadīth Cairo, 1993, First Edition, verified by Ayman ibn Ṣālih ibn Sha'bān
- Ibn Kathīr ﵀, Tafsir Ibn Kathīr, Dar Taibah for Publishing and Distribution Riyadh, 1999, Second Edition, verified by Sāmī ibn Muḥammad Salāmah

Scholarly/Other sources:

- Imām Al-Ghazālī ﵀, Letter to a Disciple (Ayyuhāl Walad), The Islāmic Texts Society, 2005, bilingual English-Arabic Edition
- Imām Al-Ghazālī ﵀, Iḥyā 'Ulūm Ad-Dīn, Dar ElMarefah Beirut, 1982
- Imām Al-Ghazālī ﵀, The Beginning of Guidance (Bidāyah Al-Hidāyah), White Thread Press London, 2010, translated by Mashad al-Allaf
- Imām Al-Ghazālī ﵀, Mīzān Al-'Amal, Dār Al-Ma'ārif Egypt, 1964, First Edition, verified by Dr Sulaymān Dunyā
- Imām As-Shafi'ī ﵀, Diwān As-Shafi'ī, Maktaba Ibn Sīna Cairo, 1988, verified by Muḥammad Ibrāhīm Salīm
- Imām An-Nawawī ﵀, Al-Adhkār, Dar Ibn Kathīr Damascus, 1990, Second Edition, verified by Muḥiyyuddīn Mastū
- Shaykh Hamza Yusuf Hanson, Purification of the Heart: Signs, Symptoms and Cures of the Spiritual Diseases of the Heart, Starlatch, 2004, Second Edition

THE HANDBOOK TEAM

Author & Project Manager
Ibn Daud
Leicester, UK

Consultation Team
Shaykh Zaqir
Director of Darul Arqam Educational Trust, Leicester, UK
Shaykh Imran bin Adam
Principal, Jame'ah Uloom Al Qur'an, Leicester, UK
Mawlānā Muhammad Yahya ibn Faruq
Director of An Nasihah Publications, Leicester, UK
Henna Parekh
San Jose, California, USA
Ammaarah Parekh
A-Level Student, Leicester, UK

Qur'ān, Ahādīth & Scholarly Referencing & Translations
Mawlānā Amaan Muhammad
Mawlānā Uthmaan Ghani Hafejee
Graduates of Darul Uloom Leicester, and students of Shaykh Ayyub Surti
Leicester, UK

Design & Artwork
Irfan Chhatbar
Director of Brandboard Creative, Leicester, UK

Editing
Mustafa Abid Russell
Leicester, UK

Along my journey, I have received invaluable support from many other kind and generous individuals.

May Allāh ﷻ compensate them all abundantly with the best of rewards in both worlds.

Āmīn.